AF838890

THE RULE OF LAW IN GERMANY

The rule of law, or *Rechtsstaatsprinzip*, is one of Germany's oldest constitutional principles and forms part of Germany's constitutional self-understanding. This book critically examines to what extent this key constitutional principle has translated into a reality for all.

The book provides a comprehensive insight into rule of law experiences and discourses in Germany. It explores Germany's long rule of law tradition and highlights where the German state has fallen short of its rule of law promise, using historical and contemporary examples. It also shows that Germany's rule of law experience is tightly interwoven with European and international rule of law debates. By integrating historical, socio-legal, and doctrinal perspectives, the book provides a nuanced account of a foundational principle in German constitutional thought.

Dedicated chapters explore the history and doctrine of the rule of law, challenges to the rule of law in today's Germany, the rule of law experience in the former German Democratic Republic and in the context of reunification, the relationship of the German rule of law practice with the rule of law on the European and international level, and the rule of law in times of crisis. This includes challenges to the rule of law through anti-terrorism measures, as well as the more recent COVID-19 pandemic and the so-called migration crisis, but also how the rule of law has been discursively (mis-)used in those situations. In concluding, the book highlights digitalisation as a challenge to the future of the rule of law in Germany.

Volume 3 in the series Rule of Law In Context

Rule of Law In Context

By exploring the rule of law in different jurisdictions around the world, the series makes an original and insightful contribution to the rule of law scholarship by moving past intractable debates over what the rule of law should mean to find out what it actually means and how it works 'on the ground', with an implicitly comparative objective as it explores these issues in the context of different legal systems.

Series Editors

Lorne Neudorf
Gabrielle Appleby

Associate Editors

Rosalind Dixon
David Landau
Lawrence McNamara
Arun Thiruvengadam

Recent titles in this series:

The Rule of Law in the United States: An Unfinished Project of Black Liberation
Paul Gowder

The Rule of Law in Brazil: The Legal Construction of Inequality
Juliano Zaiden Benvindo

The Rule of Law in Germany: Bringing the Rechtsstaat *into the 21st Century*
Hannah Birkenkötter and Dana Burchardt

The Rule of Law in Germany

Bringing the Rechtsstaat *into the 21st Century*

Hannah Birkenkötter
and
Dana Burchardt

•HART•
OXFORD • LONDON • NEW YORK • NEW DELHI • SYDNEY

HART PUBLISHING
Bloomsbury Publishing Plc
Kemp House, Chawley Park, Cumnor Hill, Oxford, OX2 9PH, UK
1385 Broadway, New York, NY 10018, USA
29 Earlsfort Terrace, Dublin 2, Ireland

HART PUBLISHING, the Hart/Stag logo, BLOOMSBURY and the Diana logo are trademarks of Bloomsbury Publishing Plc

First published in Great Britain 2025

Copyright © Hannah Birkenkötter and Dana Burchardt, 2025

Hannah Birkenkötter and Dana Burchardt have asserted their right under the Copyright, Designs and Patents Act 1988 to be identified as Authors of this work.

All rights reserved. No part of this publication may be reproduced or transmitted in any form or by any means, electronic or mechanical, including photocopying, recording, or any information storage or retrieval system, without prior permission in writing from the publishers.

While every care has been taken to ensure the accuracy of this work, no responsibility for loss or damage occasioned to any person acting or refraining from action as a result of any statement in it can be accepted by the authors, editors or publishers.

All UK Government legislation and other public sector information used in the work is Crown Copyright ©. All House of Lords and House of Commons information used in the work is Parliamentary Copyright ©. This information is reused under the terms of the Open Government Licence v3.0 (http://www.nationalarchives.gov.uk/doc/open-government-licence/version/3) except where otherwise stated.

All Eur-lex material used in the work is © European Union, http://eur-lex.europa.eu/, 1998–2025.

A catalogue record for this book is available from the British Library.

Library of Congress Cataloging-in-Publication data

Names: Birkenkötter, Hannah, author. | Burchardt, Dana, 1983- author.

Title: The rule of law in Germany : bringing the Rechtsstaat into the 21st century / Hannah Birkenkötter and Dana Burchardt.

Description: Oxford ; New York : Hart Publishing, 2025. | Series: The rule of law in context ; volume 3 | Includes bibliographical references and index. | Summary: "This book critically examines to what extent the rule of law, a principle that forms part of Germany's constitutional self-understanding, has translated into a lived experience for all. It explores Germany's long rule of law tradition and highlights where the German state has fallen short of its rule of law promise, using historical and contemporary examples"—Provided by publisher.

Identifiers: LCCN 2024036758 (print) | LCCN 2024036759 (ebook) | ISBN 9781509969296 (hardback) | ISBN 9781509969319 (paperback) | ISBN 9781509969289 (Epub) | ISBN 9781509969272 (ebook)

Subjects: LCSH: Rule of law—Germany—History. | Rule of law—Germany.

Classification: LCC KK4426 .B57 2025 (print) | LCC KK4426 (ebook) | DDC 340/.11—dc23/eng/20240813

LC record available at https://lccn.loc.gov/2024036758

LC ebook record available at https://lccn.loc.gov/2024036759

ISBN: HB: 978-1-50996-929-6
ePDF: 978-1-50996-927-2
ePub: 978-1-50996-928-9

Typeset by Compuscript Ltd, Shannon

To find out more about our authors and books visit www.hartpublishing.co.uk. Here you will find extracts, author information, details of forthcoming events and the option to sign up for our newsletters.

Contents

Introduction

In one of its earliest decisions, the German Federal Constitutional Court stated: 'The fundamental principles of the Basic Law include the principle of democracy, the principle of the federal state and the principle of the rule of law.'[1] The German constitutional order is generally regarded as founded on the rule of law – on the *Rechtsstaat*: it is safe to say that the *Rechtsstaat* forms part of Germany's constitutional identity. This volume traces how the concept of the *Rechtsstaat* developed in German constitutional thought, and how it is deployed in various contexts today. Notably, the term '*Rechtsstaat*' has recently experienced a considerable revival in German political debates. It was used over 700 times in German parliamentary speeches (or 15 times per 100,000 words of parliamentary speech) in 2018, an all-time record, with the second-highest uses in 1977 and 1991, but well below current use.[2] The Federal Constitutional Court mentions the principle in half of its decisions nowadays, although it did not mention it as much in earlier years.[3]

At the same time, the precise content and contours of the German *Rechtsstaat* are – as in any jurisdiction – anything but clear. The oft-cited characterisation that the rule of law is an 'essentially contested concept'[4] also holds true for the German context. In addition, there has been considerable disagreement as to whether the German *Rechtsstaat* can be equated at least in its fundaments to its English equivalent, the rule of law,[5] or whether it bears such unique features that it constitutes a different concept altogether.[6] In light of European integration, the question has gained prominence again, and most accounts argue for a

[1] FCC, decision of 23 October 1951, 2 BvG 1/51.

[2] *ZEIT Online*, www.zeit.de/politik/deutschland/2019-09/bundestag-jubilaeum-70-jahre-parlament-reden-woerter-sprache-wandel#s=rechtsstaat%2Crechtsstaatlichkeit%2Crechtsstaatlichen. ZEIT Online provides access to texts of speeches delivered in the German Parliament between 1949 and 2019.

[3] C Möllers, 'Rechtsstaat' in U Kischel and H Kube (eds), *Handbuch des Staatsrechts. Neuausgabe Band II* (CF Müller, forthcoming) 542.

[4] J Waldron, 'Is the Rule of Law an Essentially Contested Concept (in Florida)?' (2002) 21 *Law and Philosophy* 137.

[5] This view is perhaps most prominently held by Neil MacCormick, see DN MacCormick, 'Der Rechtsstaat und die Rule of Law' (1984) *JuristenZeitung* 65.

[6] Ernst-Wolfgang Böckenförde famously asserted that the rule of law is 'no parallel conceptualisation' to the *Rechtsstaat*, see EW Böckenförde, 'Entstehung und Wandel des Rechtsstaatsbegriffs' in H Ehmke, C Schmid and H Scharoun (eds), *Festschrift Für Adolf Arndt Zum 65. Geburtstag* (Europäische Verlagsanstalt, 1969) 53, 54 at fn 4; for a recent careful analysis against MacCormick's view, see J Meierhenrich, '*Rechtsstaat* versus the Rule of Law' in J Meierhenrich and M Loughlin (eds), *The Cambridge Companion to the Rule of Law* (Cambridge University Press, 2021) 39.

common core, emphasising historically contingent differences in how the rule of law principle plays out in different constitutional orders.[7]

This book explores some of the major developments in the history of the German *Rechtsstaat* and how it has played out in different contexts: as a principle of constitutional law, as an important slogan in difficult political situations, and in interaction with European and global rule of law discourses. In doing so, we do not presuppose a specific conceptual understanding of the rule of law or an exclusive 'thin' or 'thick' approach to this notion. Rather, we acknowledge that there are varying understandings and uses, including uses that aim at instrumentalising the notion for specific political aims. This volume does not purport to provide a clear and unequivocal definition of what the *Rechtsstaat* means and how it ought to be used in constitutional discourse. In line with the series, our aim is to address the notion from a socio-legal perspective that contextualises and explains its use from a primarily descriptive standpoint, rather than providing a specific account of the *Rechtsstaat* that we consider normatively desirable. This descriptive approach does not mean, however, an uncritical adoption of the German rule of law ideal. Rather, we examine how the rule of law has played out in various contexts. In several chapters, we use studies on the rule of law perception in Germany as starting points to examine how and to what extent this constitutional ideal translates into practice. We couple explorations of this gap between ideal and reality with analyses of the public discourse on various dimensions of the rule of law to show how the notion is used and, at times, also arguably misused. This includes explicating the varying normative connotations (positive or negative) with which actors have referred to this notion in different contexts.

I. CHANGING MEANINGS OF THE GERMAN *RECHTSSTAAT*: SOME PRELIMINARY OBSERVATIONS

The title, 'Bringing the *Rechtsstaat* into the 21st century', reflects that Germany is undergoing a shift in its understanding of the rule of law as it is facing new challenges and is in increasing dialogue with other legal orders, influenced by supranational and international legal debates. As in other states,[8] the German variety of the rule of law has not always, if ever, translated into a reality for all. We acknowledge that the German conceptualisation of the *Rechtsstaat* is rooted in a specific intellectual history and liberal tradition that centres on

[7] The most comprehensive overview is L Heuschling, *État de droit, Rechtsstaat, Rule of Law* (Dalloz, 2002); see also S Martini, 'Die Pluralität von Rule-of-Law-Konzeptionen in Europa und das Prinzip einer europäischen Rule of Law' in M Kötter and GF Schuppert (eds), *Normative Pluralität Ordnen: Rechtsbegriffe, Normenkollisionen Und Rule of Law in Kontexten dies- und jenseits des Staates* (Nomos, 2009) 303.

[8] See, eg, P Gowder, *The Rule of Law in the United States: An Unfinished Project of Black Liberation* (Hart Publishing, 2021 – in this series).

formal statutory law and its review by independent courts, which has led to a specific doctrinal understanding of the *Rechtsstaat* in German constitutional jurisprudence. Throughout the six chapters of the book, we contextualise the German rule of law understanding by highlighting specific matters that have characterised German rule of law debates over the last decades, including times of emergency and increased (perceived or real) threats to the legal order, as well as German partition and reunification.

Against this backdrop, a few terminological clarifications are in order. We will use the German term *Rechtsstaat* or *Rechtsstaatsprinzip* when referring to the German constitutional principle, both in its historical evolution and contemporary form, as used in German constitutional law scholarship and by the Constitutional Court. The equivalent English translation used in this volume is 'the German rule of law principle' or 'the principle of the *Rechtsstaat*'. In doing so, we depart from the terminology used by Donald P Kommers and Russell A Miller in their textbook on the Constitutional Jurisprudence of the Federal Republic of Germany, who translate the doctrinal principle of the *Rechtsstaat* as the 'principle of the constitutional state' while acknowledging the difficulty of translating the term *Rechtsstaat*.[9] We use a broader translation to reflect the various conceptual modifications that the term has experienced throughout constitutional history. While we agree with Kommers and Miller that the 'constitutional state' might be the most appropriate translation when discussing the principle in contemporary German constitutional jurisprudence, the broader term allows us to trace the variations in meaning across time. In turn, the German word *Rechtsstaatlichkeit* will be equated with the English term 'rule of law', bearing in mind that different institutions will adopt different notions of the rule of law, as mentioned above. For translations of the Basic Law, we use the translation by Christian Tomuschat, David P Currie, Donald P Kommers, and Raymond Kerr in cooperation with the Language Service of the German Bundestag and provided by the German Federal Government.[10]

II. OUTLINE OF THE BOOK

This book is divided into six chapters. The first chapter outlines the German concept of *Rechtsstaat*. We trace the principle's historical evolution and then turn to its use in current constitutional doctrine. An underlying theme that emerges is the German focus on formal statutory law as the primary means for state action to be both legitimised and limited and the key role that courts and judicial review occupy in the German understanding of the rule of law.

[9] See DP Kommers and RA Miller, *The Constitutional Jurisprudence of the Federal Republic of Germany*, 3rd edn (Duke University Press, 2012) eg, at 48–49, 622–23; at 48: 'The term Rechtsstaat has no exact equivalent in English'.

[10] See www.gesetze-im-internet.de/englisch_gg/englisch_gg.html.

The chapter ends with a summary of certain key features that the German *Rechtsstaat* purports to protect.

The second chapter turns from this legal notion to the reality of the rule of law in Germany, highlighting current rule of law issues. In this chapter, we ask to what extent Germany lives up to its own rule of law ambitions outlined in the previous chapter. In doing so, we address several challenges Germany faces with regard to both formal and substantive dimensions of the rule of law and examine issues of the independence of the judiciary and the prosecution, effectiveness of judicial decision-making, structural inequalities, certain fundamental rights, and transparency in lawmaking.

After these two chapters that together provide an overview of German *Rechtsstaat* doctrine and practice, the book then puts a spotlight on the German rule of law experience in specific contexts. The third chapter addresses both the rule of law experience in the former German Democratic Republic as well as the rule of law debates ensuing German reunification. Both are unique features of the German rule of law experience. The fourth chapter turns to Germany's rule of law experience in times of crisis. We examine specific challenges to rule of law principles such as due process guarantees during times of terrorism or challenges to administrative action and the separation of powers during the so-called refugee crisis of 2015/16 and the COVID-19 pandemic and observe a shift from a rule of law ideal that is concerned with limiting state action to a discursive use of the rule of law as a law and order state, at least with regard to some policy areas.

This engagement with internal German debates is followed by a broadened perspective: the fifth chapter focuses on Germany's embeddedness in the European and the international rule of law context, analysing the interactions among the rule of law understandings and practices on the various levels. We examine how the rule of law in Germany has been shaped by European influences but has also, in turn, influenced European standards and examine Germany's extensive rule of law assistance at the international level.

The sixth chapter concludes by looking ahead and discussing the challenges that the rule of law in Germany is likely to face as the world enters an age of comprehensive digitalisation. We show the impact of digitalisation on the rule of law experience today, assess the structural effect of digitalisation on the *Rechtsstaatsprinzip* as a legal principle and reflect on the future challenges that digitalisation causes for the rule of law in Germany.

1

The German Rechtsstaat: *Historical Evolution and Constitutional Doctrine Today*

THE *RECHTSSTAAT* IS often considered one of the most important contributions of German constitutional law scholarship throughout the centuries,[1] and has left its mark on neighbouring countries' constitutional thought, for example, in France.[2] It is part of the German Constitution's unamendable core, protected by the Basic Law's so-called 'eternity clause'.[3] In this first chapter, we provide an overview of the historical origins of the German *Rechtsstaat* and its development throughout the nineteenth and first half of the twentieth century (I). We then present how the *Rechtsstaat* has developed in contemporary constitutional jurisprudence and scholarship under the Basic Law since 1949 (II).

I. HISTORY OF THE *RECHTSSTAAT*

The concept of the *Rechtsstaat* in German constitutional thought is generally considered to have evolved throughout the nineteenth century, even if the core idea of a territory ruled by law goes back further, with first traces in the Middle Ages.[4]

The *Rechtsstaat*, as it marks German constitutional theory today, is intimately linked to the rise of the constitutional state in Europe. The Constitution

[1] PM Huber, 'Rechtsstaat' in M Herdegen et al (eds), *Handbuch des Verfassungsrechts* (CH Beck, 2021) 383, 384.

[2] See on this, L Heuschling, *État de droit, Rechtsstaat, Rule of Law* (Dalloz, 2002). Prominent scholars who conceptualised an *État de droit* drawing on German jurisprudence are L Duguit, *L'État, le droit objectif et la loi positive* (Fontemoing, 1901), and R Carré de Malberg, *Contribution à la théorie générale de l'État* (Sirey, 1920–1922).

[3] Art 79(3) Basic Law: 'Amendments to this Basic Law affecting the … principles laid down in Articles 1 and 20 shall be inadmissible.'

[4] The 1555 Augsburg Peace as the first step towards freedom of religion is considered key by Peter M Huber and Eberhard Schmidt-Aßmann in their treatments, Huber (n 1) 385; E Schmidt-Aßmann, 'Der Rechtsstaat' in J Isensee and P Kirchhof (eds), *Handbuch des Staatsrechts*, vol 2, 3rd edn (CF Müller, 2004) 541, 547.

is the legal form of a theoretical concept of legitimate authority exercised by the state. It is through the notion of the constitutional state that legitimate authority through law was first conceptualised.[5] Put differently, the constitutional state is legitimate only insofar as it rules through and is ruled by law.

The idea of the *Rechtsstaat* as the constitutional state based on the rule of law dates back to German idealism and a reason-based conception of the state, which aims at integrating material justice and formal law into one unified conception of the state (A). Throughout the second half of the nineteenth century, however, German legal scholars developed a formalistic understanding of the *Rechtsstaat* centered on the principle of legality of administration (*Gesetzmäßigkeit der Verwaltung*),[6] thus solving the tension between material justice and formal law in favour of formalism (B). In turn, after the failed Constitution of Weimar and the terror of the Third Reich, a substantive understanding of the *Rechtsstaat* was developed in the early days of the German Federal Republic (C).

A. Origins in German Idealism

In European legal thought, the modern nation-state is generally thought to have emerged around the end of the 30-year war and the Peace of Westphalia with its division of religion and the state. In nineteenth-century Germany, the *Rechtsstaat* was understood as its own type of state, based on and rooted in reason.[7] This notion of the *Rechtsstaat* finds its origins in German idealism, perhaps most explicitly in Immanuel Kant's writings on the state.[8] While Kant never used the term '*Rechtsstaat*', his writings influenced other scholars of his time. Kant's contemporary, Johann Wilhelm Petersen (under the pseudonym of Placidus), used the term 'Rechts-Staats-Lehrer' for those scholars who were working in the Kantian tradition and is thus believed to be the etymological source of the term '*Rechtsstaat*'.[9] Even if Kant never used the term, he marked thinking about the *Rechtsstaat*, especially in the late eighteenth and early nineteenth century, when the term was established in German constitutional law, and he continues to influence thinking about the relationship between law and the state to this date. We therefore briefly sketch his most important contributions to state theory.

[5] D Grimm, *Deutsche Verfassunsgeschichte 1776–1866* (Suhrkamp, 1988) 12.

[6] Translation taken from DP Kommers and RA Miller, *The Constitutional Jurisprudence of the Federal Republic of Germany*, 3rd edn (Duke University Press, 2012) 175.

[7] *Vernunftstaat* or *Verstandestaat*, see E-W Böckenförde, 'Entstehung und Wandel des Rechtsstaatsbegriffs' in H Ehmke, C Schmid and H Scharoun (eds), *Festschrift für Adolf Arndt zum 65. Geburtstag* (Europäische Verlagsanstalt, 1969) 53, 55–56; see also Heuschling (n 2) 43.

[8] See also C Bäcker, 'Rechtsstaat' in M Sellers and S Kirste (eds), *Encyclopedia of the Philosophy of Law and Social Philosophy* (Springer Netherlands, 2020) 1.

[9] Heuschling (n 2) 36; K Sobota, *Das Prinzip Rechtsstaat – Verfassungs- und verwaltungsrechtliche Aspekte* (Mohr Siebeck, 1997) 266, fn 11 (with reference to Stern).

Kant defines the state as 'a union of a multitude of human beings under laws of right'. Right (*Recht*) is famously understood as 'the sum of the conditions under which the choice of one can be united with the choice of another in accordance with a universal law of freedom'.[10] Notwithstanding the complicated and debated relationship between the categorical imperative (or some version of it) and the universal principle of right,[11] Kant's very definition of the law as right, that is as norms that every individual is morally compelled to follow based on reason, leads to a theory of the state that is not justified *qua* consent or utilitarian considerations but rather presents the state as a moral necessity that is grounded in reason.[12] This is the basis for the reason-based state that marks early nineteenth-century thought on the *Rechtsstaat* in Germany.

A tension central to many debates on the *Rechtsstaat* (as well as on the rule of law) is that between formal, statutory law, and morally justified principles. Kant anticipates this tension in his very definition of law: he distinguishes 'right' (*Recht*) from laws and external lawgiving (*äußere Gesetzgebung*) and asserts that 'whether what these laws prescribed is also right, and what the universal criterion is by which one could recognize right as well as wrong' is to be sought 'in reason alone', lest one ends up with a 'merely empirical doctrine of right … that may be beautiful but unfortunately it has no brain'.[13] The tension is thus resolved by privileging such external lawgiving that conforms to the categorical imperative; these are the laws of right. One should be motivated to follow such laws because it is the reasonable thing to do: the universal principle of right provides that 'any action is *right* if it can coexist with everyone's freedom in accordance with a universal law', and this is not a maxim, but rather an ethical requirement that follows from reason.[14] Kant views the establishment of the state as a moral necessity.[15] The state is not based on a de facto exercise of power but is conceived – as mentioned – as a union of human beings united under the laws of right, that is under those laws that reason requires us to follow. This leads then to a privileging of the right of the state over individual moral

[10] I Kant, *Metaphysik der Sitten* (Nicolovius, 1797) 230; see for an authoritative English translation I Kant, 'The metaphysics of morals' in MJ Gregor (trans), *Practical Philosophy* (Cambridge University Press, 1996) 353, 386–87.

[11] For an overview of the recent debates see F Tomassini, 'Right, Morals and the Categorical Imperative' (2023) 114 *Kant-Studien* 513.

[12] J Waldron, 'Kant's Theory of State' in P Kleingeld, *Toward Perpetual Peace and Other Writings on Politics, Peace, and History* (Yale University Press, 2017) 179.

[13] Kant, Metaphysik (n 10) 230 = Kant, Metaphysics (n 10) 386–87. At the same time, Kant advocates a distinction between right and virtue as fundamental to his doctrine of morals, where right relates to duties of outer freedom and virtue to duties of inner freedom, Kant, Metaphysik (n 10) 407 = Kant, Metaphysics (n 10) 534. Only the former is the subject of the external laws that make up a state, or, in Kant's words, 'laws for which there can be an external lawgiving', Kant, Metaphysik (n 10) 225 = Kant, Metaphysics (n 10) 379. The notion of 'right' then only concerns such actions that have an influence on other persons, SEP, para 1, plato.stanford.edu/entries/kant-social-political/.

[14] Kant, Metaphysik (n 10) 231 = Kant, Metaphysics (n 10) 387–88.

[15] Waldron (n 12).

judgment, which in turn explains Kant's rejection of a right to resistance or civil disobedience.[16]

It is this tradition that provides the background to the composite German term *Rechtsstaat* as the combination of *Recht* (right) and *Staat* (state). *Recht* is not understood as either formal or substantive but rather as uniting a formal, procedural dimension with a specific, liberal content.[17] Its institutional form is the constitutional state which marks legal thinking throughout the first half of the nineteenth century, influenced by the political developments of the American and French revolutions.

One of the first legal scholars to employ the term *Rechtsstaat* in the Kantian tradition is Carl Theodor Welcker, who explicitly defines the *Rechtsstaat* as a 'state of reason'. In a clear Kantian tradition (albeit without Kant's philosophical sophistication, and rather with a theological dimension), Welcker states that 'right' is only what reason dictates.[18] The law-based state (*Rechtsstaat*) results from the notion of law as right, and as such is based on reason: the state is what emerges from the general reign of reason to the benefit of all people.[19] Welcker writes from a liberal position and emphasises as indispensable elements of the *Rechtsstaat* certain fundamental liberties, such as the freedom of expression.[20] He was, however, less interested in the doctrinal import of the *Rechtsstaat*, and does not propose any specific form of the state nor a specific set of legal rules. For Welcker, a monarchy or aristocracy can be a law-based state as much as a democracy. What matters is the notion of law as right that is grounded in reason.[21] The *Rechtsstaat* in Welcker's understanding is thus the ideal, liberal state, only to be reached through historical development that leads from the despotic state through the theocratic state to, finally, the reason- and therefore law-based state.[22] Welcker's contemporary and fellow liberal lawyer Johann Christoph Freiherr von Aretin considered the state of Bavaria an example of the *Rechtsstaat* in this sense, as a state in which reason alone was reigning, pursuing the general interest.[23]

The first comprehensive doctrinal analysis of the *Rechtsstaat*, and along with it, the popularisation of the term, is found in Robert von Mohl's seminal work, titled 'Police Science According to the Principles of the Rule of Law State' (*Die Polizei-Wissenschaft nach den Grundsätzen des Rechtsstaats*). *Policeyrecht*, the law of public policy (rather than police in the modern sense of the word as law enforcement only), had been evolving since the mid-eighteenth century and

[16] Waldron (n 12) 194–197.

[17] This is Böckenförde's reading of the *Vormärz* liberals, see Böckenförde (n 7) 58.

[18] CT Welcker, *Die Letzten Gründe von Recht, Staat und Strafe: Philosophisch und nach den Gesetzen der merkwürdigsten Völker rechtshistorisch entwickelt* (Heyer, 1813) 25.

[19] Welcker (n 18) 71, esp at 80 et seq.

[20] Bäcker (n 8) 2.

[21] Sobota (n 9) 268.

[22] Heuschling (n 2) 37.

[23] ibid 38.

started to be called 'administrative law' just about the time when von Mohl's work was first published in 1832/33 – the term is thus broad and encompasses questions of the welfare state and general administration.[24] Von Mohl was both an academic as well as a legal practitioner with positions at the universities of Heidelberg and Tübingen, as a parliamentarian in the state of Baden and later as a diplomat on behalf of Baden in other German states.[25] Rooted in both practice and scholarly thought, his work was the first to systematically align administrative practice with constitutional functions; he argued for a prohibition of arbitrary administrative action, although he only required a legislative basis for restrictions on citizens' liberty or infringement of property rights.[26] Two elements that would become imperative for the further consolidation of the *Rechtsstaat* throughout the nineteenth century are present in von Mohl's work: the principle of legality of the administration, including clarity of the law, primacy of the law, the principle of necessity and proportionality, and review of administrative action at the request of the individual.[27] Later in life, von Mohl, who was familiar with the Federalist Papers, would also be the first legal scholar in Germany to publish a major legal treatise dedicated to the defence of judicial review,[28] even if in his main treatise, he defended a form of administrative review outside of ordinary courts.[29] He is also the first scholar to clearly distinguish between the constitution and the administration.[30]

While von Mohl was instrumental in introducing key formal elements of the *Rechtsstaat*, his conception remains decidedly substantive and informed by Kantian ideas on the relationship between law and the state.[31] His treatise assumes that the concept of the *Rechtsstaat* is known: there is no clear definition throughout his work, but there are clear Kantian elements where von Mohl defines the aim of a *Rechtsstaat* to organise the co-existence of people in such a way that every member of a political community can achieve greatest possible freedom, with limits on individual freedom to be found in reason.[32] Social welfare is an important factor in his work; in that sense, his conception is a substantive conception of the rule of law that is geared towards securing the greatest possible welfare of all individuals in a community whilst securing individual liberty through legal procedure.[33]

[24] M Stolleis, *Öffentliches Recht in Deutschland: Eine Einführung in Seine Geschichte (16.-21. Jahrhundert)* (CH Beck, 2014) 47, 63–64.

[25] U Scheuner, 'Der Rechtsstaat und die soziale Verantwortung des Staates: Das Wissenschaftliche Lebenswerk von Robert von Mohl' (1979) *Der Staat* 1, 10–12; Sobota (n 9) 307.

[26] Stolleis (n 24) 63–64.

[27] See Sobota (n 9) 316–318.

[28] Kommers and Miller (n 6) 5–6.

[29] Sobota (n 9) 318.

[30] Scheuner (n 25) 14.

[31] Scheuner (n 25) 16–17.

[32] Sobota (n 9) 308.

[33] Scheuner (n 25) 16–17.

Von Mohl is not only the first to provide a doctrinal analysis of the *Rechtsstaat*, but also one of the last to provide a comprehensive treatise that seeks to systematically integrate jurisprudence, political theory, and sociological observations into one single contribution that analyses all levels of the state in accordance with what was perceived as the scientific method.[34] In later treatments, we see a greater differentiation between doctrinal, legal questions on the one hand and broader, general questions on the functions of the state on the other hand, due to the development of positivist legal scholarship. Mohl was then one of the last defenders of a comprehensive conception of the rule of law in Germany in the nineteenth century, but without defending a specific form of the state. As such, he has been identified as a 'thinker between the ages'.[35] The second half of the nineteenth century in German legal thought was decidedly more formalistic. This development will be explored in the following section.

B. Formal Conceptions of the *Rechtsstaat* in the Long Nineteenth Century

As has become clear from the previous section, Robert von Mohl rejects the paternalistic state, but at the same time does not embrace a libertarian state with minimal interventionist powers, either.[36] Instead, his vision of the *Rechtsstaat* is one that is closely associated with ideas of the welfare state, which would gain prominence again over a century later.[37] However, this was not the predominant view throughout most of the nineteenth century. Mohl's contemporary, Julius von Stahl, proposed an influential formalistic conception of the term: 'By the character of *Rechtsstaat* I mean solely the steadfastness of the statutory legal order, not its content.'[38] The substantive dimension is excluded from this definition: there is no talk about properties that the statutory legal order might require, or that it needs to be related to reason. The statutory legal order is the formal legal order, irrespective of the substantive content of its laws. Stahl, a legal scholar and fervent monarchist who had taught in three Bavarian cities before being called to Berlin by Friedrich Wilhelm IV, repeatedly restated his vision of the rule of law in different writings. In its most famous iteration, it reads:

> The state shall be a rule of law state (*Rechtsstaat*), that is the slogan and is, truth be told, the development of recent times. It [the *Rechtsstaat*] shall, through the means of law, clearly determine the ways and limits of its action as well as the free sphere of

[34] Scheuner (n 25) 12; Sobota (n 9) 307.

[35] Sobota (n 9) 306; see also Scheuner (n 25) 29 ('figure of transition', '*Gestalt des Übergangs*').

[36] See also Scheuner (n 25) 19.

[37] See below section II.C on the social state.

[38] FJ Stahl, *Die Philosophie des Rechts*, 2nd edn (JCB Mohr, 1847), translation quoted after Bäcker (n 8) 2.

its citizens ... this is the notion of the *Rechtsstaat* ... not the end and content of the state, but only the nature and character through which it is realized.[39]

This quote has been understood to clearly establish the state as a formal container and guarantor of the law, and to distinguish it neatly from its substantive content.[40]

Katharina Sobota has shown that this reading is at best too simplistic and at worst misunderstanding Stahl.[41] Stahl was a deeply religious Christian and defended the monarchy based on its divine right to rule; it would have been surprising if he had nothing to say about the state's morality or had no substantive observations to make at all. Indeed, his legal philosophy contains extensive chapters on the relationship between law and morality.[42] At its helm, Stahl posits the 'Realm of God' and derives from it a 'moral realm' that animates the fields of law, but also of religion and morality.[43] In Stahl's conception, the moral realm and the legal realm interact through the (monarchic, constitutional) state in a dialectic manner; they are separate from one another but are mutually dependent.[44] Stahl is then very much a scholar of his time, animated by ideas of German idealism. That he is best known as the 'father' of the formalistic *Rechtsstaat* is due in no small part to later writers quoting Stahl selectively and disregarding his framework of morality in which he situates the law and with it, the *Rechtsstaat*.

This reception needs to be read against the political context of nineteenth-century Germany. Most nineteenth-century legal scholars were also politically active, as the example of Robert von Mohl shows. Both von Mohl as well as Welcker, the two early proponents of substantive versions of the *Rechtsstaat* inspired by German idealism, were present at the Frankfurt Parliament in 1848. The Frankfurt Parliament was the first pan-German parliamentary assembly to debate the possible adoption of a liberal constitution and the creation of a German nation state that would replace the patchwork of independent German states existing at the time. Welcker and von Mohl were actively involved in drafting the constitutional text which ultimately failed, but which remained important for future German constitutions, especially the Weimar Constitution of 1919.[45]

[39] FJ Stahl, *Die Philosophie des Rechts, Zweiter Band: Rechts- und Staatslehre auf der Grundlage christlicher Weltanschauung*, 5th edn (JCB Mohr, 1878) 137–138.

[40] This is the standard understanding of Stahl's contribution, see, eg, Bäcker (n 8) ('formal concept in its depoliticized and dematerialized formal reading'); Böckenförde (n 7) 60 ('"unpolitical" formal element').

[41] Sobota (n 9) 319–337; see also Heuschling (n 2) 74–75.

[42] The famous quote is contained in the second volume of his 'Philosophy of Law'; his general legal philosophy is contained in the first volume of the same book and comprises chapters on the 'philosophical foundations', with a first chapter titled 'God's personality as the principle of the world'.

[43] Stahl (n39) 1; Sobota (n 9) 326–328.

[44] Sobota (n 9) 300.

[45] Stolleis (n 24) 66.

The failure of the Frankfurt Constitution strengthened conservative forces in the various German states. It effectively stifled parliamentarianism until 1918.[46] Moreover, the political defeat of liberal forces, coupled with the death of republican ambitions, led to an increased focus on developing jurisprudence that followed the scientific ideals of precision and systematicity and distanced itself from non-legal (ie, historical, philosophical, and political) elements, claiming autonomy as the discipline gave itself a decidedly positivist outlook.[47] In this context, Stahl's separation of the legal realm and the moral realm and his restriction of the term *Rechtsstaat* to the legal realm, voiding this specific notion of its substantive connotation, fell on fertile ground.

The formal understanding of the rule of law is prevalent throughout the second half of the nineteenth century and intimately linked to the emergence of a body of administrative law that was subject to scholarly treatment.[48] Two elements in particular are understood as key to this formal understanding: judicial review and the principle of legality of administrative action. Two scholars are specifically associated with the idea of judicial review: Otto von Bähr, who published his short, yet highly influential book 'The rule of law state. A journalistic sketch' in 1864,[49] and Rudolf von Gneist, who was instrumental in introducing independent administrative courts in the second half of the nineteenth century. In turn, Otto Mayer's name is inextricably linked with the development of German administrative law, including the important principle of legality of the administration (*Gesetzmäßigkeit der Verwaltung*).

The question of judicial review had already occupied liberal scholars on the rule of law such as von Mohl. Given the restricted role of Parliaments in the various German states throughout the nineteenth century, even before the failed 1848 revolution, scholars paid increased attention to the role of the judge. The debate centred around who should review administrative acts, specifically whether such review should be kept within the administration or be conferred to the courts, with conservatives arguing for the former and liberals for the latter.[50] The Frankfurt Constitution of 1849, which never entered into force, provided for judicial review as a means to protect individual rights and stated in its Article X, paragraph 182: 'Administrative review shall cease; ordinary courts shall decide on any infringement of rights.'[51]

After the failure of the Frankfurt Constitution, the question of who should exercise this review remained open. Otto von Bähr, a judge from the state of Kurhessen, which had unusually extensive judicial review compared to other

[46] Grimm (n 5) 208.
[47] Stolleis (n 24) 67–68.
[48] On this development P Badura, *Das Verwaltungsrecht Des Liberalen Rechtsstaates* (Schwartz, 1967); Stolleis (n 24) ch VIII.
[49] O Bähr, *Der Rechtsstaat: eine publicistische Skizze* (Wigand, 1864).
[50] Stolleis (n 24) 61.
[51] 'Die Verwaltungsrechtspflege hört auf; über alle Rechtsverletzungen entscheiden die Gerichte.'

states at the time,[52] strongly advocated for judicial review of administrative action by ordinary courts. His book on the *Rechtsstaat* opens by quoting Stahl's famous statement on the rule of law to then show why Stahl was mistaken in rejecting judicial review: Stahl considered administrative review an entirely internal affair, not apt to the review of courts. Bähr proclaims instead: 'The law can only gain real significance and power where a court judgment backs its realisation',[53] and advocates for a unified judiciary that would be able to hear disputes in the field of public law.[54] Against this view, Prussian scholar Rudolf von Gneist is perhaps the strongest proponent of special administrative courts to carry out administrative review.[55] His main argument in favour of an independent administrative judiciary (and not submitting administrative review to the ordinary courts) can be traced back to what he considers the primary aim of such review: whereas Bähr holds that the main objective of administrative review is to secure the rights of individuals, Gneist views administrative review as a tool to guarantee the objective legal order that is administrative law.[56] Both coincide, however, in considering judicial review of administrative action as an indispensable component of the *Rechtsstaat*. In practice, Gneist's vision of independent administrative courts became a reality: the first German state to introduce administrative courts was Baden in 1863, followed by Prussia (under the influence of Gneist) in 1872/75, Hesse in 1874, Württemberg in 1876 and Bavaria in 1878.[57]

The question of administrative review and the establishment of administrative courts is closely linked to the broader development of administrative law as a distinct branch of public law and jurisprudence. In 1871, the year of German unification under Bismarck, no independent administrative law scholarship existed.[58] The first half of the nineteenth century had been important in linking administrative activity to the notion of the *Rechtsstaat*: as discussed in the previous section, Mohl's treatise is amongst the first comprehensive treatises of what would come to be called 'administrative law' throughout the second half of the nineteenth century, and he explicitly links administrative practice to the notion of the *Rechtsstaat*. But it would only be in the late nineteenth century that a fully formed scholarly treatment of administrative law had consolidated

[52] Sobota (n 9) 338.

[53] Bähr (n 49) 12.

[54] Bähr (n 49) 71–72. While Bähr considers the option of having separate administrative and civil courts in lower instances, he is adamant that at the Appeals level, there should be no division, lest the judiciary might be divided on certain issues, see p 71.

[55] R Gneist, *Der Rechtsstaat und die Verwaltungsgerichte in Deutschland* (Springer, 1879) 270–274.

[56] See AK Mangold, 'The Persistence of National Peculiarities' (2014) 21 *Indiana Journal of Global Legal Studies* 223, 228–229; Gneist (n 55) 270: 'administrative law is an objective legal order that shall be preserved independently of individual interests for the sake of public law and good'.

[57] KP Sommermann, *Die Deutsche Verwaltungsgerichtsbarkeit*, 3rd edn, (Deutsches Forschungsinstitut für öffentliche Verwaltung, 1994) 1.

[58] Badura (n 48) 11.

against the backdrop of the already mentioned positivist turn of public law jurisprudence. While the practice of administrative law had become increasingly important throughout the entire nineteenth century, a body of general administrative law only developed slowly. Treatises of general administrative law became increasingly popular after the subject of 'administrative law' had been introduced in Prussian universities in 1881, with various textbooks emerging over the following decade.[59] Amongst these textbooks, 'German Administrative Law', written by Strasbourg professor Otto Mayer, who is often dubbed the 'Father of Administrative Law' in Germany, occupies a central place. His treatise on administrative law is widely regarded as having perfected the positivist method of doctrinally penetrating administrative practice that had accumulated over almost a century.[60]

For Mayer, the administration needs to be understood as all 'state activity that is carried out to realise state objectives under its legal order'.[61] This definition already contains a close relationship to the *Rechtsstaat* understood as the state that acts through its laws, and binds the administration through law. Mayer then explicitly connects the idea that the administration is bound by law to the notion of the *Rechtsstaat*: the *Rechtsstaat*, he claims in the first edition of his treatise, provides that where the administration faces the citizen, it cannot exercise its power vis-à-vis the citizen as it pleases, but is limited by the legal order.[62] If the state wants to act vis-à-vis the citizen, it needs to do so through the legal form, namely through an administrative act.[63] Mayer asserts:

> The state that does not have neither law nor the administrative act for its administration is no *Rechtsstaat*. The state that has developed both is a more or less perfect *Rechtsstaat* depending on how much it makes use of these forms and how it secures their effective application.[64]

In Mayer's conceptualisation, the administration is a manifestation of state power, and as such it can only face the citizen *through* law.[65] Administrative law then has as its aim to bring order to the power that is the administration. In the third and last edition of his textbook, Mayer uses an oft-cited quip to summarise this idea: 'The *Rechtsstaat* is the state of *well-ordered* administrative law.'[66]

In summary, the idea of the formal *Rechtsstaat* prevalent throughout the second half of the nineteenth century rests on the central importance of law: it is through law that state action is rendered predictable for the citizen – but

[59] Stolleis (n 24) 80.

[60] Badura (n 48) 53, observes that the novelty of Mayer's treatise was not the method as such but rather the fact that he had perfected its application.

[61] O Mayer, *Deutsches Verwaltungsrecht, Band I* (Duncker & Humblot, 1895) 13.

[62] Mayer (n 61) 62–66.

[63] ibid.

[64] Mayer (n 61) 66.

[65] Badura (n 48) 24, 54.

[66] O Mayer, *Deutsches Verwaltungsrecht*, 3rd edn (Duncker & Humblot, 1924) 58, emphasis added.

understood as formal law, not as the Kantian *Recht* (right). This is, as Christoph Möllers has observed, a 'strange adoption of the Kantian concept [of *Recht*]',[67] because it is completely devoid of any substantive dimension, reduced to pure form.

C. From the Formal to the Substantive *Rechtsstaat*

i. Rechtsstaat *During the Weimar Republic*

Otto Mayer asserted that '[t]he *Rechtsstaat* is the state of well-ordered administrative law' in 1923, after the German Empire had lost World War I and the Weimar Republic had been proclaimed. For Mayer, not much had changed concerning administrative law, and with it, his understanding of the *Rechtsstaat*: 'Nothing much new had to be added', he writes in his preface to his textbook on administrative law, and: 'constitutional law passes, administrative law persists'.[68]

This is a surprising statement given the radical changes that the Weimar Republic brought with it, even if the term '*Rechtsstaat*' does not appear in the text of the Weimar Constitution of 1919. The Weimar Constitution was Germany's first democratic constitution and the first constitution to contain a bill of fundamental rights in Germany, following the example of the failed 1849 Frankfurt Constitution, but going beyond the Frankfurt Constitution in including a clear social dimension which led to important contributions to the social state.[69] The Weimar Republic was also a crucial era for German public law scholarship and was the site of the so-called 'methods dispute' between legal positivists who had primarily been trained under the Empire, and a new generation of scholars who were inspired by methods from neighbouring disciplines.[70]

Throughout the methods dispute, the concept of the *Rechtsstaat* played no explicit role and to the extent that scholars continued to use the term in a formalistic way as developed in the nineteenth century, the Weimar Republic does indeed not add much to the theoretical or doctrinal discussion of the *Rechtsstaat*.[71] Yet, the Weimar Constitution is important in the evolution of the *Rechtsstaat* to a substantive conception that is prevalent today. Specifically, the Weimar Constitution is associated with having introduced the idea of the

[67] C Möllers, *The Three Branches: A Comparative Model of Separation of Powers* (Oxford University Press, 2013) 34.

[68] Mayer (n 66) preface to the third edition (in German, the quib rhymes: 'Verfassungsrecht vergeht, Verwaltungsrecht besteht.').

[69] M Stolleis, 'Die soziale Programmatik der Weimarer Reichsverfassung' in H Dreier and C Waldhoff (eds), *Das Wagnis der Demokratie* (CH Beck, 2018) 195.

[70] For a brief overview see Stolleis (n 24) 90–105; for a translation into English of the main texts that shaped the debate, see AJ Jacobson and B Schlink (eds), *Weimar: A Jurisprudence of Crisis* (University of California Press, 2002).

[71] For this assessment Sobota (n 9) 11 ('for the Weimar constitutional law scholarship, the *Rechtsstaat* was not an issue').

social state, which acknowledged that to enjoy individual rights, certain living and economic conditions are important.[72] Similarly, the hard-fought battles on method in public law had implications for the functioning of the rule of law institutions in Weimar and beyond.[73]

Where it was explicitly addressed in scholarship during the Weimar Republic, the concept of the *Rechtsstaat* was often considered a relic of the nineteenth century. Several scholars acknowledged its centrality to the evolution of the liberal constitutional state but then used it primarily according to their widely diverging theories of law and the state. One example is Hans Kelsen. For Kelsen's Pure Theory of Law, there is no point in attempting to legitimise the state as *Rechtsstaat*, because the state is constituted through law and, in that sense, every state is a *Rechts-Staat*. The term is then simply superfluous.[74] Kelsen acknowledges that the term *Rechtsstaat* is often understood to signify a particular type of state, namely a state that provides for specific institutions such as the guarantee of liberty rights or democracy – in short, the nineteenth-century constitutional state – but dismisses this use of the term for his theory of law as a 'natural law prejudice'.[75]

Kelsen's main antagonist, Carl Schmitt, similarly designates the term *Rechtsstaat* to signify the liberal bourgeois state of the nineteenth century:

> The principles of the modern, bourgeois-Rechtsstaat constitution correspond to the constitutional ideal of bourgeois individualism, so much, indeed, that these principles are often equated with the constitution as such and 'constitutional state' is given the same meaning as the 'bourgeois *Rechtsstaat*'.[76]

On the one hand, Schmitt acknowledges the peculiarity and strength of the *Rechtsstaat* as it had developed throughout the nineteenth century ('The state … is subordinated to a closed system of legal norms, or it is simply identified with this system of norms, so that it is nothing but norm or procedure'). On the other hand, he ultimately asserts that the state cannot be only a *Rechtsstaat* because it is also, and primarily, 'a *state*, so it still contains another distinctly *political* component besides the bourgeois Rechtsstaat one'.[77] Both scholars thus view the term as a concept intimately linked to a liberal-bourgeois idea of the state and advocate for a lesser role of it – in the case of Kelsen, because every state is a *Rechtsstaat* and therefore the term is a pleonasm and theoretically useless; in

[72] For such a reading of the importance of the Weimar Republic in the development of the *Rechtsstaat*, see B Pieroth, 'Historische Etappen des Rechtsstaats in Deutschland' (2011) 33 *Juristische Ausbildung* 733; Bäcker (n 8) 2.

[73] Huber (n 1) 387, even though he, like Sobota, asserts that 'there was no fundamental change in the concept of the rule of law [as a consequence of the Weimar method dispute]'.

[74] H Kelsen, *Reine Rechtslehre. Einleitung in Die Rechtswissenschaftliche Problematik* (Mohr Siebeck, reissue 2008, orig 1934) 127.

[75] Kelsen (n 74) 127.

[76] C Schmitt, *Constitutional Theory*, J Seitzer (transl and ed) (Duke University Press, 2008) 169.

[77] ibid (emphasis in the original.).

the case of Schmitt, because the *Rechtsstaat* in its bourgeois liberal tradition is insufficient to describe the essence of the state, which lies in the political.

While the term *Rechtsstaat* and the debate over it might have lost popularity throughout the Weimar Republic, the Weimar Constitution was indebted to earlier ideas of the *Rechtsstaat*. The principle of the legality of administration, as Mayer's quote shows, was an important structuring principle as much under the Weimar Constitution as it had been under the German Empire.[78] In addition, the issue of judicial review was a very contentious issue throughout the Weimar Republic. Articles 102 to 108 of the Weimar Constitution were dedicated to the administration of justice and the judiciary and called for the establishment of a State Court (*Staatsgerichtshof*). This State Court, a non-permanent court with competence to adjudicate certain constitutional questions, was, however, not competent for constitutional review of laws,[79] and the Weimar Constitution was silent on the issue. Given this silence, several federal high courts and the Imperial Court of Justice (*Reichsgericht*) asserted their competence to review the constitutionality of laws. The Imperial Court of Justice found in a controversial judgment that the Weimar Constitution's provision that 'judges are only bound by the law' (Article 102) did not preclude judges from considering higher-ranking provisions, especially the Constitution. It then found that because the Constitution was silent on the matter and did not provide for a special jurisdiction for constitutional review, such review needed to be accorded to the courts, with a 'right and a duty of the judge to review the constitutionality of federal laws'.[80] This meant that laws could be reviewed against the substantive guarantees of the Weimar Constitution in the fields of fundamental rights and the social state. Thus, the Weimar Constitution paved the way for a more substantive understanding of the *Rechtsstaat* which comprised these contents.[81] Yet, the term itself was not necessarily tied to such substantive guarantees.

ii. The Rechtsstaat *and the Third Reich*

The standard narrative in German constitutional law today holds that the *Nazi* regime made absolutely no contribution to the concept of the *Rechtsstaat*, but rather perverted the very idea.[82] The Kantian dimension of the word *Rechtsstaat* as encompassing a concept of law as right, a concept of law that cannot be reduced to its mere formal container, is perhaps best seen in its opposite, the *Unrechtsstaat (Un-Rechts-Staat)*, which translates to 'unjust state' or, more

[78] B Grzeszick, 'VII. Rechtsstaat' in G Dürig, R Herzog and R Scholz (orig eds), *Grundgesetz-Kommentar*, 99th EL (CH Beck, 2022) para 14.

[79] See the Law on the State Court (*Gesetz über den Staatsgerichtshof vom 9. Juli 1921*, Reichsgesetzblatt Nr 74 (194)).

[80] *Reichsgericht*, judgment of 4 November 1925, V 621/24, RGZ 111, 320, 323.

[81] Bäcker (n 8) 2.

[82] Huber (n 1) 388, para 11.

literally, to 'non-right-state' (see also chapter three). *Unrechtsstaat* is a common designation for the Nazi regime in contemporary German constitutional jurisprudence and more generally in public discourse. The term highlights its absolute opposition to prior ideas of the *Rechtsstaat*,[83] and indeed, the substantive concept of the *Rechtsstaat* under the Basic Law was primarily forged in contradistinction to the Third Reich. It is also plausible to argue that the problem of the *Rechtsstaat* under the Weimar Constitution was not that it had no substantive content, but rather that the substantive contents enshrined in the Weimar Constitution were not linked closely enough to the formal guarantees of the *Rechtsstaat*.[84]

Yet, it appears too easy to simply dismiss the Third Reich as an interruption of an otherwise linear and unequivocally positive development of the *Rechtsstaat* concept. While some writers, perhaps most prominently and clairvoyantly Hermann Heller, viewed fascism and the emerging Nazi regime as the opposite of the *Rechtsstaat*,[85] Carl Schmitt suggested in 1934 that a national socialist understanding of the *Rechtsstaat* was entirely possible.[86] To be sure, in this essay, Schmitt argues against the traditional understanding of the *Rechtsstaat* as a liberal idea that in his view, led to a formalistic understanding, a *Law-State* (*Gesetzesstaat*) and did not sufficiently consider arguments of justice, which he saw secured only in the new National-Socialist State.[87] But even if he later rejected the term *Rechtsstaat*, Schmitt re-defined and thus ultimately defended the term *Rechtsstaat* at the outset of the Third Reich with a new meaning, all while institutions of the previous *Rechtsstaat* collapsed. The national-socialist understanding of the *Rechtsstaat* was characterised by a decidedly non-positivist outlook and focused on notions of justice as understood by the national-socialist regime.[88] The national-socialist understanding of the *Rechtsstaat* that Schmitt proposes clearly juxtaposes what he calls the 'formal legislative state' to 'justice and law that is good on the merits'.[89] This implies a collapse of the executive and the legislative powers and a subordination of traditional principles of separation of powers and proportionality to the 'will of the *Führer*'.

[83] See, eg, Grzeszick (n 78) para 15. The term was first coined by Gustav Radbruch in his seminal article on 'Statutory Injustice and Suprastatutory Law'. See G Radbruch, 'Gesetzliches Unrecht und übergesetzliches Recht' (1946) 1 *Süddeutsche Juristenzeitung* 105, 107.

[84] Schmidt-Aßmann (n 4) 551, para 15.

[85] H Heller, *Rechtsstaat oder Diktatur?* (Mohr Siebeck, 1930). Heller advocated not only against the fascist state, but also against the liberal *Rechtsstaat*, as he considered the liberal *Rechtsstaat* not taking sufficiently into account social inequalities. Instead, he proposed a *social Rechtsstaat*, a concept that would be codified in the Basic Law, but without much traction in constitutional jurisprudence, as we shall see below (section II.C).

[86] C Schmitt, 'Nationalsozialismus und Rechtsstaat' (1934) in C Schmitt, *Gesammelte Schriften 1933–1936: Mit Ergänzenden Beiträgen aus der Zeit des Zweiten Weltkriegs* (Duncker und Humblot, 2021) 131.

[87] ibid.

[88] See Bäcker (n 8) 3.

[89] Schmitt (n 86) 146.

Perhaps the most important change to the Weimar constitutional order was eliminating the separation of the legislative and the executive powers, based on an emergency decree and the Enabling Act of 1933, which Schmitt explicitly welcomed as an achievement of the new national socialist leadership.[90] Ernst Fraenkel's seminal work on the dual state captures these developments by making a distinction between what he calls the 'prerogative state' and the 'normative state'. In Fraenkel's understanding, the 'prerogative state' is characterised by the exercise of unchecked arbitrariness, the selective application of the law, and a collapse of various institutions of the *Rechtsstaat*, including the principle of proportionality, the principle of the separation of powers, and the possibility of judicial review, for example of acts by the Nazi special police (the *Gestapo*).[91] In other words, the prerogative state is what Schmitt hails as a turn to 'justice and law that is good on the merits'.[92] Yet, as Fraenkel astutely observes, a 'normative state' characterised by a legal order 'as expressed in statutes, decisions of the courts, and activities of the administrative agencies' continues to exist in parallel, with courts as important guardians. This normative state does, however, not apply equally to all people; it is limited to 'constructive force'. While there might be a presumption of jurisdiction for the normative state, the prerogative state always has the possibility of attracting jurisdiction by declaring a matter as political. As Fraenkel puts it: 'The jurisdiction over jurisdiction rests with the Prerogative State', and: 'One reservation always lurks in the background of the Normative State: considerations of political expediency.'[93] This means that certain legal institutions continued to exist during the Third Reich, at least in its earlier years and until World War II, albeit always under the threat of being abolished or superseded by the prerogative state.

Given the possibility of adopting laws at will, there was little coherence and ever-increasing arbitrariness in Nazi legislation, which was considered to be legitimated through the will of the *Führer*.[94] This development has been described by Fraenkel's former co-attorney, Franz Neumann, in his seminal book *Behemoth*.[95] Unlike Fraenkel's normative state, *Behemoth* argues that law played no role whatsoever, and that ultimately, the Nazi regime was best characterised as unbridled terror. This interpretation has been criticised recently as not giving enough credit to remaining elements of the Weimar *Rechtsstaat*.[96] Another interpretation of the relationship between the *Dual State* and *Behemoth* is that both works assess different periods of Nazi rule: whereas the *Dual State* focuses

[90] Schmitt (n 86) 139–143; see also Bäcker (n 8) 3.

[91] E Fraenkel, *The Dual State: A Contribution to the Theory of Dictatorship*, E Shils, E Lowenstein, KE Knorr and J Meierhenrich (transl) (Oxford University Press, 2017) part I, ch I.

[92] Schmitt (n 86) 146.

[93] Fraenkel (n 91) 57, 65.

[94] Stolleis (n 24) 117–120.

[95] FL Neumann, *Behemoth: The Structure and Practice of National Socialism, 1933–1944* (Ivan R. Dee, reissue 2009, org 1942).

[96] J Meierhenrich, *The Remnants of the Rechtsstaat* (Oxford University Press, 2018) ch 2.

on the early years of the Nazi regime, from 1933 until roughly Fraenkel's emigration in 1938, *Behemoth* primarily addresses the immediate pre-war and wartime regime.[97] Yet, all of this shows that the notion of a *Rechtsstaat*, even if emptied of its previous content, was still present throughout at least the early years of the Nazi regime and was used even by its most notorious legal practitioners, including radical Nazi judge Roland Freisler.[98]

iii. The Post-War Notion of Rechtsstaat*: Towards a Substantive Conception*

While it is thus untrue that the *Rechtsstaat* played no role during the Third Reich and reckoning with the role of lawyers and law during the Third Reich is far from concluded in contemporary Germany, it is also clear – and Fraenkel's concept of the prerogative state illustrates just that – that the Third Reich was marked by a high degree of arbitrariness and terror, which are generally seen as antipodes to any rule of law conception. It is therefore not surprising that discussions surrounding the Basic Law (*Grundgesetz*), the constitutional text adopted in the western part of Germany after the end of World War II, were marked by calls for a 'return' to the traditional elements of the *Rechtsstaat*: independence of justice, no extraordinary courts, no double punishment, protection from arbitrary deprivation of liberty.[99] The rule of law thus played an important role during the drafting of the Basic Law and animated both Articles 20 and 28 that enshrine the current *Rechtsstaatsprinzip* (see section II below), as well as Articles 92 et seq which address the judiciary and establish the Federal Constitutional Court as well as other supreme federal courts.[100] The Basic Law as a whole and the focus on the *Rechtsstaat* as not only a law-based state but also a constitutional state is a clear normative reaction to the atrocities of the Third Reich. In 1946, two years before the drafting of the Basic Law began, Gustav Radbruch argued influentially that any conflict between positive law and material justice needed to be solved in favour of positive law, 'unless the contradiction between the positive law and material justice is unbearable to the point that the positive law, as "false law", needs to give way to justice'.[101] In part influenced by notions of natural law, such as advocated by Radbruch, the concept of the *Rechtsstaat* in the Basic Law has a distinct substantive dimension and is intended to protect material justice. Carsten Bäcker has described this development as a shift from *Rechtsstaat* to *Gerechtigkeitsstaat*, which roughly translates to a shift from a law-based state

[97] A von Brünneck, 'Vorwort des Herausgebers zur 2. Auflage' in E Fraenkel (ed), *Der Doppelstaat*, 5th edn (Europäische Verlagsanstalt, 2019).

[98] Meierhenrich (n 96) ch 5.

[99] Stolleis (n 24) 144.

[100] Schmidt-Aßmann (n 4) 551, para 16.

[101] Radbruch (n 83) 107 (authors' translation; the expression 'false law', which seems to be a common translation, is 'unrichtiges Recht' in German, which might also be translated as 'unright law' if one wanted to make the connection to a Kantian notion of law as right). See ch 3 on the application of this formula in the controversial 'border guard trials' after German reunification.

to a 'state of justice'.[102] He questions, however, whether this is the right lesson, as this conception risks displacing existing laws, and therefore the value of legal certainty, by overriding justice considerations.[103] The matter is further complicated by the fact that the *Rechtsstaat* is not a standalone principle, but interacts with other fundamental principles of the Basic Law, importantly with the principle of democracy, of the social state, and with fundamental rights and human dignity. We will address these tensions in the next section when discussing core elements of the *Rechtsstaat* and how the *Rechtsstaat* relates to other fundamental principles of the Basic Law.

II. THE *RECHTSSTAAT* DOCTRINE IN GERMAN CONSTITUTIONAL LAW

In contemporary German constitutional jurisprudence, the *Rechtsstaatsprinzip* is a structuring principle that is part of Germany's constitutional identity as well as an umbrella term for several specific constitutional guarantees. In its first major decision in 1951, the German Constitutional Court affirmed: 'The fundamental principles of the Basic Law include the principle of democracy, the principle of the federal state, and the principle of the rule of law.'[104] It also specified some important tenets of the rule of law principle, including the principles of legality and of constitutional primacy. This section addresses first the nature of the rule of law as a structuring principle of the Basic Law (A). In a second step, we identify core elements of the German *Rechtsstaat* widely accepted in constitutional jurisprudence (B). Lastly, we discuss substantive dimensions of the *Rechtsstaat* and how the *Rechtsstaat* relates to other core principles of the Basic Law, in particular to democracy and fundamental rights (C). Throughout all sections, it will become clear that the history of the *Rechtsstaat*, which emphasises the central role of statutory, formal law, has left a clear imprint on the conceptualisation of the *Rechtsstaat* in contemporary jurisprudence.

A. *Rechtsstaat* as a Guiding Principle of the Basic Law

In Anglo-American scholarship, the rule of law has famously been characterised as an 'essentially contested concept'.[105] Similarly, in Germany, the *Rechtsstaat* is often described as a dazzling concept[106] and, famously, as a 'gateway concept: formulated in a manner that is vague and that does not fully

[102] Bäcker (n 8) 4.
[103] ibid.
[104] 'Das rechtsstaatliche Prinzip', see FCC, decision of 23 October 1951, 2 BvG 1/51.
[105] J Waldron, 'Is the Rule of Law an Essentially Contested Concept (in Florida)?' (2002) 21 *Law and Philosophy* 137.
[106] Eg, T Holterhus, *Der Rechtsstaat* (Bundeszentrale für Politische Bildung, 2022) 4, ('Schillernder Begriff').

lend itself to interpretation based on wording, and incapable of being conclusively defined in "objective" and intrinsic terms; instead, such terms are open to the influx of evolving notions of constitutional theory and theory of state'.[107] As we have seen before, the Weimar Constitution of 1919 did not contain any explicit reference to the *Rechtsstaat*. This changed with the Basic Law of 1949 – even though explicit references to the term *Rechtsstaat* are scant. The *Rechtsstaatsprinzip* is typically found to be rooted in Article 20(3) of the Basic Law, but this article does not explicitly mention the term. Article 20(3) contains elements of the *Rechtsstaat*, namely the principle of legality of the administration, a long-time core element of the German *Rechtsstaat*, as well as the principle of constitutionality.[108] To the extent that the *Rechtsstaat* is protected by Article 20, it is unamendable according to the Basic Law's 'eternity clause' in Article 79(3).[109]

The *Rechtsstaat* is explicitly mentioned in Article 28 of the Basic Law, which contains structuring principles for the German federated states (*Länder*) and ought to be read as a parallel provision to Article 20.[110] Article 28(1) provides: 'The constitutional order in the *Länder* must conform to the principles of a republican, democratic and social *state governed by the rule of law* within the meaning of this Basic Law.'[111] Lastly, Article 23(1) of the Basic Law on European integration explicitly commits the German state to contribute to a 'European Union that is committed to democratic, social and federal principles, to the rule of law and to the principle of subsidiarity and that guarantees a level of protection of basic rights essentially comparable to that afforded by this Basic Law'.[112] Except for the principle of subsidiarity, which is a principle that was

[107] Böckenförde (n 7) 53–54; cited by FCC Judge König in her Separate Opinion to FCC, order of 15 December 2015, 2 BvL 1/12, paras 1–26.

[108] Art 20 [Constitutional principles – Right of resistance]

(1) The Federal Republic of Germany is a democratic and social federal state.
(2) All state authority is derived from the people. It shall be exercised by the people through elections and other votes and through specific legislative, executive and judicial bodies.
(3) The legislature shall be bound by the constitutional order, the executive and the judiciary by law and justice.

[109] Art 79 [Amendment of the Basic Law]

(3) Amendments to this Basic Law affecting the division of the Federation into Länder, their participation in principle in the legislative process, or the principles laid down in Articles 1 and 20 shall be inadmissible.

[110] Art 28 [Land constitutions – Autonomy of municipalities]

(1) The constitutional order in the Länder must conform to the principles of a republican, democratic and social state governed by the rule of law within the meaning of this Basic Law.

[111] Art 28 Basic Law; emphasis added.

[112] Note that Art 23 was introduced with the Treaty of Maastricht. Until 1990, Art 23 contained a provision on reunification, stating that the Basic Law was applicable in the *Länder* of the German Federal Republic. After reunification, the provision was abolished and then reinstated in 1992 as

first developed in EU law, the other principles are all principles that are covered by the Basic Law's eternity clause: democracy, social and federal principles, the rule of law, and fundamental rights guarantees.

In part because of the scant explicit references in the constitutional text, in part because of the long trajectory of the notion of *Rechtsstaat*, German constitutional doctrine has long struggled with characterising its legal nature. There is considerable disagreement about the precise contours and the doctrinal import of the *Rechtsstaatsprinzip*. As early as 1954, Wolfgang Abendroth claimed that the 'unamendable constitutional principle of the democratic and social rule of law is a structural principle of the constitutional order … but not a positive legal norm'.[113] It is difficult to pin down the principle of the *Rechtsstaat* from a doctrinal point of view and there is agreement that there is no unequivocal definition of what precisely the *Rechtsstaat* entails. Rather, it has been described as consisting of 'different structural layers'.[114]

Philip Kunig is perhaps the most prominent voice to have argued that the rule of law has no separate doctrinal function in constitutional jurisprudence and that there is no separate 'legal norm' of the *Rechtsstaat* that would exist independently of its component parts. Instead, he suggests a terminological shift from a doctrinal principle of the rule of law (*Rechtsstaatsprinzip*, which translates to 'rule of law principle') to the rule of law as a concept that animates political thought (*Rechtsstaatlichkeit*, which loosely translates to 'rule of law-ness') and is an underlying idea (as opposed to a legal principle) of the German Basic Law insofar as it serves as an umbrella term that bridges the tension between material justice and legal certainty.[115] Katharina Sobota, in turn, has emphasised the doctrinal valence of the *Rechtsstaat* and proposed no fewer than 17 norms that she considers fundamental to the rule of law principle as it is codified in the German Basic Law, including restraining and enabling elements as well as the proportionality principle.[116] These two extremes illustrate the contested nature of the rule of law in German constitutional doctrine.

The Federal Constitutional Court (FCC) had no issue citing both of the abovementioned works to characterise the *Rechtsstaatsprinzip* as a 'general principl[e] and guiding concep[t]' of the Basic Law.[117] The Court views the *Rechtsstaatsprinzip* as one of those principles that provide inner cohesion to the Basic Law even if it does not consist of one single positive legal constitutional

the main article of the Basic Law relating to European integration, see *Gesetz zur Änderung des Grundgesetzes vom 21. Dezember 1992*, BGBll I 1992 58 2086–2087.

[113] W Abendroth, 'Zum Begriff des demokratischen und sozialen Rechtsstaates im Grundgesetz der Bundesrepublik Deutschland' in M Buckmiller, J Perels and U Schöler (eds), *Wolfgang Abendroth, Gesammelte Schriften – Band 2: 1949–1955* (Offizin Verlag Hannover, 2008) 338.

[114] Schmidt-Aßmann (n 4) 542.

[115] P Kunig, *Das Rechtsstaatsprinzip: Überlegungen Zu Seiner Bedeutung Für Das Verfassungsrecht Der Bundesrepublik Deutschland* (Mohr Siebeck, 1986) 481 et seq.

[116] Sobota (n 9) 517–18.

[117] FCC, decision of 15 December 2015, 2 BvL 1/12, para 78 – English translation provided by the FCC at www.bverfg.de/e/ls20151215_2bvl000112en.html.

norm. Rather, the *Rechtsstaatsprinzip* is derived from the abovementioned Article 20(3) of the Basic Law, read in conjunction with Article 1(3) on the direct applicability of the basic rights to all three powers, Article 19(4) which secures a person's right to access to justice in case of a violation of rights by public authority, the abovementioned Article 28(1) on the *Länder*, and the 'overall design' (*Gesamtkonzeption*) of the Basic Law. The Court found this as early as 1953, where it held that the *Rechtsstaat* was both a guiding principle of the Basic Law and a norm on the basis of which the Court could invalidate statutory laws.[118] It is settled case law of the Court to trace the core of the *Rechtsstaat* to Article 20(3) of the Basic Law, and to characterise it as a broad and indeterminate principle that 'does not contain legal obligations or prohibitions that are clearly defined in every detail',[119] but that it can at the same time be at the basis of invalidating of a legal or administrative act.

Eberhard Schmidt-Aßmann has suggested that there are thus two dimensions of the *Rechtsstaat*. Insofar as it comprises guarantees that are specified elsewhere in the Basic Law and that are considered an integral part of the rule of law principle, the term has a declaratory function serving as a catch-all phrase. In addition, it has a constitutive function where it is used as an expression of a general and systematic principle that informs the Basic Law as a whole. Schmidt-Aßmann also points out that most often, the term is used in order to link these two dimensions.[120]

The German *Rechtsstaatsprinzip* is based on three fundaments: it posits the constitutional state and human dignity, and that law as a form has specific abilities to order social relations.[121] Based on these assumptions, the *Rechtsstaat* comprises several core elements that will be explored in more depth in the following section. While there is a continuous debate as to which elements precisely are comprised by the rule of law in German constitutional doctrine, it is largely consented that the formal law-based state comprises the principle of legality and primacy of the law (*Vorbehalt und Vorrang des Gesetzes*) including the state's obligation to respect fundamental rights; the proportionality principle; and due process obligations including a general obligation to grant judicial review. We will outline the content of these core elements in the following section.

B. Core Elements of the *Rechtsstaat*

In this section, we focus on a range of core elements that are typically associated with the rule of law principle in German constitutional jurisprudence

[118] FCC, decision of 1 July 1953, 1 BvL 23/51.

[119] FCC, decision of 24 July 1957, 1 BvL 23/52; see also FCC, decision of 22 November 1983, 2 BvL 25/81; decision of 17 June 2004, 2 BvR 383/03.

[120] Schmidt-Aßmann (n 4) 546, para 9; see also Grzeszick (n 78) para 45, for a similar view.

[121] Schmidt-Aßmann (n 4) 554, para 21.

and scholarship. Contemporary constitutional scholars generally assert that the *Rechtsstaat* comprises a formal and material, or substantive, dimension, even if this distinction has recently been criticised as confused, because there is little justification as to why certain substantive values ought to pertain to the rule of law whereas others do not.[122] There is some debate about whether the material dimension of the *Rechtsstaat* refers to specific content of the Basic Law, especially to the fundamental rights guarantees, or whether it relates to the source of law and the fact that the Basic Law provides for the *Rechtsstaat* as a fundamental principle and binds not only all branches of the state, but even the constitutional legislator.[123] In this latter sense, the material *Rechtsstaat* is understood to comprise specific institutions guaranteed by the Basic Law, such as the separation of powers or the principle of proportionality, whereas the former understanding is equivalent to a substantive, or thick, notion of the rule of law.[124]

In this section, we briefly outline those component parts of the *Rechtsstaat* that are related to procedure and institutional guarantees (typically considered the 'formal' dimensions of the *Rechtsstaat*): the principle of legality including primacy of the law and the Constitution; properties of the law and provisions related to legal certainty; procedural guarantees; and the principle of proportionality. We close by briefly addressing how the component parts of the *Rechtsstaat* can be invoked in proceedings before the FCC. To the extent that the *Rechtsstaat* is considered to contain specific substantive guarantees or a general notion of substantive justice, these are addressed in section C, which also looks at how the *Rechtsstaat* relates to other fundamental constitutional principles, in particular to fundamental rights, the separation of powers, democracy and the social state.

i. The Principle of Legality: Primacy of the Law and Public Acts Grounded in Law

German constitutional doctrine traditionally distinguishes two dimensions of the principle of legality: the primacy of the law (*Vorrang des Gesetzes*) and the general requirement that any exercise of public authority must have a formal basis in statutory law (*Vorbehalt des Gesetzes*). While these elements are typically considered to form part of the 'formal' *Rechtsstaat*, they are closely related to the notion of law as right, rooted in German idealism, and are thus not to be understood as purely formalistic.[125]

[122] C Möllers, 'Rechtsstaat' in U Kischel and H Kube (eds), *Handbuch des Staatsrechts. Neuausgabe Band II* (CF Müller, forthcoming) 517, 536.

[123] Grzeszick (n 78) paras 37 et seq.

[124] On the distinction between formal and substantive understandings, see PP Craig, 'Formal and Substantive Conceptions of the Rule of Law: An Analytical Framework' (1997) *Public Law* 467. On situating different rule of law conceptions on a spectrum from thin to thick, see BZ Tamanaha, *On the Rule of Law. History, Politics, Theory* (Cambridge University Press, 2004) 91.

[125] Schmidt-Aßmann (n 4) 552, para 18.

The principle of primacy of the law comprises both statutory law and the Constitution. We have seen that throughout Germany's constitutional history, the principle of constitutional primacy, and relatedly, of constitutional review, was contentious. Under the Basic Law, there is now an explicit constitutional basis: the primacy of the Constitution is rooted in Articles 1(3) and 20(3) of the Basic Law. Article 20(3) of the Basic Law explicitly states that 'the legislature shall be bound by the constitutional order'. This provision thus establishes the primacy of the constitutional order; it extends to all norms of the Basic Law and binds both state and federal legislatures. The primacy of the Constitution for the legislative power means that legislative acts violating a constitutional norm are generally null and void.[126] However, the Constitutional Court has found that simple procedural errors only lead to invalidation if the error is evident.[127] This is due to the principle of legal certainty, which we discuss in the next section.

The term 'law' (*Gesetz*) in Article 20(3) refers to all statutory law that is adopted in accordance with the procedures of the Basic Law and also comprises the Constitution. Generally, it provides that all parts of the state are bound by the provisions of statutory law. This means that all administrative and legal acts need to conform with all higher-ranking provisions, including the Constitution. Article 20(3) thus establishes a principle of primacy of the law that includes constitutional primacy for all three branches.[128] In addition, Article 1(3) of the Basic Law provides that the 'basic rights [codified in the German Basic Law] shall bind the legislature, the executive and the judiciary as directly applicable law'.

If an act does not conform with higher-ranking provisions, it is generally considered null and void.[129] However, an exception applies again to procedural errors. German administrative procedure, for example in the field of construction and planning law, provides that under certain circumstances, the principle of legal certainty and trust in public acts (legitimate expectations) supersedes a strict application of formal legality, such that certain procedural errors do not result in the nullification of administrative acts unless they are invoked within a specific time frame.[130] This has been criticised by the Court of Justice of the European Union (CJEU) as a far-reaching exception to the principle of legality,[131] showing that the specific content of the *Rechtsstaat* today is also the result of constitutional struggles between the domestic and the European level.[132]

[126] HD Jarass and B Pieroth, *Grundgesetz für die Bundesrepublik Deutschland: Kommentar*, 17th edn (CH Beck, 2022) Art 20, para 46.

[127] See, eg, FCC, decision of 15 January 2008, 2 BvL 12/01, para 71.

[128] Jarass and Pieroth (n 126) para 53.

[129] ibid 54.

[130] Huber (n 1) 391, para 20.

[131] See, eg, CJEU, *Altrip*, decision of 7 November 2013, C-72/12, ECLI:EU:C:2013:712; *Alcan II*, decision of 20 March 1996, C-24/95, ECLI:EU:C:1997:163.

[132] For further discussion of this tension see ch 5.

There is some debate as to what the Basic Law means when it states that the executive and the judiciary are bound by 'law and justice'. The translation adds to the confusion, as the German text speaks of statutory law (*Gesetz*) and right (*Recht*). While some people consider the phrasing 'bound to statutory law *and* right' to be a mere tautology, others argue that the formulation suggests a dimension of material justice beyond the statutory positive law.[133] We address this question below in section C. In summary, though, the principle of the primacy of the law and, relatedly, the legality of administrative action is a dimension of the *Rechtsstaat* that can be traced back to the nineteenth century. This becomes even more obvious when considering the second dimension, the principle that public acts need to be grounded in law (*Vorbehalt des Gesetzes*).

The principle that public acts must have a legal basis in formal statutory law (*Vorbehalt des Gesetzes*) is a constitutional requirement. It is based on the idea that the law does not only have a restraining function, but also a legitimising function, an idea that, as we have seen, has a long tradition in Germany. In fact, the very idea of the constitutional state in the German tradition is linked to its legal basis; the state cannot exist without being grounded in law. These are two sides of the same coin: the state and its actions cannot exist without being grounded in law, but they are also limited by law. This goes back to the Kantian idea of the centrality of law as right.[134] Traditionally, this idea was rooted only in the notion of *Rechtsstaat* and was primarily geared at guaranteeing fundamental liberties – where state action was to limit individual liberty, it needed to be grounded in statutory law. This was the essence of the *Rechtsstaat*. Today, the principle has evolved. State action is no longer limited exclusively to intervention in the sense of intrusion upon a space of liberty but also comprises public services and other types of public acts. For such acts, the requirement of a statutory basis according to the *Vorbehalt des Gesetzes* also applies if they concern essential areas of regulation.

With regard to these essential areas of regulation, the Constitutional Court has developed a doctrine of essentiality or fundamentality (*Wesentlichkeitsgrundsatz*). This doctrine holds that the state has a responsibility to regulate via statutory law all issues that are essential or fundamental to it. An obvious issue of fundamental importance is such state action that infringes upon fundamental rights.[135] But the essentiality doctrine is a more expansive notion that, in the words of the Constitutional Court, extends to all issues 'that are of fundamental importance to the state and society'.[136] The leading case in which the Court

[133] Jarass and Pieroth (n 126) para 52.

[134] See section I.A.

[135] FCC, decision of 24 October 2017, 2 BvF 1, 2/15, para 194. See also FCC, decision of 8 August 1978, 2 BvL 8/77.

[136] ibid. The Court explicitly distinguishes between fundamental rights issues on the one hand and questions that are of fundamental importance to the state and society on the other hand.

developed this principle concerned the right of a specific profession, namely specialised medical doctors, to self-legislate questions relating to their specialist status. Here, the Court found that specialised medical doctors exercised an important function in society and therefore could not self-legislate entirely. At least some fundamental norms relating to how to acquire the status of 'medical specialist' needed to be established through formal, statutory law. The Court derives this from the *Rechtsstaat* in conjunction with fundamental rights and the principle of democracy.[137] We will come back to the relationship between the *Rechtsstaat*, democracy, and fundamental rights in the following section. For our purposes here, the case illustrates the importance that German constitutional jurisprudence attaches to formal law and how this is considered an integral dimension of the *Rechtsstaat*. The Court holds that each area of life needs to be regulated by a legislative organ that can be traced back to the people and asserts that 'the legislature may not leave its noblest task at the free disposal of other entities within or outside the state order'.[138]

ii. Legal Certainty and Trust in the Legal Order

Predictability of a legal order, also known as legal certainty, is a fundamental attribute of the law and has been considered an integral component of the *Rechsstaat* by the FCC early on.[139] In German constitutional doctrine, legal certainty relates first and foremost to formal, legal acts (both statutory law and administrative action). Legal certainty has different dimensions. We briefly highlight the following aspects: the principle of clarity and specificity, the principle of coherence, which is particularly important for the judiciary, and the protection of legitimate expectations, which affects both the legislative and executive power.

Legal certainty provides that laws must be made public, accessible, sufficiently clear, and specific so as to provide predictability for its citizens. It is the legislator's task to formulate laws in a sufficiently clear and precise manner. At the same time, the principle of specificity does not imply that there cannot be any vague terms at all. Rather, the requisite degree of specificity depends on the intensity of the measure in question: the more a legal act infringes upon individual rights, the higher the threshold. This applies to both individual acts as well as to general statutory laws and is considered an integral part of the *Rechtsstaat*. We see here that fundamental rights play an important role in determining the requirements of the principle of specificity. This shows the intimate connection of fundamental rights protection with the contemporary understanding of the *Rechtsstaat*.

Legal certainty further demands that individual legal rules as well as the legal order as such be free of contradictions. The FCC has explicitly stated that

[137] FCC, decision of 9 May 1972, 1 BvR 518/62 und 308/64.
[138] ibid.
[139] FCC, decision of 1 July 1953, 1 BvL 23/51.

it considers this as an integral part of the *Rechtsstaat*.[140] The judiciary and doctrinal jurisprudence play an important role in interpreting legal rules in such a way that there are no contradictions. We can only speak of a violation of the *Rechtsstaatsprinzip* where there is a genuine conflict that cannot be resolved through legal interpretation.[141]

Moreover, legal certainty generally requires for laws not to be applied retroactively. For criminal law, this principle is codified in Article 103(2) of the Basic Law, which provides that '[a]n act may be punished only if it was defined by a law as a criminal offence before the act was committed'.[142] In German constitutional jurisprudence, the principle of non-retroactivity is also shaped by fundamental rights, which entails that the legislator is free to *improve* the legal position of an individual retroactively but is generally prohibited from retroactively disadvantaging an individual legal position.[143] Exceptions are provided for cases where the present law is unclear or contradictory, where the change is minor, where the individual was not justified in trusting the continued existence of a legal rule, or where there are overriding common good considerations.[144]

This last justification illustrates that legal certainty often conflicts with other fundamental principles, specifically with requests for substantive justice. Here, it is typically not the judiciary that is called upon to solve the conflict. Rather, the FCC found early on that it is the task of the legislator to resolve tensions between substantive justice and legal certainty through formal law, again underlining the importance that statutory law plays for the German understanding of the *Rechtsstaat*. The Court held that, as long as the legislator has made a non-arbitrary choice through the normal legislative procedure, substantive justice may take precedence over legal certainty.[145] One example of such a statutory regulation is the legislation on rescinding administrative acts in the Federal Administrative Procedure Act: here, the legislator enacted an elaborate rule that differentiates between lawful and unlawful administrative acts, and between lawful acts which burden or benefit the individual, and put into place clear and restrictive criteria under which lawful administrative acts that benefit the individual can be rescinded.[146]

iii. Procedural Guarantees

The rule of law and the *Rechtsstaat* are typically associated with a set of procedural rights and fair trial guarantees, several of which have been given

140 FCC, decision of 12 February 1969, 1 BvR 687/62; decision of 23 June 1998, 1 BvR 2306, 2314/96, 1108, 1109, 1110/97.

141 Jarass and Pieroth (n 126) para 89.

142 On the controversial application of this provision after German reunification see ch 3.

143 Grzeszick (n 78) para 75.

144 Jarass and Pieroth (n 126) paras 100–103.

145 FCC, decision of 18 December 1953, 1 BvL 106/53.

146 Sections 48, 49 German Federal Administrative Procedures Act (*Verwaltungsverfahrensgesetz*). This example is used, eg, by Schmidt-Aßmann (n 4) 588, para 83.

constitutional rank in the German Basic Law. Article 19(4) of the Basic Law states: 'Should any person's rights be violated by public authority, he may have recourse to the courts.' This extends to all public acts of the legislative and the executive branches of government, regardless of their form.[147] In addition, Article 103 of the Basic Law contains a set of specific fair trial rights, namely that in court, every person shall be entitled to a hearing (para 1), *nullum crimen sine lege* – an act can only be punished if it was defined as a crime by law before commission (para 2), and *ne bis in idem* – no punishment for the same act more than once under general criminal laws (para 3). Article 104 of the Basic Law provides for specific guarantees with regard to the deprivation of liberty. Importantly, deprivation of liberty may only be ordered by a judge, law enforcement 'may hold no one in custody on their own authority beyond the end of the day following that of the arrest' (Article 104(2) Basic Law). Article 101 of the Basic Law prohibits extraordinary courts; Article 102 prohibits capital punishment.

To the extent that the Basic Law does not provide for specific procedural guarantees – this is the case especially in private and labour law – German constitutional jurisprudence finds that the *Rechtsstaat* provides for a general right of access to justice in the form of effective access to formal court proceedings that result in a comprehensive evaluation of the factual and legal questions and result in a legally binding decision by a judge.[148] This jurisprudence highlights the importance that German constitutional law accords to the role of courts in defining the *Rechtsstaat*.

The main organisational structure of the federal courts is outlined in the Basic Law. In addition to establishing the FCC and grounding its competence for specific procedures (Articles 93, 94), the Basic Law specifies that there shall be the Federal Court of Justice, the Federal Administrative Court, the Federal Fiscal Court, the Federal Labour Court and the Federal Social Court as supreme courts of ordinary, administrative, financial, labour and social jurisdiction (Article 95). All judges, irrespective of the court they serve on, 'shall be independent and subject only to the law' (Article 97).

iv. Proportionality

Proportionality is a cornerstone of German constitutional doctrine, even though the principle is not explicitly mentioned in the Basic Law. The principle of proportionality predates the Basic Law and was first developed by the Prussian High Court in the late nineteenth century in cases where police action would infringe on an individual's liberty or property.[149] The proportionality principle addresses the central problem of how to resolve conflicts between

[147] Pieroth (n 72) 734.
[148] FCC, decision of 12 February 1992, 1 BvL 1/89; Grzeszick (n 78) para 135.
[149] Pieroth (n 72) 730; B Schlink, 'Proportionality in Constitutional Law: Why Everywhere But Here?' (2012) 22 *Duke Journal of Comparative & International Law* 291, 294.

different rights, especially between individual rights on the one hand and public interests on the other hand. While the proportionality principle evolved slowly in the Court's early jurisprudence and over several judgments that applied the administrative law principle of proportionality to the Basic Law, there is today virtually no decision by the FCC on fundamental rights where the principle of proportionality does not play a decisive role.[150] The FCC has held that the principle of proportionality has constitutional rank and that it is an expression of the *Rechtsstaatsprinzip* as well as of the very nature of fundamental rights.[151]

The underlying idea of the principle of proportionality is that public acts that infringe on an individual's right must have limits: public authorities need to justify restrictions to fundamental rights, and citizens must not be subject to arbitrary decision-making. Constitutional jurisprudence applies a four-pronged test to determine whether a measure is proportionate or not: any measure that affects fundamental rights is only permissible if it pursues a legitimate end (1); the measure needs to be generally appropriate to achieve that end (2); it must be necessary, that is the least restrictive measure is adopted: no measure that has the same effect but is less intrusive must be available (3); and lastly, it must be proportionate given the weight of the intrusion, measured against the aim that is pursued (4). This last prong is often called 'proportionality in the narrow sense', but has also been labelled 'appropriateness' or 'reasonability'. It is this last part in particular that might be called a 'German' specificity.[152] The proportionality test, especially 'proportionality in the narrow sense', was popularised beyond Germany and normatively defended by Robert Alexy (not without criticism from within and outside Germany).[153]

v. Invoking the Rechtsstaat *in Court: Germany's Extensive Judicial Review*

As we have seen in the preceding sections, the German understanding of *Rechtsstaat* gives central importance to public acts being grounded in formal law, while also having a long tradition of emphasising the judiciary as an inherent component of the *Rechtsstaat*. Under the Basic Law, these principles are extended to the Constitution, and constitutional review by the German

[150] Pieroth (n 72) 735. See generally on the principle the contributions in M Jestaedt and O Lepsius (eds), *Verhältnismäßigkeit – Zur Tragfähigkeit eines verfassungsrechtlichen Schlüsselkonzepts* (Mohr Siebeck, 2015).

[151] FCC, decision of 15 December 1965, 1 BvR 513/65.

[152] Kommers and Miller (n 6) speak of a three-pronged test (p 67) as they address legitimate end and general appropriateness together, which in practice happens often. The focus of a proportionality analysis will typically be on whether the measure is necessary and proportionate in the narrow sense.

[153] For a normative critique of Alexy see J Habermas, *Between Facts and Norms*, W Rehg (transl) (MIT Press, 1996) 253–61; for an overview of Alexy's understanding of proportionality and a critique of his reconstructive theory, see N Petersen, 'Alexy and the "German" Model of Proportionality: Why the Theory of Constitutional Rights Does Not Provide a Representative Reconstruction of the Proportionality Test' (2020) 21 *German Law Journal* 163.

Constitutional Court is a crucial feature of Germany's contemporary understanding of the *Rechtsstaat*. This is perhaps best expressed by the quip that the *Rechtsstaat* needs to be a *Verfassungsstaat*: the law-based state of the nineteenth century is today a constitutional state with constitutional supremacy. It is therefore no surprise that the FCC has extensive faculties to review the constitutionality of laws as well as the constitutionality of administrative acts insofar as they infringe on fundamental rights.

In an early decision, the German Constitutional Court found that an individual has no general right to either claim a specific legislative act or to invoke the illegality of a law without being personally affected.[154] In other words, there is no *actio popularis* that could be derived from the *Rechtsstaat*. Rather, individuals must base their claims on the fundamental rights and guarantees that are enshrined in Articles 1 to 19 of the Basic Law; these fundamental rights spell out and concretise the more abstract principle of the rule of law.[155] This means among other things that a constitutional complaint by an individual cannot be based solely on an alleged violation of the *Rechtsstaat*. Rather, specific rights or due process guarantees need to be invoked.

At the same time, the rights that an individual can invoke are broad. The constitutional complaint (*Verfassungsbeschwerde*), an important procedure before the FCC, makes it possible for individuals to have the constitutionality of a law or an act of the administration or the judiciary reviewed (for the latter, the individual first needs to exhaust other remedies before turning to the Constitutional Court). The FCC found early on that Article 2(1) of the Basic Law, which enshrines an individual's right to 'free development of [their] personality' should be understood as a right to general freedom of action and as a residual right.[156] Coupled with Article 19(4), which, as we have seen, guarantees access to justice if a right is infringed, virtually any human action that is directly or indirectly impacted by public authority can serve as a basis to file a complaint. Individuals can thus in principle attack all public acts, including legislative acts, that impact any of their fundamental rights, including the residual right of general freedom of action. This gives the courts, and ultimately the FCC, great power in determining the constitutionality of public acts.

In addition, the Basic Law provides for specific procedures through which statutory law can be submitted to constitutional review (*Normenkontrolle*), namely abstract judicial review and concrete judicial review. Abstract judicial review is provided for in Article 93(1)[2] of the Basic Law, which holds that the FCC shall rule 'in the event of disagreements or doubts concerning the formal or substantive compatibility of federal law or *Land* law with this Basic Law'. The Federal Government, any state government, or a quarter of the members of

[154] FCC, decision of 19 December 1951, 1 BvR 220/51.
[155] Jarass and Pieroth (n 126) para 40.
[156] FCC, decision of 16 January 1957, 1 BvR 253/56.

the German Parliament can apply for abstract judicial review. Concrete judicial review in turn is the prerogative of courts: 'If a court concludes that a law on whose validity its decision depends is unconstitutional, the proceedings shall be stayed, and a decision shall be obtained … from the Federal Constitutional Court where this Basic Law is held to be violated.' (Article 100(1) Basic Law).

Abstract judicial review emphasises the importance that German constitutional jurisprudence gives to the principle of constitutionality. Unlike in the US, abstract judicial review can take place where there is a difference of opinion on the constitutionality of a statutory law and does not require adverse parties and a real controversy.[157] And unlike in France, where abstract judicial review is limited to the preventive control of constitutionality before a law enters into force, abstract judicial review in the German constitutional order can be invoked after a law has come into force.[158] Courts, and in particular the FCC, thus play a crucial role in the German *Rechtsstaat*. As former Constitutional Court judge Peter M. Huber puts it, politics in Germany has, for a long time, gone beyond the struggle to gain democratic majorities and also encompasses problem-solving through law and courts.[159] He asserts: 'The more intensive the judicial review, the stronger the *Rechtsstaat*.'[160] This is a good example of the prevailing view that equates the *Rechtsstaat* with the rule of statutory law and strong courts to watch over the legality, and, today, the constitutionality of all public acts.

C. The Material Dimensions of the *Rechtsstaat* and Relations with Other Fundamental Principles in German Constitutional Law

As mentioned at the outset of this section, the German Constitutional Court affirmed in its first major decision that the principle of democracy, the principle of the federal state, and the principle of the rule of law were all fundamental principles of the German Basic Law. In addition, the Basic Law also codifies a principle of the social state: Article 20(1) provides that 'the Federal Republic of Germany is a … social federal state', even if the Basic Law does not contain many individual social rights.[161]

It is not entirely settled to what extent the principles discussed in this section can be severed from the *Rechtsstaat* or whether the different fundamental principles need to be read together. For example, some authors discuss the separation of powers as part of the material *Rechtsstaat*.[162] In contrast, other commentators link the separation of powers to the principle of democracy and root it

[157] Kommers and Miller (n 6) 15.
[158] N Marsch, 'Verfassungsgerichtsbarkeit' in N Marsch, Y Vilain and M Wendel (eds), *Französisches und Deutsches Verfassungsrecht: Ein Rechtsvergleich* (Springer, 2015) 275, 291.
[159] Huber (n 1) 419.
[160] ibid 421.
[161] Pieroth (n 72).
[162] Schmidt-Aßmann (n 4) 565–572, paras 46–57; Huber (n 1) 394–395.

in Article 20(2) of the Basic Law, rather than Article 20(3), which is typically considered the constitutional basis of the *Rechtsstaat*.[163] Similarly, human dignity and fundamental rights protection are today considered integral parts of the material *Rechtsstaat*,[164] but at the same time, rights violations need to be brought to the courts in their own name and cannot be brought forward primarily as violations of the principle of the *Rechtsstaat*.

It is clear that the Basic Law considers different fundamental principles to be in interaction with one another. In the same early decision in which the FCC declared the *Rechtsstaat* to be a fundamental principle, the Court also stated:

> An individual constitutional provision may not be analyzed and interpreted in an isolated manner. Every provision finds itself in a context of meaning with the other constitutional provisions which provide for an inner unity.[165]

It has been pointed out that the idea of an 'inner unity', of integrating all constitutional provisions into a coherent whole, can be traced back to Smend's 'integration' theory, in which the constitution functions to integrate and unify a nation around common values that animate the constitution.[166]

What is less clear is the extent to which each of the principles can be normatively justified independently from one another and to what extent the normative justification of the *Rechtsstaat* feeds on other principles, and vice versa. In the following sections, we provide a brief overview of four principles that are all protected by the Basic Law's eternity clause and that are frequently invoked jointly with the *Rechtsstaat*. Fundamental rights and the separation of powers are often characterised as constitutive of the material *Rechtsstaat*; we discuss them first. Democracy and the social state are principles in their own right, even though they are closely related with the *Rechtsstaat*: democracy, because the separation of powers is also partly justified by the idea of democratic self-determination; the social state, because there is a textual basis in the Basic Law that links the social state to the constitutional state (*sozialer Rechtsstaat*).

i. The Rechtsstaat *as a Rights-Protecting State: Fundamental Rights in the German Basic Law*

Fundamental rights protection is often considered as an integral part of the contemporary German *Rechtsstaat*.[167] Today's understanding of the *Rechtsstaat* in Germany is a substantive understanding that comprises fundamental rights protection. The Basic Law's strong focus on fundamental rights and human

[163] Jarass and Pieroth (n 126) paras 32, 32a. Art 20(2) reads: 'All state authority is derived from the people. It shall be exercised by the people through elections and other votes and through specific legislative, executive and judicial bodies.'

[164] See, eg, Grzeszick (n 78) para 24; Huber (n 1) 395, para 31.

[165] FCC, decision of 23 October 1951, 2 BvG 1/51.

[166] Kommers and Miller (n 6) 57.

[167] Grzeszick (n 78) para 24; Huber (n 1) para 31.

dignity is generally considered as marking a clear departure from the Third Reich's injustice. However, it is the *idea* of strong fundamental rights that forms part of the *Rechtsstaat*, rather than every individual human right.[168] The individual fundamental rights of the Basic Law are treated separately from the *Rechtsstaat* in constitutional law and procedure as they form their own basis for judicial proceedings and are not typically invoked jointly with the *Rechtsstaat*. To the extent that the *Rechtsstaat* is a principle that carries its own, independent valence, fundamental rights can be severed.

Among the fundamental rights guaranteed by the Basic Law, the provisions related to human dignity and to access to justice have a particularly pronounced rule of law dimension. The Basic Law codifies a principle of human dignity in Article 1(1), and thus at the very beginning of the constitutional text: 'Human dignity shall be inviolable. To respect and protect it shall be the duty of all state authority.' Article 1(3) provides that all three branches of government shall be bound by the fundamental rights and thus establishes the principle of the constitutional state and the basis for judicial review of all public acts. Article 19 contains requirements for limiting fundamental rights: fundamental rights that explicitly provide that they may be restricted on the basis of a law may only be restricted on the basis of a *general* law (Article 19(1)); such laws must not affect the very essence of the right in question (Article 19(2)); and the same article also provides for access to justice in case of a rights infringement (Article 19(4)). Once again, we see that the rule of law understanding promoted by the Basic Law is one that emphasises the importance of two things: formal statutory law as the basis for the exercise of legitimate authority, and judicial review and access to courts to review the legality and constitutionality of public acts.

ii. Rechtsstaat *and the Separation of Powers*

There is a clear connection between the rule of law and the separation of powers: if the rule of law is characterised by the absence of arbitrary rule of men, there must be some mechanism of control, some form of checks and balances, which in turn necessitates that different powers exist in the first place.[169] In that sense, the separation of powers is the other side of the coin of the sovereign state with a monopoly of force.[170] The separation of powers in the German Basic Law is clearly expressed in Article 20(2) of the Basic Law, which provides that '[a]ll state authority is derived from the people. It shall be exercised by the people through elections and other votes and through specific legislative, executive and judicial bodies'. This provision links the separation of powers in the German constitutional order explicitly to the democratic exercise of state power. This

[168] Schmidt-Aßmann (n 4) 559, para 31.

[169] C Möllers, *Gewaltengliederung: Legitimation und Dogmatik im nationalen und internationalen Rechtsvergleich* (Mohr Siebeck, 2005) 76.

[170] Schmidt-Aßmann (n 4) 565, para 47.

is so even though historically, the separation of powers is as much linked to the protection of individual freedom as it is to democratic self-determination, and theoretically, both individual freedom and democratic self-determination have been considered intrinsically linked, so as to provide for a normative justification of the separation of powers.[171]

Beyond the checks and balances dimension, the separation of powers doctrine in German constitutional law also has a functional dimension: its aim is to ensure that the state power that is best suited to a given task executes that task. As a result, the division of legislative and executive powers is less strict than in a Presidential system.[172] In fact, chancellors derive their legitimacy from the Parliament, which elects them (Article 63 Basic Law). The relationship between Parliament and the executive has thus been described as a 'creative tension'[173] rather than a strict separation of powers.

The relationship between the *Rechtsstaat* and the separation of powers in the German understanding finds its clearest expression in the role of the judiciary. The key reference point here is formal statutory law.[174] As discussed above, the executive is bound by law, and the judiciary's role is to independently and impartially control that executive acts stay within the bounds of law. Further, the lawmaking authority rests with the legislative power, but the law that it produces must integrate into a coherent system of rules, and it is the judiciary that is considered the appropriate power to ensure this coherence through the application of rules of interpretation.[175] It is also the task of the judiciary to ensure the constitutionality of statutory lawmaking. The functional dimension of the separation of powers, by which each power must do what it is best positioned to do, thus demands that the judiciary ensure the principle of legality. To that extent, the separation of powers is related – some argue: inherent – to the rule of law.

iii. Rechtsstaat *and Democracy*

The separation of powers, as mentioned in the previous section, is codified in the Basic Law in conjunction with the democratic principle. The Basic Law provides for a representative model of democracy: whereas Article 20(1) stipulates that the German Federal Republic is a democratic state, Article 20(2) explicitly states that the people exercise their authority 'through elections and other votes', with the German Parliament as the primary representative organ.

We also mentioned in the previous section when discussing the primacy of the law that the principle of grounding state action in formal, statutory law has

[171] Möllers, Branches (n 67).
[172] Huber (n 1) 394–395, para 29.
[173] Kommers and Miller (n 6) 153–54.
[174] Schmidt-Aßmann (n 4) 573, para 58.
[175] Kommers and Miller (n 6) 164–65.

been justified not only with regard to the *Rechtsstaat*, but also with regard to democracy. The formal, statutory law under the contemporary constitutional order is necessarily a law passed by Parliament.[176] The essentiality doctrine, which requires the state to regulate all essential issues via statutory law, is rooted both in a *Rechtsstaat* tradition that values formal, statutory law, but also in a democratic tradition because under the Basic Law, it requires action of the elected Parliament, which is the representative of the people. The Constitutional Court has explicitly held that justification for the essentiality doctrine has a 'democratic component' and requires regulation not only where there is an act of public authority that infringes upon a right, but rather extends to 'all fundamental normative areas'.[177] Because the statutory law is by definition a parliamentary law, every act of public authority grounded in a formal statutory law is also considered to have democratic legitimacy. Unlike other parliamentary democracies, there is no parliamentary supremacy in German constitutional law. As stated in the previous section, laws passed by Parliament are subject to constitutional limits and judicial review by the FCC. This is another clear connection between democracy and the *Rechtsstaat*.

To the extent that the essentiality doctrine is grounded both in the principle of democracy and the *Rechtsstaat*, it might seem difficult to distinguish between both. While statutory law is at the core of both, the principles provide different justifications for the importance of the statutory legal act: the principle of democracy is primarily concerned with an individual right to democratic self-determination, channelled through Parliament, whereas the *Rechtsstaat* addresses ways through which state power can be contained.[178] In this sense, the democratic principle and the *Rechtsstaat* are complementary: the *Rechtsstaat* provides for formal processes (how the Parliament is elected, how laws are adopted, how they are reviewed), whereas the democratic principle states that laws need to be adopted by a body that represents the people, that is the Parliament.[179] This underscores again the central role that the formal law plays at the intersection of the democratic principle and the *Rechtsstaat*.

iv. The Social Rechtsstaat

While the social state and the *Rechtsstaat* are closely related in the text of the Basic Law, German constitutional jurisprudence treats them as largely separate principles. We have discussed above that elements of what is today called 'the social state' were first introduced in the Weimar Constitution. The Basic Law links the social state and the *Rechtsstaat* in Article 28, which provides

[176] Jarass and Pieroth (n 126) para 69.
[177] FCC, decision of 8 August 1978, 2 BvL 8/77.
[178] Huber (n 1) 408–9, paras 59, 60, using Jellinek's distinction between *status activus* (democratic principle) and *status negativus* (*Rechtsstaat* principle) to differentiate between both.
[179] Schmidt-Aßmann (n 4) 598, para 96.

that the federated states need to conform inter alia with the principle of the 'social state governed by the rule of law' – the German *Rechtsstaat* is a social *Rechtsstaat* (*sozialer Rechtsstaat*), a 'social constitutional state'.[180] Similarly to the *Rechtsstaat*, the Basic Law thus elevates the principle of the social state to a fundamental structuring principle, but is silent as to its specific content. What is more, the Basic Law joins the two principles, which led to heated debates as to the relationship between the two principles in the early days of the Federal Republic. Wolfgang Abendroth traced the origins of the social constitutional state in the Basic Law back to social democrat Carlo Schmid and to Hermann Heller, who had advocated for a social *Rechtsstaat* in dual opposition to the fascist conception as well as the liberal *Rechtsstaat*, which he considered to be blind to economic inequalities and thus at the root of rising fascism in the Weimar Republic.[181] In this reading, the social state principle, and specifically linking it to the *Rechtsstaat*, is a response to the Third Reich in the same way as the anchoring of the Basic Law in human dignity and the fundamental rights protection afforded by the Basic Law and can ultimately lead to a redistribution of wealth through law.

Yet, in constitutional doctrine, it is unclear to what extent the two principles ought to be considered together. During the early years of the Federal Republic, one of the annual meetings of German public law professors was dedicated to the 'concept and nature of the social *Rechtsstaat*' in 1953. Main rapporteur Ernst Forsthoff adamantly defended the primacy of the *Rechtsstaat* and cautioned against uniting both principles at the expense of rule of law guarantees.[182] Instead, he argued that the social state needed to be realised through legislation and administrative action rather than at the constitutional level through individual social rights and other constitutional provisions. The social state ought to be considered a state objective (*Staatszielbestimmung*) and as such, is a binding norm for the legislative and the executive branches of government that they need to consider when exercising their discretionary power.[183] Forsthoff's view was subsequently confirmed and defended by Ernst-Wolfgang Böckenförde in what can be considered a seminal text on the history and content of the *Rechtsstaat*. Böckenförde subscribed to Forsthoff's view that the only way in which the social state principle could be realised without rolling back protections afforded on the basis of the *Rechtsstaat* was through delegating it to the

[180] This last translation is from Kommers and Miller (n 6) 622.

[181] Abendroth (n 113); Heller (n 85).

[182] Appointing Forsthoff rather than Abendroth as the main rapporteur for this topic had important ramifications for the understanding of the social state and its relation to the *Rechtsstaat* in German constitutional doctrine, as Abendroth would have certainly advocated for a stronger operationalisation of the social state in constitutional law, see J Perels, 'Der Soziale Rechtsstaat Im Widerstreit: Zur Verfassungsinterpretation Wolfgang Abendroths Aus Anlass Seines 100. Geburtstags' (2006) 39 *Kritische Justiz* 295.

[183] E Forsthoff, 'Begriff und Wesen des sozialen Rechtsstaates' (1973) 12 VVDStRL 1.

legislator and the administration, lest it lead to a redistribution of wealth based on the Constitution, a view that Böckenförde unequivocally rejected.[184]

While the social state principle is today recognised as a constitutional principle in its own right and on an equal footing with the *Rechtsstaat*, constitutional jurisprudence still provides for a primary role of the legislator in realising the social state, and individual rights are generally not derived from the social state.[185] In more recent decisions, the FCC has given way to constitutional complaints on the basis of the social state principle in conjunction with human dignity to provide for a minimum standard of living and a right to health derived from the right to bodily integrity.[186] There is thus a closer relationship today between fundamental rights and the social state principle and to the extent that fundamental rights are considered an inherent condition of the contemporary *Rechtsstaat*, we might find some links today. Yet, the social state and the *Rechtsstaat* continue to be treated as largely separated, despite the textual link in the Basic Law.

III. CONCLUSION

This chapter has traced the origins of the German *Rechtsstaat* in constitutional history and theory. Two mainstays throughout the history of the German *Rechtsstaat* remain important for jurisprudence today: formal statutory law, and the review of the legality of public acts by courts. Today, this includes broad constitutional review. The legislator is bound to the Constitution, including importantly to the Constitution's fundamental rights guarantees, and courts can review to what extent public power's infringements of such rights are justified under the Constitution. This is why the contemporary *Rechtsstaat* principle has been translated as 'constitutional state' in important works on German constitutional law.[187] The German *Rechtsstaat* further needs to be linked with other structuring principles of the Basic Law. The material dimensions of the *Rechtsstaat* comprise fundamental rights protection, the separation of powers, democracy, and the social state, even if these principles have their own constitutional grounding and can be separately justified.

While there has been an exchange between the German and other rule of law traditions, notably the English and the French traditions, for centuries, the German *Rechtsstaat* has evolved in its own right. There may be some common themes across different conceptions of the *Rechtsstaat* and its equivalents, the

[184] Böckenförde (n 7) 69.

[185] HM Heinig 'The Political and the Basic Law's *Sozialstaat* Principle – Perspectives from Constitutional Law and Theory' (2011) 12 *German Law Journal* 1887.

[186] See, eg, FCC, decision of 9 February 2010, 1 BvL 1, 3, 4/09. We address some of these decisions in more detail in ch 2.

[187] Notably by Kommers and Miller (n 6).

rule of law, and the French état de droit.[188] Yet, there are considerable differences as well, perhaps the most important being the German focus on statutory law as the *Rechtsstaat*'s linchpin that can be traced back to a Kantian tradition of German idealism but has weaker democratic traction than in other European countries, expressed today through the absence of parliamentary sovereignty in German constitutional jurisprudence.[189]

Recent years have led to an increase in the exchange of varying rule of law conceptions, especially in the European context. We address EU and Council of Europe influences on the German understanding of the rule of law in greater detail in chapters two and five. At this point, suffice it to say that European influences have challenged traditional components of the German *Rechtsstaat*, especially in the field of due process guarantees, but have also led to subtle shifts in the understanding of this important concept.

[188] DN MacCormick, 'Der Rechtsstaat und die Rule of Law' (1984) *JuristenZeitung* 65; Heuschling (n 2).

[189] Similarly questioning whether the rule of law and the *Rechtsstaat* truly boil down to the same fundamental principles J Meierhenrich, '*Rechtsstaat* versus the Rule of Law' in J Meierhenrich and M Loughlin (eds), *The Cambridge Companion to the Rule of Law* (Cambridge University Press, 2021) 39.

2

Between Aspiration and Reality: Realising the Rule of Law Ideal

In this chapter, we ask how Germany's rule of law ambitions outlined in chapter one are implemented in practice. As shown in chapter one, the rule of law in contemporary German constitutional theory and doctrine comprises both elements that are related to a thin, or formal, conception as well as elements integrated in a thick, or substantive, conception of the rule of law. We have also highlighted the importance of statutory law and judicial review for Germany's rule of law understanding. In this chapter, we assess how the de jure status of the rule of law translates into legal reality, whether it converges with the de facto implementation of rule of law standards, and where deficiencies and obstacles for reform exist. This sets up the stage for the in-depth discussions of two specific rule of law issues in Germany, namely German reunification and the rule of law in times of crisis, which we address in chapters three and four. At the same time, the aspects discussed in the present chapter show the close interrelation between European and domestic rule of law standards, an aspect addressed in detail in chapter five. The present chapter thus has a bridging function. It links the constitutional law notion of *Rechtsstaat* and *Rechtsstaatsprinzip* as outlined in chapter one to the rule of law practice in Germany and the focal points of its rule of law discourse.

The chapter proceeds in two steps. First, courts and the structural features of the judicial system have long been an integral part of the formal understanding of the *Rechtsstaat*. In the first part of this chapter, we address two features of the German judicial system that have raised controversies: judicial independence and the effectiveness of court proceedings. Second, today's rule of law notion in German constitutional law is thickly imbued with substantive values: the rule of law is understood to entail the protection of fundamental rights and democratic governance as guaranteed by the German Basic Law. We look at these dimensions in the second part of this chapter. While the selection of issues we discuss in this chapter does not claim to be exhaustive, it does reflect persisting challenges in translating the rule of law into a reality for all in Germany.

I. FORMAL DIMENSION OF THE RULE OF LAW: THE JUDICIAL SYSTEM

The judicial system is a key element of the German rule of law structure – and of course of the (international) rule of law notion more generally. It has long been accepted, as chapter one has outlined, as a cornerstone of the formal German *Rechtsstaat*. This can appear as both a blessing and a curse. On the one hand, attacks against the rule of law and the judiciary are vehemently opposed. The importance of a well-functioning judicial system for bringing the rule of law to the people as well as for guaranteeing the separation of powers necessary for a *Rechtsstaat* is deeply entrenched in the German self-understanding. Yet, on the other hand, the long history of the formal dimension of the rule of law in Germany has arguably contributed to a certain inertia and inflexibility of formal rule of law structures. That which has been accepted as an adequate rule of law standard for the judicial system for decades or (for some elements) even for more than a century, is barely ever reformed and adjusted to modern standards. This has also made it difficult for the German judicial system to keep up with the demands of European law and institutions. While the judicial system is a good example of how the European level influences the rule of law understanding and practice in Germany – an aspect that will be addressed in more detail in chapter five – it also shows how difficult this interaction can be when facing a rule of law culture that is set in its ways.

The present section highlights this phenomenon. It shows that, while the German judicial system is – by global comparison – considered to be well-functioning and does not fall short of general rule of law requirements, certain aspects of this system can be perceived as problematic under current rule of law standards. These aspects relate to the independence of the judiciary and the criminal prosecution as well as to the effectiveness of judicial decision-making. Both in the German rule of law discourse and the related European discourse, these aspects play a prominent role and are critically discussed. We present each of these aspects to highlight how they shape the rule of law experience in Germany with regard to both defensibility and limited possibilities of reform.

A. Independence of the Judiciary and Criminal Prosecution

A functioning judiciary is crucial to the rule of law, and judicial independence is key to a functioning judiciary. In Germany, judicial independence is a constitutional principle enshrined in Articles 97, 92, and 20(2) of the Basic Law. It is implemented in the legal framework that governs the judiciary (in particular the German Judges' Act [*Deutsches Richtergesetz*, DRiG] and the respective legal acts of the *Länder*). In global comparison, the level of independence of the German judiciary is high. The 2023 Freedom House Report rates the independence of the judiciary with 4/4 points.[1] The perceived independence among the courts' constituencies is also high. According to the EU Justice Scoreboard of 2023, 77 per cent of the general public and 71 per cent of companies considered the independence of the German judiciary to be fairly good or very good.[2]

However, certain aspects of the independence of judges and prosecutors in Germany are controversial in nature. This includes the relatively low level of judicial self-governance, especially concerning judicial appointments and promotions (i), and the lacking independence of public prosecutors in Germany (ii). These are long-existing characteristics of the German judicial system that are cherished as such by some while being considered by others to have become artifacts that do not represent a modern understanding of the rule of law. The judiciary-related rule of law debate in Germany has revolved around these aspects for decades. They have also come to the forefront due to the fact that Germany is embedded in the rule of law structure of the Council of Europe and the EU which both monitor the judicial independence of their Member States. As the following outline shows, the European legal input on these matters however encountered German rule of law inertia.

i. Judicial Self-Governance

The limited extent of judicial self-governance is a controversial particularity of Germany. The country is one of the few Member States of the Council of Europe that still allow for a considerable influence of the other branches of government on the internal governance of the judiciary. Although the German judicial system includes some elements of self-governance, this characteristic is less pronounced than in other countries. While judges themselves manage aspects such as the distribution of cases within a court, they do not – like in many other countries – govern the appointment and promotion of judges independently of the other branches of government.

Due to the federal structure of Germany, the appointment and promotion regimes differ among the federated states (*Länder*) as well as at the federal level. Regarding the appointment of judges, several *Länder* have a selection committee composed of members of the judiciary and the parliament of the respective *Land* (*Richterwahlausschuss*) that makes a recommendation as to the persons to be appointed into the judicial office.[3] The final decision is made by the Minister of Justice of the respective *Land* who then formally appoints the judge. The possibility to create such selection committees is provided by Article 98(4) Basic Law – however only as an option. Thus, in other *Länder*, the Ministers of

[1] Available at freedomhouse.org/country/germany/freedom-world/2023.

[2] Available at ec.europa.eu/info/policies/justice-and-fundamental-rights/upholding-rule-law/eu-justice-scoreboard_en.

[3] Judicial Selection Councils exist for example in Berlin, Brandenburg, Bremen and Hamburg.

Justice are directly in charge of the entire selection and appointment procedure (without any selection committee being involved) or select together with certain high courts of the respective *Land*. Selection committees also exist for the appointment of judges on the federal level.[4] A special – openly politicised – regime exists for the appointment of judges to the Federal Constitutional Court (FCC).[5] The regime for promotions is based on the appointment regime so that actors from the executive are involved here as well, in addition to further judicial actors such as the presidential council of the respective court.[6]

This appointment and promotion regime has resulted in doubts about the independence of judges in Germany. In a survey on the independence of judges conducted by the European Network of Councils for the Judiciary in 2019 among a representative sample of practicing lawyers, many suspected undue influence on appointment and promotion decisions. 31 per cent agreed that judges in Germany have entered the judiciary on first appointment other than solely based on ability and experience; 61 per cent agreed to this statement regarding first appointments to high courts; and 38 per cent agreed to that statement regarding judicial promotions.[7] Among the judges participating in the survey, the scepticism was less pronounced yet still considerable, especially regarding first appointments to high courts (34 per cent) and regarding promotions (28 per cent).[8] As compared to other aspects of the judiciary and judicial decision-making in Germany, these opinions stand out as very critical. These results show that the limited self-governance regarding appointments and promotions affects the rule of law perception in Germany.

Whether or not to increase judicial self-governance is a long-standing discussion in Germany. While already before the First World War, some voices called for the introduction of self-governance elements such as the election of the court presidents and the presiding judges by a college of judges, the – more salient – post-war starting point of this debate was a speech of the President of the High Administrative Court of the state of North-Rhine-Westphalia, Paulus van

[4] See Art 95(2) Basic Law and Judges' Election act (*Richterwahlgesetz*).

[5] According to Art 94(1) Basic Law, half the members of the FCC shall be elected by the Federal Parliament (*Bundestag*) and half by the Federal Council (*Bundesrat*). The selection process is de facto based on an informal understanding among the major political parties as to which party selects a judge in case of a vacancy. See on the related legitimacy considerations, C Landfried, 'The Selection Process of Constitutional Court Judges in Germany' in K Malleson and PH Russell (eds), *Appointing Judges in an Age of Judicial Power* (University of Toronto Press, 2006) 196.

[6] *Präsidialrat*, see Art 75 DRIG.

[7] ENCJ/CCBE Survey among lawyers on the independence of Judges 2018–2019, available at pgwrk-websitemedia.s3.eu-west-1.amazonaws.com/production/pwk-web-encj2017-p/Reports/ENCJ%20Survey%20on%20Independence%20Accountability%20of%20the%20Judiciary%20among%20lawyers%20%202019.pdf.

[8] ENCJ Survey on the independence of Judges 2019 – Independence and Accountability of the Judiciary, available at pgwrk-websitemedia.s3.eu-west-1.amazonaws.com/production/pwk-web-encj2017-p/Reports/Data%20ENCJ%202019%20Survey%20on%20the%20Independence%20of%20judges.pdf.

Husen, in 1951.[9] In this speech, he demanded that the influence of the executive on the appointment of judges, the supervision of judges, and the budget of the judiciary should be limited. For this purpose, he suggested that a judicial body or council should be created that is competent to govern these aspects. This proposition triggered an intense debate among German lawyers in the following years as to whether – and if so, to what extent – judicial self-governance is politically desirable and legally possible or even required by the principle of judicial independence.[10] Yet, the discussion did not lead to any reform. In the following decades, this debate was only occasionally taken up.[11] But it reached a renewed intensity at the turn of the millennium when the 'economisation of the judiciary' put judges under pressure. This novel phase of the debate was initiated by a proposal of the German Association of Judges in 2001.[12] The German Association of Judges put forward a model of judicial self-governance based on an 'administrative council of the judiciary' (*Justizverwaltungsrat*) composed either of the court presidents or of elected members of the judiciary. This council was suggested to be in charge of appointments and supervision of judges, while promotions would be pronounced by Parliaments of the *Länder* at the suggestion of the council. However, despite fuelling anew the discussion about judicial self-governance, this reform proposal was not implemented.

The key dissent has always been on diverging understandings of democratic legitimacy and separation of powers.[13] Those who oppose judicial self-governance generally refer to the limited and indirect democratic legitimacy of the judiciary. They argue that the influence of the democratically legitimised executive and legislative branches on appointments and promotions provides – according to them much-needed – legitimacy for judges. Calls for judicial self-governance are often perceived by them as an attempt of judges to obtain privileges and detach themselves from any control. This reflects a long-standing fear among non-judicial actors in Germany of a judiciary that becomes too strong. Preserving the status quo is perceived as imperative, because, according to this approach, it is only just acceptable as to the thin democratic legitimacy of the judiciary.

[9] P van Husen, 'Die Entfesselung der Dritten Gewalt' (1952/53) 78 *Archiv des öffentlichen Rechts* 49.

[10] See, eg, the various contributions on the topic in *Verhandlungen des 40. Deutschen Juristentages 1953* (1954).

[11] Eg, G Reinschmidt, 'Zur Legitimationsfrage bei der Richterwahl' (1972) *Zeitschrift für Rechtspolitik* 160; W Pötter, 'Die aktuellen Probleme des Richterstandes im Lichte der historischen Betrachtung' in *Die Unabhangigkeit des Richters: ein Cappenberger Gespräch* (Grote, 1969) 9.

[12] See on this proposal, F Wittreck, *Die Verwaltung der Dritten Gewalt* (Mohr-Siebeck, 2006) 655 et seq.

[13] Eg, Wittreck (n 12) 662 et seq; H-J Papier, 'Zur Selbstverwaltung der Dritten Gewalt' (2002) *Neue Juristische Wochenschrift* 2585; B Kramer, 'Die Selbstverwaltung der Dritten Gewalt' (2009) *Neue Juristische Wochenschrift* 3079; H Mertin, 'Selbstverwaltung der Justiz als Verfassungsauftrag?' (2002) *Zeitschrift für Rechtspolitik* 332; T Schulte-Kellinghaus, 'Die begrenzte Macht der Dritten Gewalt – Zur Notwendigkeit der Selbstverwaltung der Gerichte' (2008) *Zeitschrift für Rechtspolitik* 205.

In contrast, those who argue for more judicial self-governance put a high value on the separation of powers as an element of the rule of law. Any influence especially from the executive is perceived as an issue for a rule of law-based functioning of the judiciary. They frequently refer to comparative arguments, pointing to the judicial self-governance models in other European states such as Italy or Spain.[14] They also invoke international instruments and standards on judicial independence that recommend a judicial council model. Such instruments include for example the Universal Charter of the Judge adopted by the International Association of Judges which requests in its Article 2.3 that for the recruitment, training, appointment, promotion, and discipline of judges, a Council for the Judiciary should be competent which 'must be completely independent of other State powers'. Similarly, the 'Magna Carta of Judges' drafted by the Consultative Council of European Judges, an advisory body to the Council of Europe, states that 'each State shall create a Council for the Judiciary or another specific body, itself independent from legislative and executive powers'.

Against this backdrop, the limited judicial self-governance in Germany has been explicitly criticised by the Council of Europe. In a resolution from 2009, the Parliamentary Assembly of the Council of Europe called on Germany to 'consider setting up a system of judicial self-administration, taking into account the federal structure of the German judiciary, along the lines of the judicial councils existing in the vast majority of European states, as a matter of securing the independence of the judiciary in future'.[15] Although this resolution has fuelled the legal policy debate in Germany about increasing judicial self-governance, yet again no structural reforms have been initiated.

More recently, a comparative dimension has shed new light on the existing debate. Two factors have triggered novel debates about the limited self-governance in Germany: on the one hand, the erosion of judicial independence in Poland, including the regime for selection, appointment, and promotion that the PIS Government had put, to a significant extent, under its control; and on the other hand, the expanding jurisprudence of the CJEU on judicial independence, including with regard to Poland. The situation in Poland has increased the awareness of this issue in the general public as well as the sensibility for potential influence on the judiciary by the executive.[16] The debates about judicial self-governance are thus likely to go on. Yet, they will also continue to

[14] Such comparative reference had already been used by van Husen (n 9); for a detailed comparative analysis in the German literature, see, eg, M Jeschke, 'Modelle einer selbstverwalteten Dritten Gewalt in Europa' (2010) 93 *Kritische Vierteljahresschrift für Gesetzgebung und Rechtswissenschaft* 233.

[15] Resolution 1685 (2009) 'Allegations of politically motivated abuses of the criminal justice system in Council of Europe member states', para 5.4.1., available at assembly.coe.int/nw/xml/XRef/Xref-XML2HTMLen.asp?fileid=17778&lang=en.

[16] Eg, according to a 2019 survey, 63% of judges and prosecutors believed that it is possible that the executive might interfere in their work in the future similar to what has happened in Poland. See Roland Rechtsreport 2019, p 11, available at www.roland-rechtsschutz.de/media/rechtsschutz/pdf/unternehmen_1/ROLAND_Rechtsreport_2019.pdf.

take place against the backdrop of the inertia of the existing structures which constrain any reform attempts.

ii. Independence of Public Prosecutors

A second long-standing topic of debate is the (lacking) independence of criminal prosecutors in Germany, that is of the public prosecutors' offices. This issue has been discussed among legal practitioners for about 200 years.[17] The discussion relates to the fact that, under the current and longstanding legal regime (Paragraph 147 of the Courts Constitution Act [*Gerichtsverfassungsgesetz*, GVG]), executive actors, including the Minister for Justice, have the power to issue directions or instructions in a specific case to a public prosecutor. This power has led to a range of controversial cases. This includes, for example, a case in which the minister of justice of one of the *Länder* had instructed the public prosecutor's office to interrupt the prosecution of one of its political opponents and to resume it at a point in time that suited the minister politically; and a scandal much discussed in the media according to which public servants from a justice department exercise pressure on the prosecutors in charge of corruption cases.[18] These examples highlight how the power of instructions by the executive impedes – directly and indirectly – the independence of the public prosecutor, an issue that has been controversially discussed repeatedly over the past decades.

In German constitutional law and jurisprudence, the focus is on the independence of judges. Public prosecutors are not included in the constitutional guarantee of independence. While for judges, an executive power to issue instructions to actors of the judiciary would be clearly incompatible with the notion of substantive independence,[19] the Constitution does not provide the same protection for public prosecutors. According to the FCC, public prosecution is a part of the executive branch of government, even if it is integrated into the judiciary.[20]

Due to this constitutional understanding, the lack of independence of the public prosecutors has been discussed predominantly in terms of legal policy rather than constitutional law. Classical arguments in support of the current regime include the fact that this is a long-existing regime which has not given rise to much abuse because, as a matter of practice, such instructions are hardly ever issued; that prosecutors are bound by the principle of legality and thus do not have to implement instructions that are not in line with the law; and that the

[17] ES Carsten and EC Rautenberg, *Die Geschichte der Staatsanwaltschaft in Deutschland*, 3rd edn (Nomos, 2015).

[18] See on these and further examples, Carsten und Rautenberg (n 17) 510–512.

[19] See, eg, FCC, decision of 22 March 2018, 2 BvR 780/16, para 57; decision of 11 June 1969, 2 BvR 518/66; decision of 9 May 1962, 2 BvL 13/60.

[20] FCC, decision of 20 February 2001, 2 BvR 1444/00, para 41; decision of 19 March 1959, 1 BvR 295/58.

power to issue instructions is an element of democratic legitimacy.[21] In contrast, opponents of this instruction right, including judges and prosecutors, have argued that the legal possibility of such instructions suffices to shed an unfavourable light on decisions of the prosecution, creating a perception of dependence even if, de facto, the decision has not been influenced.[22] Furthermore, not only have such instructions indeed been issued,[23] but the right to instructions also creates a professional culture in which informal influence by the ministers of justice is facilitated.[24] The professional associations of judges and prosecutors have thus made proposals as to how to reform the system in view of enhancing independence.[25] However, the legislator has remained inactive in this regard. In particular, a proposal in 1978 that suggested to at least restricting the right to instructions failed.[26]

The independence deficit of public prosecutors in Germany has been critically assessed by various European institutions. To start with, the already mentioned resolution of the Parliamentary Assembly of the Council of Europe from 2009 which reviewed the criminal justice system in certain Council of Europe Member States, including Germany, addressed this issue explicitly.[27] The Assembly 'calls on Germany to: … abolish the possibility for ministers of justice to give the prosecution instructions concerning individual cases'.[28] Similarly, the GRECO group of the European Council asked Germany in 2014 to consider the abolition of the right of the minister of justice to issue case-specific instructions.[29] In fact, the majority of European states (as well as the EU in the context of the European Public Prosecutor's Office) have adopted a system of independent prosecutors so that Germany is by now one of the few countries with such an explicit de jure dependency. Germany, however, did not take these requests as an opportunity to enhance the independence of the public prosecutors. Instead, in a statement on this issue in 2014, the Federal Ministry

[21] See for an overview of the various arguments, EC Rautenberg, 'Deutscher Widerstand gegen weisungsunabhängige Staatsanwaltschaft' (2016) *Zeitschrift für Rechtspolitik* 38.

[22] Already in 1970, the German Association of Judges had argued for an abolition of the instruction right (in its proposal for an amendment of the GVG). This association has repeatedly called for such a reform and still does so at present.

[23] Carsten and Rautenberg (n 17) 509 et seq.

[24] Rautenberg (n 21).

[25] See, eg, the proposal of the German Association of Judges (which includes public prosecutors) from 2010 for a legal act regulating the self-administration of the judiciary ('*Entwurf für ein Landesgesetz zur Selbstverwaltung der Justiz*'), available at www.drb.de/positionen/themen-des-richterbundes/selbstverwaltung-der-justiz. Interestingly, the association of (defence) attorneys has taken a difference stance, as they feared for independent prosecutors to take more intrusive and coercive measures than is currently the case, see, eg, statement 58/2015 of the German Bar Association, of November 2015, p 4.

[26] See on this proposal, W Maier, 'Wie unabhängig sind Staatsanwälte in Deutschland?' (2003) *Zeitschrift für Rechtspolitik* 387.

[27] Resolution 1685 (2009) 'Allegations of politically motivated abuses of the criminal justice system in Council of Europe member states', available at assembly.coe.int/nw/xml/XRef/Xref-XML2HTMLen.asp?fileid=17778&lang=en.

[28] ibid para 5.4.3.

[29] Greco Eval IV Rep (2014) 1 E.

of Justice referred to the aforementioned arguments in support of the power of instruction. The Ministry further emphasised that, due to the federal structure of Germany in which the *Länder* are competent for most of the regulation regarding the public prosecution, the *Länder* must agree on such a reform – which they had not done at this point.[30] The federal structure is thus presented as one of the factors that contribute to the difficult reformability of the system.

Yet, this issue has again come to the forefront due to a decision of the CJEU in 2019.[31] In this case, the Irish Supreme Court and High Court addressed the CJEU via the preliminary reference procedure under Article 267 TFEU, asking whether two European Arrest Warrants (EAWs) issued by public prosecutors in Germany can be enforced under the EAW framework decision. This legal act requires the EAW to be issued by 'judicial authorities'. The CJEU concretised this notion in the light of EU fundamental rights guarantees and demanded that the judicial authority issuing the EAW must not be 'exposed to the risk that its decision-making power be subject to external directions or instructions, in particular from the executive'.[32] According to the Court,

> independence requires that there are statutory rules and an institutional framework capable of guaranteeing that the issuing judicial authority is not exposed, when adopting a decision to issue such an arrest warrant, to any risk of being subject, inter alia, to an instruction in a specific case from the executive.[33]

Against this yardstick, the Court assessed the legal framework in Germany enabling executive instructions to prosecutors. Although taking note of several safeguards existing in the law that aim at limiting the use and abuse of this instrument, the Court concluded that the fact remains, that the 'power to issue instructions enables that minister to have a direct influence on a decision of a public prosecutor's office to issue or, in some cases, not to issue a European arrest warrant'[34] and that accordingly, the public prosecutor's office is not an independent judicial authority fit to issue EAWs.[35]

[30] Statement of the Federal Ministry of Justice and Consumer Protection of 28 November 2014 regarding a query of Member of Parliament Marieluise Beck concerning Resolution 1685 (2009) of the Council of Europe, available at www.drb.de/positionen/themen-des-richterbundes/selbstverwaltung-der-justiz.

[31] CJEU, decision of 27 May 2019, joint cases C-508/18 and C-82/19 PPU, ECLI:EU:C:2019:456. As to the reception of this decision in German academia, see, eg, K Ambos, 'The German Public Prosecutor as (no) judicial authority within the meaning of the European Arrest Warrant: A case note on the CJEU's judgment in OG (C-508/18) and PI (C 82/19 PPU)' (2019) 10 *New Journal of European Criminal Law* 399; J Eisele and C Trentmann, 'Die Staatsanwaltschaft – "objektivste Behörde der Welt"?' (2019) *Neue Juristische Wochenschrift* 2365; W Kluth, 'Systemische Mängel im deutschen Rechtsstaat wegen fehlender Unabhängigkeit der Staatsanwaltschaften?' (2019) *Neue Juristische Wochenschrift* 1175. For an overview of the jurisprudence of the CJEU on the independence of the authority that issues the EAW, T Niedernhuber, 'How Much Independence is Necessary to Issue a European Arrest Warrant?' (2020) 10 *European Criminal Law Review* 5.

[32] ibid 73.

[33] ibid 74.

[34] ibid 77.

[35] ibid 88.

In the aftermath of the CJEU decision, the preliminary reaction of Germany was to solve the problem on a practical level and only in the context of the EAW. While keeping the executive power to issue instructions in place, each EAW is no longer issued by prosecutors alone but confirmed by a judge. The EU law requirement of an independent authority is thus fulfilled because judges are involved. However, as the instruction power has been discussed controversially for a long time, the CJEU decision has been taken as an occasion for a novel attempt to structurally reform the independence of the public prosecutor's office. In early 2021, the Ministry of Justice drafted a legislative amendment proposal which, although not entirely abolishing the executive power to issue instructions to prosecutors, aimed at enhancing the safeguards against an abuse of this power.[36] It included a provision regarding the legality principle as standard for instructions as well as requiring instructions to be issued in a written (rather than merely oral) form. For cases concerning international legal assistance in criminal matters, instructions were to be excluded. After having triggered controversial reactions by interest groups and during expert hearings, the reform proposal has however not been adopted before the end of the legislative period. This reform attempt thus has become yet another manifestation of the inertia that constrains changes in the judiciary-related rule of law structures.

B. Effectiveness of Judicial Decision-making

The second aspect of the judicial system, which has been prominent in the rule of law debate in Germany, is the effectiveness of judicial decision-making. This notion pertains to the efficacy of court proceedings as well as to the compliance with judgments. A closer look at the effectiveness of judicial decision-making in Germany and its development over time exemplifies further how arduous it can be to reform the German judicial system and for European rule of law standards to be implemented on the domestic level. Yet, it also highlights how the *Rechtsstaat* is deeply entrenched in the German self-understanding when attacks against the rule of law-based functioning of the judiciary trigger vehement reactions in support of the latter.

Two structural challenges to the effectiveness of judicial decision-making in Germany are addressed here. Although in global comparison, the effectiveness of judicial decision-making in Germany is for the most part adequate, certain issues exist. This includes the length of proceedings before German courts which has been perceived as a key problem of the German judiciary (i). Less widespread, but all the more impactful and controversially debated are instances of non-implementation of judicial decisions in Germany (ii).

[36] Available at www.bmjv.de/SharedDocs/Gesetzgebungsverfahren/Dokumente/RefE_Unabhaengigkeit_Staatsanwaltschaften.pdf;jsessionid=88FF6983759CE23491D67C9ECB087661.1_cid297?__blob=publicationFile&v=1.

i. Length of Proceedings

As compared to international standards, the average length of proceedings before German courts is not excessively high. For civil proceedings, Germany ranks 4/142 on the World Justice Project's Rule of Law Index with a rate of 0.83;[37] and for criminal proceedings, it ranks 6/142 with a rate of 0.78 on this index.[38] For example, the average length of proceedings for first instance decisions in civil and criminal cases is roughly around five to eight months, with cases before administrative courts currently taking longer inter alia due to a backlog.[39]

However, despite these average lengths of proceedings, there has been a non-negligible number of cases in which judicial proceedings have been very long. Around 40 per cent of the decisions of the ECtHR against Germany finding a violation concern this issue. Since the decision *König v Germany* from 1978,[40] the ECtHR has repeatedly found violations of the right to a fair trial (Article 6 ECHR) and/or right to an effective remedy (Article 13 ECHR) in cases in which proceedings before German courts took too long. In the *König v Germany* case, a physician whose authorisation to run his clinic as well as his authorisation to practise was withdrawn complained about proceedings before an administrative court that took more than ten years to decide on the legality of these administrative decisions. It is telling that in this case, one of the arguments brought forward by the representative of Germany as the respondent state was that the 'long tradition' of the administrative procedure, including its complexity, needs to be taken into account when assessing whether the length of the procedure is appropriate.[41] This reflects, here again, how the long-standing nature of various features of the German judicial system can undermine a critical reflection on its rule of law adequacy.

Lengthy proceedings continue to be an issue. For example, in 2021, it took longer than 24 months to obtain a decision in 11.1 per cent of civil cases before the district court (first instance) and in 7.6 per cent of criminal cases before the district court (first instance). 12.9 per cent of cases before administrative courts in 2020 took between 24 and 36 months and 17.2 per cent took longer than 36 months.[42]

[37] Available at worldjusticeproject.org/rule-of-law-index/country/2023/Germany/Civil%20Justice/.

[38] See worldjusticeproject.org/rule-of-law-index/country/2023/Germany/Criminal%20Justice/.

[39] Eg, in civil proceedings, the average length in 2020 to obtain a judicial decision in first instance cases was 8.4 months (local court [*Amtsgerichte*]) and 13.4 months (district courts [*Landgerichte*]); and for decisions in second instance cases 7.8 months (district courts) and 13.2 months (higher district court [*Oberlandesgerichte*]). For criminal proceedings, the average length in 2020 to obtain a judicial decision before local courts was 5.3 months, before district courts (first instance) 8.3 months and 6.3 months (second instance). Before administrative courts, proceedings in 2020 took an average 17.9 months which is longer than in previous years and due to a backlog in asylum cases that came in in high numbers for several years starting from 2015. All statistics cited here are available at www.destatis.de/DE/Themen/Staat/Justiz-Rechtspflege/_inhalt.html#sprg235918.

[40] ECtHR, *König v Germany*, decision of 28 June 1978, no 6232/73.

[41] ibid para 100.

[42] What is more, one can detect an unfavourable trend over time as to the length of proceedings, at least in certain branches of the judiciary. For example, the average length of civil proceedings

As a consequence, the German judiciary has been criticised in this regard by both domestic and external actors. To start with, lengthy proceedings are a topic that is salient in the general public perception. In a survey from 2024, 82 per cent of the general public hold the opinion that judicial proceedings in Germany take too long, an impression that has existed for many years now and is a commonly voiced critique.[43] This is not surprising. For a country with an overall high rule of law standard, the general public and thus the parties to judicial proceedings will have the legitimate expectation that such a high standard also applies to managing the length of proceedings. This includes both the average length of proceedings as well as instances of excessive duration.

The FCC has clarified the legal standards regarding the length of proceedings. It recognised that Article 19(4) of the Basic Law which guarantees the right to an effective remedy also includes the right to timely delivery of justice and a prohibition of excessively long judicial proceedings.[44] The latter obliges, on the one hand, the legislator to organise the judiciary and design the procedural law in a way that enables speedy delivery of justice; and on the other hand, it obliges judges to use the procedural means available to speed up proceedings where necessary. However, despite these constitutional law standards, the length of proceedings has remained an issue.

The ECtHR has played an important role in reforming the procedural law to reduce lengthy proceedings in Germany. Starting from the *Sürmeli* case of 2006, the Court has repeatedly addressed the then non-existing remedy against unduly long proceedings in German procedural law.[45] In this case, the applicant had been involved in a series of civil proceedings to obtain a pension due to the injuries he had suffered in an accident in 1982, a saga of proceedings that took more than 20 years. The applicant in the case had even repeatedly addressed the FCC, arguing that the delay violated the rule of law, yet without success. The ECtHR ruled in particular that, even if it had been successful, a constitutional complaint to the FCC (which cannot take measures to speed up proceedings before other courts) cannot be regarded as an effective remedy for the excessive length of pending civil proceedings, and neither can special complaints alleging inaction.[46] However, despite this jurisprudence, Germany did not create such an effective remedy in the following years. To induce a reform more forcefully, the ECtHR issued a pilot judgment in 2010 characterising the lacking remedy as a structural deficiency of the German judicial system and setting a deadline for

has increased continuously over the last 25 years, in particular on the level of the district courts. See statistics available at www.destatis.de/DE/Themen/Staat/Justiz-Rechtspflege/_inhalt.html#_hp3yzsq52.

[43] Roland Rechtsreport 2024, available at www.roland-rechtsschutz.de/media/roland-rechtsschutz/pdf-rr/042-presse-pressemitteilungen/roland-rechtsreport/roland_rechtsreport_2024.pdf.

[44] See, eg, FCC, decisions of 27 September 2011, 1 BvR 232/11, para 21; 7 December 2011, 2 BvR 2500/09, 1857/10, para 114; 2 March 1993, 1 BvR 249/92, paras 21 et seq; 16 December 1980, 2 BvR 419/80; 8 July 1973, 1 BvR 23, 155/73.

[45] ECtHR, *Sürmeli v Germany*, decision of 8 June 2006, no 75529/01.

[46] ibid paras 103–112.

the state to correct that issue.[47] The legislator then did in fact react and made the necessary amendments. Since 2011, parties to a dispute can file a complaint against the court that, according to their perception, does not decide their case with sufficient speed; and it is possible to claim damages for excessive length of proceedings.[48]

Despite the now existing remedy, the issue of delay persists. To address this problem, the government has recently adopted strategies to improve the situation by increasing resources for the judiciary. An important tool in this regard has been the 'Pact for the Rule of Law'.[49] In this pact, the Federal Government and the governments of the *Länder* have agreed to expand the judicial and non-judicial staff in the judiciary to improve the quality of the decision-making. In fact, between 2017 and 2021, the *Länder* have created about 2,700 new judicial and about 3,800 non-judicial positions, partially financed by the federal level. In addition to better staffing of courts, the legal framework has been amended to speed up proceedings. For example in criminal procedural law, the amended provisions enable the judge to dismiss abusive applications to produce evidence (Section 244 Criminal Procedural Code) or to reject a judge for lack of impartiality (Section 29 Criminal Procedural Code).[50] In private law litigation, the legislative modifications broaden inter alia the possibility to decide without an oral hearing about secondary issues such as accessory claims or provisional enforceability.[51] In administrative proceedings, the legislator has particularly addressed infrastructure-related cases, limiting inter alia the suspensive effect of legal remedies.[52]

The nature of the 'Pact for the Rule of Law' points to one of the underlying challenges in addressing the issue of lengthy proceedings: Germany's federal structure. The organisation and equipment of the judicial system lie, to a considerable extent, in the competence of the *Länder*. This has made it difficult in the past to initiate major Germany-wide reforms of the judiciary such as the one needed to avoid structural deficiencies as to the length of judicial proceedings. In this context, and similar to what has been mentioned above for reforming the public prosecution, the federal structure has been a double-edged sword with regard to improving the rule of law in Germany.

[47] ECtHR, *Rumpf v Germany*, decision of 2 September 2010, no 46344/06.

[48] *Gesetz über den Rechtsschutz bei überlangen Gerichtsverfahren und strafrechtlichen Ermittlungsverfahren vom 24. November 2011*, BGBl 2011 I 60. The ECtHR has considered this novel remedy as compliant with the Convention, see ECtHR, *Taron v Germany*, decision of 29 May 2012, no 53126/07.

[49] *Pakt für den Rechtsstaat*, Federal Ministry of Justice and Consumer Protection (2019), Pact for the Rule of Law.

[50] *Gesetz zur Modernisierung des Strafverfahrens vom 10. Dezember 2019*, BGBl. I S. 2121.

[51] *Gesetz zur Regelung der Wertgrenze für die Nichtzulassungsbeschwerde in Zivilsachen, zum Ausbau der Spezialisierung bei den Gerichten sowie zur Änderung weiterer prozessrechtlicher Vorschriften vom 12. Dezember 2019*, BGBl. I S. 2633.

[52] *Gesetz zur Beschleunigung von Investitionen vom 3. Dezember 2020*, BGBl. I S. 2694.

ii. Non-implementation of Judgments

A further risk for the effectiveness of judicial decision-making lies in the non-implementation of judgments. In Germany, this risk has been low for the most part. As a matter of separation of powers, judicial decisions are generally respected by the executive and the legislative branch of government. In global comparison, Germany ranks 7/142 on the World Justice Project's Rule of Law Index as to the effective enforcement of civil judgments[53] and 3/142 for criminal judgments.[54]

However, despite this common practice, there have been several prominent cases in which judicial decisions have been ignored by the other branches of government. When this has happened, it has regularly triggered an outcry in the general discourse by actors such as the Association of Judges or Lawyers, high-level politicians including the Minister of Justice and the President of the Federal Republic, and the concerned courts themselves. For example, the President of the Republic cautioned in 2019 that

> [it] should make us vigilant when the executive ignores a decision by the Federal Constitutional Court; when administrative courts are outmanoeuvred and presented with a fait accompli before they can decide; when courts have to think aloud about the use of means of coercion against authorities to enforce their decision, as the Bavarian Administrative Court recently did in a case.[55]

Such reactions reflect a high sensitivity of the German legal and political system to threats to the rule of law. They are thus an indicator for the rule of law being well-engrained both in professional and public perception.

Nonetheless, the instances of non-implementation that have occurred have raised concerns as to whether they indicate a trend towards non-implementation becoming a structural problem. The most salient and heavily criticised are cases in which judicial decisions have been disregarded by executive actors. One of the most prominent and lengthy cases of the recent past involves the refusal, for almost a decade, of the government of the state of Bavaria to implement judgments of the administrative courts of this state. In these judgments, the courts had ordered the government to take measures concerning air quality, in particular the adoption of traffic bans, measures required under European environmental law.[56] The Bavarian Government openly refused to do so. The dispute went so far that the litigant – a non-governmental organisation promoting environmental protection – asked for the coercive detention of certain members of the government of Upper Bavaria, the Minister for the Environment and Consumer

[53] Ranking available at worldjusticeproject.org/rule-of-law-index/country/2023/Germany/Civil%20 Justice/.

[54] ibid.

[55] Speech at the occasion of the hundred's anniversary of financial courts in Germany on 1 October 2018.

[56] Decision of the Administrative Court Munich of 9 October 2012, no M 1 K 12.1046 and subsequent decision of the Higher Administrative Court of Bavaria of 9 November 2018, no 22 C 18.1718.

Protection of the state of Bavaria or the Minister-President of that state to induce them to implement the decisions. When this enforcement dispute reached the Higher Administrative Court of Bavaria, this court requested a preliminary ruling from the CJEU. The latter decided that domestic courts have to order coercive detention of 'office holders involved in the exercise of official authority where provisions of domestic law contain a legal basis for ordering such detention'.[57] Where domestic law does not provide for this possibility, EU law does not provide a substitute for a legal basis. As a result, and given that the Bavarian Court considered that such a possibility was lacking in domestic law, it did not order coercive detention.

In this dispute, courts have been not only the victims of a state government's behaviour that is contrary to the rule of law but also actors supporting the rule of law by discursive statements and legal actions. In its preliminary reference, the High Court of Bavaria finds strong words condemning the executive behaviour. It deplores the 'deliberate disregard of legally binding judicial decisions by the executive power'.[58] It further cites the above statement of the President of the Federal Republic and a press interview with the former President of the FCC, Hans-Jürgen Papier, who criticised the non-implementation of judgments in this case. Beyond rhetorically condemning the executive actors in charge, the Court also made a specific effort to explore all the legal means available. By its preliminary reference to the CJEU, it tried to overcome the limitations of domestic law, hoping for an EU law basis for coercive measures – measures that, if it had been legally possible, it was clearly ready to take. This self-perception of the court as an enforcement institution against the executive branch of government has indeed a legal basis in German procedural law. As the FCC confirmed in a decision of 1999 regarding the enforcement of a judgment against the Berlin city administration, the procedural law allows taking the full range of severe coercive measures also against public entities.[59]

Further high-profile cases of recent years in which judicial decisions have been ignored by the executive include a case of 2018, in which the German authorities ignored administrative court decisions regarding the deportation of the Tunisian citizen Sami A. suspected of terrorist activities.[60] In violation of procedural law and of the deportation ban issued by the court, Sami A. was deported to Tunisia. The court then ordered the authorities to fly him back to Germany. This escalation of the relationship between courts and the executive branch has triggered controversial reactions in public discourse. On the one

[57] CJEU, decision of 19 December 2019, C-752/18, ECLI:EU:C:2019:1114, para 56.

[58] High Administrative Court of Bavaria (VGH München), decision of 9 November 2018, 22 C 18.1718, para 119 ('gezielte Missachtung rechtskräftiger gerichtlicher Entscheidungen durch die vollziehende Gewalt').

[59] FCC, decision of 9 August 1999, 1 BvR 2245/98, para 9.

[60] Decision of the Administrative Court Gelsenkirchen of 12 July 2018, no 7a L 1200/18A and subsequent decision of the Higher Administrative Court Münster of 15 August 2018, no 17 B 1029/18.

hand, voices such as the then Minister of Justice warned that it would be 'the end of the *Rechtsstaat*' if administrative authorities could choose which judicial decision to implement.[61] The minister further emphasised that those who reject judicial remedies against the decision of the state attack the foundation of the *Rechtsstaat*. On the other hand, right-wing politicians exploited that case to juxtapose the rule of law and 'common sense', as the latter is claimed to require that Sami A. be deported – which, according to them, makes courts 'the grave-digger of the *Rechtsstaat*'.[62]

What is more, even the FCC has not been spared when it comes to its decisions being disregarded by other branches of the government. The widespread resistance against the implementation of a decision in 1995 regarding a matter of religious freedom is a prominent example. Further, in a case of 2018, the court had decided as an interim remedy that the administrative authorities of the city of Wetzlar had to give a political party (the National Democratic Party of Germany (NPD)) access to a public event location.[63] The city administration openly ignored this decision, refusing access as a political statement against this (right-wing) party. The court formally reacted to its decision being disregarded by the city administration. It asked the higher administrative authority competent for reviewing the city administration's actions to investigate the matter and take the necessary means to ensure compliance by the city.[64] This was a highly unusual reaction of the court as it does not have a monitoring function as to the implementation of its judgments.

Yet, the FCC has not only been the target of a non-implementation of judicial decisions, but it has also done so itself. In its much-criticised judgment of 5 May 2020 on the Public Sector Purchase Programme (PSPP) of the European Central Bank, it disregarded a decision of the CJEU by declaring it to be ultra vires, that is in violation of the CJEU's competences.[65] The CJEU's decision that the Constitutional Court had requested via a preliminary reference confirmed the compatibility of the PSPP with primary Union law, an assessment that the Constitutional Court did not accept. In the vivid debate about this judgment, many political actors[66] as well as academic commentators – including at a special parliamentary hearing on the issue[67] – have condemned the Constitutional

[61] Statement by then Minister of Justice Katarina Barley of 15 July 2018, reported eg, here: www.sueddeutsche.de/politik/extremismus-barley-mahnt-im-fall-sami-a-zur-einhaltung-des-rechts-dpa.urn-newsml-dpa-com-20090101-180715-99-159146.

[62] Statements of the then parliamentary group leaders of the right-wing party AfD, Alice Weidel and Alexander Gauland – reported at ibid.

[63] FCC, decision of 24 March 2018, 1 BvQ 18/18.

[64] See press release no 16/2018 of 24 March 2018, available at www.bundesverfassungsgericht.de/SharedDocs/Pressemitteilungen/DE/2018/bvg18-016.html;jsessionid=D970EEEA305BDD8BEF862DC4F1AF5EDC.1_cid507.

[65] FCC, decision of 5 May 2020, 2 BvR 859/15.

[66] See, eg, statement by the Commission, available at ec.europa.eu/commission/presscorner/detail/en/statement_20_846.

[67] EU affairs committee, Committee documents 19(21)97 (C Walter), 99 (B Wegener), 100 (C-D Classen), 101 (C Calliess) and 103 (FC Mayer).

Court's judgment as undermining the rule of law in Europe.[68] It also caused the EU Commission to commence an infringement procedure against Germany – which, however, was closed after Germany 'formally declared that it affirms and recognises … the values laid down in Article 2 TEU, including in particular the rule of law'.[69]

In sum, these cases illustrate the high sensitivity in Germany to non-implementation of judgments as a serious risk to the rule of law. They also show, however, that in a country like Germany that has a generally high rule of law standard, such significant issues can occur – and that not all political, societal, and even judicial actors in Germany agree that the unconditional implementation of judicial decisions should be 'lived' as a basic element of the rule of law.

II. SUBSTANTIVE DIMENSIONS OF THE RULE OF LAW: INEQUALITY AND DEMOCRATIC GOVERNANCE

The first section of this chapter highlighted persistent rule of law challenges concerning the judiciary, which is one of the most important formal rule of law institutions in Germany. While courts are an indispensable element of the German rule of law understanding – also visible in Germany's advocacy for a stronger judiciary at the international level, as we discuss in chapter five – German contemporary rule of law doctrine squarely embraces substantive elements. As discussed in the previous chapter, most commentators today consider fundamental rights protection and their implementation by courts integral to the German *Rechtsstaat*.[70] This is particularly true for fundamental rights that relate to access to justice, and the protection of specific groups. The *Rechtsstaat* is further understood to be of a social and democratic nature, as expressed in Article 28(1) of the Basic Law. This section addresses to what extent this commitment to a substantive rule of law that promises equal rights protection for all in a democratic state plays out in contemporary Germany.

We first focus on persistent structural inequalities which Germany's legal system has been unable to tackle. This is in line with other books in this series and rests on the assumption that the rule of law requires that no groups be continually disadvantaged and therefore excluded from legal institutions. The volume on the US focuses on the exclusion of different groups from the rule of

[68] An overview of the intensive academic and media debate about this judgment is provided by FC Mayer, 'The Ultra Vires Ruling: Deconstructing the German Federal Constitutional Court's PSPP decision of 5 May 2020' (2020) 16 *European Constitutional Law Review* 733. See also the special section of (2020) 21 *German Law Journal* 944–1127.

[69] See statement on the closure decision of the European Commission of 2 December 2021, available at ec.europa.eu/commission/presscorner/detail/en/inf_21_6201?fbclid=IwAR1w6wbHhdcA5vxlqXTohUjxcgF7mJbpSBxTXjxaNWXpMJ0MIzb9Zyuwv7I.

[70] C Möllers, 'Rechtsstaat' in U Kischel and H Kube (eds), *Handbuch des Staatsrechts. Neuausgabe Band II* (CF Müller, forthcoming) 517.

law, but especially on the structural exclusion of Black people.[71] The Brazilian contribution, in turn, addresses specifically the structural socio-economic inequality, which has remained virtually unchanged as the country has experienced different transitions through starkly diverging political regimes.[72] We take up these themes and apply them to the German context. It bears mentioning that structural inequalities are not typically discussed as a rule of law challenge in German legal discourse. Yet, we submit that they pose a de facto challenge to the rule of law.

We first focus on socio-economic inequality. Germany is subject to increasing socio-economic inequality, and neither the concept of the social rule of law state (*Sozialer Rechtsstaat*) nor fundamental rights protection has been able to tackle this issue. In addition, socio-economic inequality is also increasingly leading to unequal access to justice. The second section turns to identity-based inequality, which, under the influence of EU law, has increasingly been addressed through antidiscrimination law. In the last section, we pivot to a different substantive dimension of the German rule of law concept: transparency in legislative processes. This is an important dimension of the German rule of law experience due to the democratic dimension of the separation of powers and the weight that the German *Rechtsstaat* gives to formal legislation.

A. Socio-economic Inequalities as a Challenge for the Rule of Law

Germany is a highly industrialised and wealthy country with a long life expectancy, good public education, a well-functioning public health care system, and overall high levels of income and wealth. It is the world's fourth-largest economy if measured by gross national income, and it ranks sixth on the UN Development Programme's Human Development Index.[73] While overall economic growth and declining unemployment rates suggest that Germany is doing well economically speaking, this upward trend is very unevenly distributed. Wealth inequality in Germany is high, with 64 per cent of the total net wealth held by only 10 per cent of the population.[74] This is the highest wealth inequality amongst EU states. Similarly, the number of people who remain permanently either in the highest socio-economic category (very affluent) or the lowest category (poverty) rises steadily, and the likelihood of staying poor has risen from 40 to 70 per cent since the end of the 1980s.[75]

[71] P Gowder, *The Rule of Law in the United States: An Unfinished Project of Black Liberation* (Hart Publishing, 2021).

[72] JZ Benvindo, *Rule of Law in Brazil: The Legal Construction of Inequality* (Hart Publishing, 2022).

[73] UN Development Programme, Human Development Index, available at hdr.undp.org/en.

[74] 'Life Situations in Germany. The German Federal Government's Sixth Report on Poverty and Wealth', Executive Summary, pp XVI-XVII.

[75] ibid at p XIX. Poverty is defined here through a combination of income below the risk-at-poverty threshold, unemployment, and low work intensity.

Statistics show that socio-economic inequalities and identity-based inequalities typically coincide: socio-economic inequalities often disproportionately affect specific social groups. Thus, people with a migrant background face unemployment rates that are twice as high as the rate for the population without a migrant background, and the income gap has widened considerably over the past decade.[76] Similarly, the unemployment rate for people with disabilities is more than twice as high as for the population as a whole, and their wages increased at a lower speed, exposing people with disabilities to a higher than average risk of permanently facing a low-income level.[77] Women still earn less than men: the unadjusted gender pay gap stands at 18 per cent in 2020, and the adjusted gender pay gap is around 6 per cent.[78] The gender care gap currently stands at 52.4 per cent, that is, women spend on average one and a half times, or 87 minutes, more on unpaid household and care work every day.[79] The OECD-wide PISA study has shown that socio-economic status in Germany strongly impacts school performance (above OECD average) and that, for example, the gap in reading performance between advantaged and disadvantaged students has grown in recent years.[80]

A specific aspect of regional socio-economic inequality relates to the East and West German regions. Especially rural areas in East Germany are experiencing a permanent structural crisis, including a shrinking population due to infrastructural deficits such as lack of access to health care services, transportation or high-speed internet.[81] Thirty years after reunification, considerable economic differences remain between East and West Germany. Unemployment and low-wage employment in East Germany are higher than in West Germany, people from East Germany occupy considerably fewer top positions than West Germans (less than 2 per cent for all Germany, and even in East Germany, the rate is low at 23 per cent), and especially East German men rarely experience upward occupational mobility whilst many experience downward mobility. In terms of net income, the income gap between East and West Germany has widened over the past decade.[82] We will discuss some of the developments that

[76] Report on Poverty and Wealth (n 74), Executive Summary, p LI. 'Migrant background' is a category that has long been used in German public discourse and German statistics, including in the Report on Poverty and Wealth. It denotes a person who was born or has at least one parent born without German citizenship. The category has been subject to debate as it has been perceived as stigmatising and not reflective of reality. An interministerial conference of federal integration ministries decided in 2021 to explore alternative categories, see Protocol of the 16th Conference of Integration Ministers, 29 April 2021, available at www.integrationsministerkonferenz.de/documents/ergebnisprotokoll_16_intmk_2020_bremen_1623323131.pdf.

[77] Report on Poverty and Wealth (n 74), Executive Summary, pp XLVIII-XLIX.

[78] ibid p XLI.

[79] This number varies widely, depending, amongst other things, on whether there are children that need to be cared for. In couple households with children, the gender care gap stands at 83.3%, ie, women spend on average two hours and a half more time than men on unpaid care work, see for all data 'Zweiter Gleichstellungsbericht der Bundesregierung' (2017) at p 96.

[80] OECD, Programme for International Student Assessment (PISA), Country Note 2018.

[81] ibid.

[82] Report on Poverty and Wealth (n 74), Executive Summary, pp XXXIII-XXXIV.

led to economic disadvantages in the former GDR, particularly the process of privatisation administered by the German Trusteeship Agency (*Treuhand*), and its impact on rule of law perceptions in more detail in chapter three.

From the aforementioned, it is clear that socio-economic inequality is a structural and multidimensional challenge in Germany. The German legal system does not, however, provide efficient tools to address socio-economic inequality through legal procedures and puts an undue burden on socio-economically disadvantaged people. We highlight two main challenges. First, few social and economic rights can be enforced in German courts, and socio-economic inequality is generally not considered a constitutional rights issue. There are only a few exceptions where people that are economically disadvantaged have found a remedy in constitutional law, and only in the gravest of cases. Second, socio-economically disadvantaged persons systematically lack access to justice and suffer, for example, greater conviction rates and prison times. Both issues are rooted in the fact that socio-economic inequality has long been neglected as a fundamental rights concern in German constitutional jurisprudence.

While socio-economic inequality de facto affects a range of human rights, it has proven difficult in German legal practice and scholarship to frame socio-economic inequality as a rights issue.[83] Article 3(1) of the Basic Law contains a general equality clause, but this clause ensures formal equality before the law and does not provide a legal basis for material redistribution.[84] Socio-economic equality is instead primarily discussed as part of the German Constitution's commitment to being a welfare state. The social state principle (*Sozialstaatsprinzip*), enshrined in Article 20(1) of the Basic Law, is a structuring principle of German constitutional law.[85] It is connected to Germany's rule of law conception in the form of the notion of the 'social state governed by the rule of law' (*sozialer Rechtsstaat*).[86]

Realising the social state principle has, however, long been considered a prerogative of the legislative with a considerable measure of discretion. The FCC has clarified that the state has a constitutional duty to implement a 'just social order' and social equity but is free to choose the means through which to comply with this basic obligation.[87] In the few cases in which the Court has declared that

[83] C Röhner, *Ungleichheit und Verfassung. Vorschlag für eine relationale Rechtsanalyse* (Velbrück, 2019).

[84] HD Jarass and B Pieroth, *Grundgesetzkommentar, 16th edn* (CH Beck, 2020) Art 3(1), para 16.

[85] The general commitment to the social state principle (*Sozialstaatsprinzip*) is subject to the Basic Law's 'eternity clause', Art 79(3), and cannot be changed through constitutional amendment, see FCC, decision of 23 April 1991, 1 BvR 1170, 1174, 1175/90.

[86] See on this, the presentations at the 1953 German Public Lawyer's Annual Meeting on 'The notion and nature of the social law-based state' in (1953) 12 VVDStRL 8-128; for a recent affirmation of the social dimension as inherent in the German rule of law notion T Wihl, 'Rechtsstaatlichkeit' in M Festl (ed), *Handbuch Liberalismus* (JB Metzler, 2021) 183, 184.

[87] FCC, decision of 18 July 1967, 2 BvF 3, 4, 5, 6, 7, 8/62; 2 BvR 139, 140, 334, 335/62; confirmed eg, in decision of 30 June 2009, 2 BvE 2, 5/08, 2 BvR 1010, 1022, 1259/08, 182/09, para 257: 'The principle of the social state establishes a duty on the part of the state to ensure a just social

there are concrete measures to be carried out based on the social state principle, it has relied on the additional fundamental right of human dignity (Article 1(1) of the Basic Law). In 2010, in a case concerning welfare benefits for long-term unemployed persons, the Court ruled that the German legislator had to devise a procedure that would 'realistically ascertain the benefits needed in line with needs which are required to ensure a subsistence minimum that is in line with human dignity' because the guarantee of human dignity in conjunction with the social state principle required to provide 'each person in need of assistance the material prerequisites which are indispensable for his or her physical existence and for a minimum of participation in social, cultural and political life'.[88] Similarly, the Court ruled in 2012 that the benefits paid to asylum seekers, which had not been changed since 1993, were evidently too low and thus infringing upon human dignity, which guarantees a dignified minimum existence encompassing not only physical existence but a minimal degree of participation in social, cultural and political life.[89]

Beyond ensuring this minimal level of dignified existence, the social state principle does not provide for positive obligations to ensure socio-economic equality that could be claimed by individuals. It has even been deemed 'dangerous' to redefine fundamental freedoms into state obligations to provide specific goods or services.[90] In this sense, and despite the formal equal rank of the social state principle and the rule of law, there is an underlying rationale that privileges a liberal conception of the rule of law based on individual liberty rights over a social rights perspective that would focus on redistribution as a constitutional matter.[91] As a consequence, the social state principle has a role to play primarily in justifying interference with classical liberal rights, especially the right to property.[92] This means that constitutional litigation can address structural inequality and questions of redistribution in only very limited circumstances. Rather, these questions remain a prerogative of the legislative power with very little normative guidance or limits coming from constitutional doctrine. Cara Röhner has pointed out that the social state principle thus remains vague and abstract, little more than a 'formulaic commitment'.[93] Where socio-economically disadvantaged groups have no possibility to claim equal treatment

order … The state must carry out this obligation on the basis of a broad discretion … The principle of the social state sets the state a task, but it does not say anything about the means with which the task is to be accomplished in individual cases.'

[88] FCC, decision of 9 February 2010, 1 BvL 1, 3, 4/09, para 211 and guiding principle 1.

[89] FCC, decision of 18 July 2012, 1 BvL 10/10, 1 BvL 2/11.

[90] H Zacher, 'Das soziale Staatsziel' in J Isensee and P Kirchhof (eds), *Handbuch des Staatsrechts* (CF Müller, 1987) vol 1, 1045, para 99.

[91] Röhner (n 83) ch 2, especially at 153–155.

[92] DP Kommers and RA Miller, *The Constitutional Jurisprudence of the Federal Republic of Germany*, 3rd edn (Duke University Press, 2012) 623; HM Heinig, *Der Sozialstaat im Dienst der Freiheit* (Mohr-Siebeck, 2008).

[93] Röhner (n 83) 153.

as a matter of constitutional law, this can create a sense of being left behind and being left out, which constitutes a challenge to the rule of law.

Socio-economically disadvantaged persons are not only facing the impossibility of claiming economic rights under the principle of the social rule of law state. They are, in fact, severely disadvantaged in accessing justice. Ronen Steinke has shown that economically disadvantaged people typically do not have access to defence lawyers, especially with regard to petty crimes, that they receive higher sentences and go to prison more often.[94] The German Criminal Code provides that people who have been condemned to pay a fine for a petty crime, but do not pay, must serve a prison sentence instead.[95] Steinke points out that in the early 2020s, default imprisonment because of a lack of payment was the most common reason for serving a prison sentence in Germany.[96] On average, there were a bit over 4,000 persons imprisoned for not paying a fine each year on the day of data collection, out of which one in four was in prison for riding public transport repeatedly without a ticket.[97] In response to a renewed debate of what Steinke calls 'new class justice', the Criminal Code was reformed to reduce the default imprisonment time by half.[98] Yet, the figure of default imprisonment for non-payment of a fine remains intact, albeit with shorter prison times. There had been debate on abolishing default imprisonment altogether, but this was ultimately rejected in the reform process.

B. Identity-based Inequality and the Importance of EU Law

While it is very difficult under the current German legal order to address socio-economic inequality as a constitutional rights issue, a somewhat less bleak picture emerges for equality claims that aim at the recognition of diverse identities.[99] Identity-based inequality has recently, and under the influence of EU law, been addressed through antidiscrimination law, attempting to counter the longstanding exclusion of certain racial, ethnic, and religious minorities. Yet, because equality claims are typically dressed in liberal rights terms, not

[94] R Steinke, *Vor dem Gesetz sind nicht alle gleich. Die neue Klassenjustiz* (Berlin Verlag, 2022).

[95] Section 43 German Criminal Code (*Strafgesetzbuch*).

[96] Steinke (n 94) 15.

[97] Statista, 'Wer nicht zahlen kann, wird eingesperrt', de.statista.com/infografik/26348/anzahl-der-menschen-die-in-deutschland-wegen-einer-ersatzfreiheitsstrafe-im-gefaengnis-sitzen/. Because default imprisonment for non-payment is short but statistics are only collected once a year, the actual numbers are estimated to be much higher than 4,000.

[98] *Gesetz zur Überarbeitung des Sanktionenrechts – Ersatzfreiheitsstrafe, Strafzumessung, Auflagen und Weisungen sowie Unterbringung in einer Entziehungsanstalt* (SanktRÜG), BGBl 2023 I Nr 203. Whereas one daily rate used to correspond to one day in prison, the current law provides that two daily rates correspond to one day in prison.

[99] On the distinction between identity-based and redistributive claims and their different treatment in constitutional law see Röhner (n 83) 13.

as equality issues, certain structural advantages and disadvantages remain.[100] A special case is the privileged position of Christian churches in Germany vis-à-vis other religious communities, and relatedly, debates surrounding the freedom of religion.

Antidiscrimination law, understood as a field of law that seeks to address inequalities spanning both public and private law relations, is a relatively recent development in Germany.[101] Two provisions of the Basic Law are relevant: Article 3(2) of the Basic Law contains a gender equality clause, whereas Article 3(3) provides for a list of specific prohibitions of discrimination, which includes prohibitions of discrimination on the basis of sex, origin, religion, and disability.[102] Beyond these constitutional guarantees, there is only limited state-level legislation in the field of anti-discrimination.[103] In turn, at the European level, several anti-discrimination directives were introduced in the early 2000s,[104] but only reluctantly implemented in Germany.[105] In 2006, Germany finally introduced a General Act on Equal Treatment to implement the EU directives.[106] The Act is geared at private law relations, especially employment relations. As such, it was controversially discussed, as some considered it an undue restriction of private autonomy and the liberty to enter contractual relations at one's will.[107] Here again, we can observe Germany's rule of law understanding privileging a liberal conception focused on individual freedom rather than on material equality.

The General Act on Equal Treatment has been an important tool in emphasising equality claims. As such, it has a great potential to curb racial discrimination,

[100] This is not to say that there necessarily has to be a dichotomy between the two frames, but rather that in public law discourse in Germany, such a dichotomy is often drawn. For a unified theoretical conception from a comparative perspective see T Wihl, *Aufhebungsrechte. Form, Zeitlichkeit und Gleichheit der Grund- und Menschenrechte* (Velbrück, 2019).

[101] AK Mangold, 'Von Homogenität zu Vielfalt. Die Entstehung von Antidiskriminierungsrecht als eigenständigem Rechtsgebiet in der Berliner Republik' in T Duve and S Ruppert, *Rechtswissenschaft in der Berliner Republik* (Suhrkamp, 2018) 461.

[102] Art 3(2) reads: '(2) Men and women shall have equal rights. The state shall promote the actual implementation of equal rights for women and men and take steps to eliminate disadvantages that now exist.'; Article 3(3) reads: 'No person shall be favoured or disfavoured because of sex, parentage, race, language, homeland and origin, faith or religious or political opinions. No person shall be disfavoured because of disability.' The two second sentences of each paragraph were added in 1994, see *Gesetz zur Änderung des Grundgesetzes (Artikel 3, 20a, 20b, 28, 29, 72, 74, 75, 76, 77, 80, 87, 93, 118a und 125a) vom 27. Oktober 1994*, BGBl. I S. 3146.

[103] Berlin was the first federated state to introduce a state-level Antidiscrimination Act in 2020, which applies to all acts of public authority and includes – exceptionally in German law – a right for associations to file collective lawsuits (*Verbandsklagerecht*), see Section 9 of the *Landesantidiskriminierungsgesetz (LADG)* of 11 June 2020, 76 Gesetz- und Verordnungsblatt für Berlin 29, p 532.

[104] Council Directives 2000/43/EC, 2000/78/EC, 2002/73/EC, 2004/113/EC.

[105] This resulted in an infringement procedure at the CJEU against Germany, see decision of 28 April 2005, C-329/04, ECLI:EU:C:2005:263.

[106] *Allgemeines Gleichbehandlungsgesetz* of 14 August 2006, BGBl I S 1897. An English translation is available at www.gesetze-im-internet.de/englisch_agg/englisch_agg.html.

[107] See the debate at the German Public Law Professors Annual Meeting on the topic of 'protection from discrimination and private autonomy' in (2004) 64 VVDStRL 403–435.

even if, in practice, it has been more successful with regard to other discrimination categories, in particular discrimination on the basis of gender. Here, we see a confluence of the constitutional prohibition of racial discrimination in Article 3(3) and the private law-oriented General Act on Equal Treatment in legal practice. In public law, several cases of racial profiling by police forces have been brought to courts in recent years. While the FCC has yet to rule authoritatively on what constitutes racial profiling, two Higher Administrative courts have found that plaintiffs had been subjected to racial discrimination because they were singled out for identity control by the police, at least partly because of their skin colour.[108] In private law, a Higher District court has ruled in favour of plaintiffs of colour on the basis of the General Act on Equal Treatment, because the two plaintiffs were denied access to a nightclub.[109]

While individual claims against racial discrimination, both from public and private actors, might be increasingly successful, they do not solve a broader concern over racial discrimination in Germany. There has been a long-standing debate specifically on anti-muslim racism in Germany, and Germany has faced criticism for not effectively addressing racial discrimination in international treaty monitoring bodies and the United Nations Human Rights Council.[110] One particularly stark example occurred in the context of the so-called 'National Socialist Underground' (NSU), a right-wing terrorist group that had killed ten people, nine of whom had a migrant background and had been murdered for racist motives.[111] As we will further expose in chapter four, the investigations as a whole can be considered a major challenge to the *Rechtsstaat*. In the current context of racial discrimination, it is significant to highlight that the investigations into the nine murders failed to suspect right-wing terrorism in the first place. Instead, blame had been put on the victims, and family members of the murder victims gave scarring accounts of how the victims had been suspected by the police of being involved in organised crime and, therefore, having been murdered.[112] This points to deeply seated institutional racism amongst parts of the German police force, an issue that has until recently not been investigated systematically in Germany.[113] Racist violence and racist stereotyping are

[108] See judgments by the Higher Administrative Court of Rhineland-Palatinate of 21 April 2016, 7 A 11108/14, and Higher Administrative Court of North-Rhine Westphalia of 7 August 2018, 20 K 7847/13. On the unconstitutionality of racial profiling under Art 3(3) Basic Law, see S Baer and N Markard, in *H v Mangoldt*, F Klein, C Starck (orig eds), *Grundgesetz: Kommentar* (CH Beck, 2018) Art 3 (2,3), 451, para 478.

[109] Higher District Court of Stuttgart, judgment of 12 December 2011, 10 U 106/11.

[110] See, eg, Committee on the Elimination of Racial Discrimination, Communication No 48/2010 of 4 April 2013, UN Doc CERD/C/82/D/48/2010; UN Human Rights Council, Report of the Working Group on the Universal Periodic Review Germany, UN Doc A/HRC/39/9.

[111] Appellate Court of Munich, judgment of 11 July 2018, 6 St 3/12.

[112] See D Koehler, *Right-Wing Terrorism in the 21st Century: The 'National Socialist Underground' and the History of Terror from the Far-Right in Germany* (Routledge, 2016) chs 5 and 6.

[113] See Research Project 'KviAPol', Rassismus und Diskriminierungserfahrungen im Kontext polizeilicher Gewaltausübung, Zweiter Zwischenbericht, kviapol.rub.de/images/pdf/KviAPol_Zweiter_Zwischenbericht.pdf.

especially prevalent against people of colour, people who are viewed as having a Turkish, Arab, or Asian background, and people who can be identified as Muslims.[114] The latter then suffer discrimination on the basis of race and on the basis of their religious views.

One important religious symbol that has been subject to public debate and constitutional court rulings is the Muslim headscarf when worn by representatives of the state, such as teachers, judges, or prosecutors. Several federated states, amongst them the states of Baden-Württemberg, Bavaria, Berlin, Bremen, Hesse, and the Saar region, prohibited teachers from wearing headscarves at school. Some of these states prohibit the wearing of any religious symbol (eg, Berlin), whereas others privilege symbols of the Christian faith (eg, Bavaria and Baden-Württemberg). In 2003, a first constitutional complaint brought by a teacher in Baden-Württemberg who refused to not wear the headscarf was decided in her favour, but on the ground that there was no sufficiently clear legal basis for a headscarf ban, leaving unanswered the question of whether such a ban was an unjustified interference with freedom of religion or constituted discrimination on the basis of religion.[115] This question was addressed in a case brought by a teacher from North-Rhine Westphalia: in its decision of 2015, the FCC found that an abstract danger to school peace was insufficient to justify a general headscarf ban. Rather, justifying a headscarf ban requires a 'sufficiently specific risk of danger to or impairment of the peace at school or the neutrality of the state'; if this is proven, then bans for specific school districts can be envisioned.[116] This means that a blanket ban on the headscarf for teachers in schools is unconstitutional, in part because the FCC envisions schools as places where 'religiously pluralistic society is mirrored'.[117] Different standards apply to public entities where 'the state exercises public authority vis-à-vis the individual in the classic hierarchical sense'.[118] The Court ruled that it was constitutional to ban legal trainees wearing the headscarf from reading out indictments and/or judgments as part of their legal training in courtrooms, due to the state's obligation to observe neutrality.[119] All of these judgments and the underlying legislative processes are subject to public debate, and it is to be expected that headscarf bans in different contexts will be subject to further litigation in different courts.

In the headscarf cases, the legal question was framed as one of religious freedom pitted against state neutrality. In contrast, the non-discrimination clause

[114] Baer and Markard (n 108) 452, para 481.
[115] FCC, decision of 24 September 2003, 2 BvR 1436/02, paras 1–138.
[116] FCC, decision of 27 January 2015, 1 BvR 471/10, paras 1–31.
[117] ibid para 105.
[118] FCC, decision of 14 January 2020, 2 BvR 1333/17.
[119] ibid. On the issue of 'neutrality' and 'objectivity' as categories that come from a specific cultural viewpoint see S González Hauck, '*Weiße* Deutungshoheit statt Objektivität: Der 'objektive Dritte' und die Systematische Abwertung Rassismuserfahrener Perspektiven' (2022) 42 *Zeitschrift für Rechtssoziologie* 153.

in Article 3(3) Basic Law did not play a role. This is bound to change with the increasing importance of EU law and the CJEU, which intervened in several cases concerning freedom of religion and the workplace, especially church employers. In Germany, the Lutheran protestant church and the Roman Catholic church enjoy a special status under the Basic Law as corporations under public law, which allows them to issue internal law for themselves, to employ personnel under public law rules, and levying taxes through the state tax system. The two main churches earn revenues in the billions through the church tax, which allows them to build schools, hospitals, nursing homes, and other charitable facilities – all of which are entities where people work. The Catholic and Protestant churches are the second-largest employer in Germany (the biggest being the state), and they hold more real estate than any other non-state entity.[120] In many cases, church employers prefer, or even make it a mandatory requirement, that their employees adhere to their faith. In two preliminary ruling procedures, the CJEU clarified that religious employers could not invoke their religious autonomy to justify unequal treatment of employees or candidates for jobs based on their faith.[121] As a consequence, the Federal Labor Court gave way to complaints against discrimination on the basis of faith.[122] These cases have been considered to contribute to a paradigm shift where non-discrimination will play an increasingly important role in structuring the relationship between individual freedom of belief and state-church-relations, at the intersection of domestic and EU law.[123]

To conclude, identity-based inequalities are much better addressed through legal procedures than socio-economic inequalities, even if structural discrimination, especially racial discrimination in conjunction with discrimination on the basis of religion, persists. The fact that racial and religious discrimination are increasingly framed as inequality issues rather than as liberty issues is in part due to the impact of EU law and international institutions on the German legal order. In chapter five, we will further discuss the impact of European institutions on the German concept of *Rechtsstaat*.

C. Transparency of the Legislative Process as a Concern for the Democratic *Rechtsstaat*

In this last section, we shift gears from inequality considerations and address another substantive dimension of the rule of law: democratic governance

[120] See Kommers and Miller (n 92) 590–591. In 2020, both churches combined raised over €10 billion in taxes.

[121] CJEU, decision of 17 April 2018, C-414/16, ECLI:EU:C:2018:257; decision of 11 September 2018, C-68/17 (IR) ECLI:EU:C:2018:696.

[122] Federal Labour Court, decision of 25 October 2018, 8 AZR 501/14; decision of 20 February 2019, 2 AZR 746/14.

[123] A Tischbirek, 'A Double Conflict of Laws: The Emergence of an EU "Staatskirchenrecht"?' (2019) 20 *German Law Journal* 1066.

standards. Germany's commitment to being a democratic constitutional state is enshrined in Article 20 of the Basic Law and forms part of the unamendable body of constitutional norms under the 'eternity clause'. Article 28(1) of the Basic Law emphasises 'the principles of a republican, democratic and social state governed by the rule of law' and thus puts democracy and the rule of law into a close relationship.[124] We showed in chapter one that this relationship between democracy and the rule of law is not a necessary connection and that historically, Germany's *Rechtsstaat* predates its democratic evolution.[125] Today, however, democracy and the rule of law are seen as interdependent[126] and in need of a unifying interpretation.[127] One important connection between the rule of law and democratic governance is the legislative act: democratically legitimate statutory law, adopted through a formal procedure, is the most important governing tool in the German *Rechtsstaat*.[128]

This connection is also emphasised in Germany's international rule of law assistance work, which we will address in more detail in chapter five. Germany's 2018 rule of law assistance strategy emphasises improving the legislative process as a primary aim of rule of law assistance, which entails the participation of experts and civil society organisations.[129] Transparency and anti-corruption are important related fields that Germany's rule of law assistance targets. From an inverse perspective, corruption and transparency matters are considered an integral part of the EU Rule of Law Mechanism to which Germany is subjected as an EU Member State. This mechanism includes the yearly Rule of Law Reports which closely monitor the anti-corruption framework as well as the transparency of public decision-making processes in Germany.[130] Transparency of the legislative process and its actors are thus important concerns for the rule of law experience in Germany, as they provide the foundation for trust in the legislative process.

Transparency of the parliamentary process and conflicts of interests are increasingly perceived as problematic within Germany. In the following, we highlight three issues that have been subject to recent public debate and legislative action: 'cooling off' periods for public officials and parliamentarians before transitioning into the private sector, disclosure obligations regarding

[124] Art 28 addresses the minimal requirements for Germany's federated states and as such provides a succinct statement of the Basic Law's structuring principles.

[125] See ch 1.

[126] PM Huber, 'Rechtsstaat' in M Herdegen et al (eds), *Handbuch des Verfassungsrechts* (CH Beck, 2021) 383, 407.

[127] 'vereinheitlichende Deutung', see E Schmidt-Aßmann, 'Der Rechtsstaat' in J Isensee and P Kirchhof (eds), *Handbuch des Staatsrechts*, vol 2, 3rd edn (CF Müller, 2004) 541, 597.

[128] Schmidt-Aßmann (n 127) 598.

[129] German Federal Government, *Ressortgemeinsame Strategie zur Rechtsstaatsförderung im Bereich Krisenprävention, Konfliktbewältigung und Friedensförderung*, 2018, p 20, available at www.auswaertiges-amt.de/de/aussenpolitik/themen/krisenpraevention/rechtsstaatsfoerderung/2245908.

[130] Available at ec.europa.eu/info/policies/justice-and-fundamental-rights/upholding-rule-law/rule-law/rule-law-mechanism/2021-rule-law-report_en.

remunerated side activities, and the impact of lobby groups and other stakeholders in parliamentary processes in Germany, including the recent introduction of a detailed lobby register.

Germany has a long track record of high-ranking politicians transitioning into the private sector through the 'revolving door', that is, almost immediately after stepping down from public office. Former chancellor Gerhard Schröder is perhaps the most prominent and the most extreme example. A mere three weeks after Schröder had put down his parliamentary mandate in November 2005, having failed to secure his re-election in September 2005, news reports emerged that he was to take up the position of head of the advisory committee of the gas pipeline project Nord Stream which had been signed off between Germany and Russia in the last weeks of his tenure as chancellor.[131] This led to massive criticism from all sides of the political spectrum.[132] Another example of a quick turnover from politics to industry is former Minister-President of the state of Hesse Roland Koch. Two months after Koch stepped down from his political office, he was appointed as CEO of Bilfinger Berger, a civil and industrial construction company, a move that was heavily criticised by Transparency International, recommending a cooling-off period of at least three years.[133] These cases, along with others, resulted in a legislative change where a cooling-off period of 18 months is recommended, although not mandatory.[134]

A related concern is transparency with regard to parliamentarians' interactions with various stakeholder groups, especially with a view to ties to the private sector. This is in part due to the emergence of non-governmental organisations that use big data to provide information to the public on industry ties, side activities exercised by parliamentarians, and remuneration that they receive outside of their usual wage.[135] The Christian Democratic Union receives by far the most money through on-the-side additional income.[136] Several politicians

[131] 'Schröder To Build Putin's Pipeline', *SPIEGEL International*, 12 December 2005, available at www.spiegel.de/international/letter-from-berlin-schroeder-to-build-putin-s-pipeline-a-389965.html.

[132] Criticism renewed in 2022, when it became known in early February 2022 that Schröder was to take up a position on the advisory board of Russia's state-owned gas conglomerate Gazprom, and later failed to distance himself from Putin's aggression in Ukraine. See, 'Gerhard Schröder soll in Gazprom-Aufsichtsrat einziehen', *SPIEGEL Online*, 4 February 2022, available at www.spiegel.de/ausland/gerhard-schroeder-soll-in-gazprom-aufsichtsrat-einziehen-a-12350b39-af36-4e52-ad4b-47fecb894cfd.

[133] 'Koch geht auf den Bau', *Die Tageszeitung*, 29 October 2010, available at taz.de/!5133155/.

[134] *Gesetz zur Änderung des Bundesministergesetzes und des Gesetzes über die Rechtsverhältnisse der Parlamentarischen Staatssekretäre*, BT-Drs 306/15. According to this law, any transition occurring less than 18 months after the end of a parliamentary position needs to be notified and under specific conditions, the transition can be prohibited.

[135] The most important such entity in Germany is the platform www.abgeordnetenwatch.de, an interactive platform with information on side activities and remuneration, ties to the industry, but also interactive features allowing to ask questions to parliamentarians.

[136] According to statistics for the last legislative period (2017–2021), politicians from the Christian Democratic Union and the Christian Social Union received more than €20 million through ancillary revenue, followed by the Liberal Democrats with over 7 million euros, see de.statista.com/statistik/daten/studie/1219831/umfrage/bruttoeinkuenfte-von-bundestagsabgeordneten-aus-nebentaetigkeiten-nach-parteien/.

from the Christian Democratic Union were involved in various scandals, many of which came to light in 2021: several politicians had received a commission for brokering deals to procure medical masks during the COVID-19 pandemic for several hundred thousand euros.[137] As a consequence of this and related affairs, parliamentarians are now subject to stricter disclosure obligations and need to report any additional revenue that exceeds €1,000 per month or €3,000 per year to the cent.[138]

Last, there has been a longstanding debate on the role of lobby groups in the parliamentary process. The Basic Law provides for political parties as the main entity through which political will should be formed.[139] At the same time, everyday life at the Parliament involves many other actors and interest groups as well as a high number of experts who all impact legislative processes. This is not in and of itself problematic. It is important that parliamentarians interact for example with groups that are going to be directly affected by laws in the making and/or with experts when they themselves cannot possibly be experts on all the topics they need to address and vote upon. The relevant question then becomes whether the processes through which individual and collective actors intervene in legislative processes are transparent. Debates on introducing a lobby register date back to the mid-2000s when various parties committed to introducing such a register.[140] Yet, it was not until April 2021 that a 'Lobby Register Act' was adopted.[141] This was not least due to the renewed attention surrounding the abovementioned 'mask affair' which showed a clear lack of transparency regarding interaction between parliamentarians and the private sector.

Before the introduction of the lobby register in 2021, there was very little regulation of lobby groups in Germany. According to an annex to the rules of procedure of the German Parliament, all groups who intend to represent specific interests vis-à-vis Parliament or the government need to register in a public list which is held by the President of the Parliament.[142] According to this rule, interest groups need to provide name and seat, the composition of board and leadership, membership numbers, names of external representatives, and address, but no information on financial means or types of contacts with the Parliament. Providing this minimal information is a prerequisite to applying for passes to the Parliament building and, in theory, also to speak at parliamentary hearings. The latter part of the rule has little practical impact, however, as it was

[137] See for an overview of different allegations, 'Welche Affären die Union gerade beschäftigen', *Sueddeutsche Zeitung*, 26 March 2021, available at www.sueddeutsche.de/politik/cdu-csu-korruptionsaffaere-ueberblick-1.5240578.

[138] See Section 45 Members of the Bundestag Act (*Abgeordnetengesetz*).

[139] Art 21(1) of the Basic Law. This article further provides that parties need to account publicly for their assets and use of funds.

[140] H-J Schmedes, 'Mehr Transparenz wagen? Zur Diskussion um ein gesetzliches Lobbyregister beim Deutschen Bundestag' (2009) 3 *Zeitschrift für Parlamentsfragen* 543, 545–547.

[141] Lobby Register Act (*Lobbyregistergesetz*, LobbyRG) of 16 April 2021, BGBl 2021 I Nr 19, S 818. The Act entered into force on 1 January 2022.

[142] *Geschäftsordnung des Deutschen Bundestages, Anlage II* of 2 July 1980, BGBl I S 1237.

interpreted in such a way that the Parliament could, on its own initiative, invite and hear representatives of groups not registered in the list if this was conducive to the Parliament's interest. In practice, many interest groups not registered with the Parliament's President have been heard by parliamentarians.[143]

The 2021 Lobby Register Act comprises not only lobbying at the Parliament, but also with the Executive, which is important given that most legislative projects are prepared in the respective ministries. The new lobby register requires information on financial expenses, public and private funds, and donations received. It is mandatory for such groups that regularly and/or permanently represent interests at the Parliament, that are remunerated for the representation of interests, or that have had more than 30 different contacts in the past three months. At the time of writing, the lobby register includes over 6,200 entries, with roughly 50 per cent of the registered lobby groups from the private sector.[144]

In conclusion, the transparency of the legislative process, and especially the impartiality of parliamentarians as the main actors in the legislative process, have received increased attention in recent decades in Germany. The relatively recent introduction of a mandatory lobby register shows that there is a perceived need to increase transparency regarding private actors' activities in the legislative process, which, if left unsupervised, might even pose a challenge to the separation of powers. This is a concern that will become even more pronounced with digitalisation, as we discuss in the concluding chapter of the book (see chapter six).

III. CONCLUSION

The *Rechtsstaat* is an important part of Germany's constitutional identity, and it is deeply entrenched in the German self-understanding of being a society governed by the rule of law. Germany even perceives itself to be an expert in the matter, offering rule of law assistance to other countries through its development cooperation and international engagement. Yet, as this chapter has sought to highlight, several issues challenge Germany's rule of law aspirations. Legal reality reflects controversies and deficiencies for which reforms are difficult to achieve and often only see change when European law and institutions push in this direction. While this chapter does not claim to exhaustively review all the rule of law challenges that Germany faces, it has highlighted some persistent topics of public discourse to provide a general overview of the rule of law as it plays out in practice.

Courts and a functioning judiciary are arguably the most important element of the formal rule of law understanding in Germany. Here, we find a certain

[143] Schmedes (n 140) 555.
[144] See www.lobbyregister.bundestag.de/suche-im-lobbyregister?lang=de.

inertia with regard to long-standing controversial features of the German judiciary, such as the appointment system for judges, which has raised doubts as to their independence, and the independence of public prosecutors. European institutions have been unable to induce change, even with sometimes harsh criticism. At the same time, the court system is cherished in Germany and where judgments, especially from the FCC, are disregarded, this is clearly and publicly denounced.

Similarly, there are several persisting structural deficiencies regarding the substantive dimensions of the rule of law in Germany. While equality claims are becoming more important due to the influence of European law, socio-economic inequality is still inadequately addressed as a constitutional rights issue. Lastly, democratic governance is closely linked to Germany's substantive rule of law notion – here, relations between the parliament and the private sector and undue influence on the legislative process through lobby groups have been particularly controversial issues for some time now.

The following chapters will address some issues that we briefly alluded to in this chapter in more depth. Chapter three addresses the rule of law in the former GDR and its portrayal as a state where the rule of law was wholly absent ('*Unrechtsstaat*') by West German authorities following reunification. The experience of reunification affects Germany until this day, as economic inequalities between regions in the former GDR and West Germany persist and political frictions along regional lines have come to the fore, which might at least in part be related to the experience of reunification without a constitutional moment for the former GDR. Chapter four will pick up the issue of discursive use and misuse of the rule of law notion in times of crisis, along with a more in-depth discussion of emergency powers, which are the subject of much controversy, in part conditioned by German history and abuse of powers. We have already highlighted, for the subject matters discussed in this chapter, how European law has impacted the rule of law debate in Germany. This dimension of the German rule of law reality is taken up in chapter five which will assess in an in-depth manner the structural shifts within the German rule of law infrastructure initiated by European and international input.

3

The Rule of Law Experience in the GDR and after the Reunification: 'Rechtsstaat *vs* Unrechtsstaat'?

THIS CHAPTER HIGHLIGHTS the German rule of law experience in the context of partition and reunification. The chapter aims, on the one hand, to provide an inclusive account of the rule of law in post-war Germany by referring to both its western and eastern parts. This allows us to understand how the rule of law experiences in the Federal Republic of Germany (FRG) and the German Democratic Republic (GDR) diverged. The chapter first outlines the rule of law experience of people who lived in the GDR (I). On the other hand, the reunification has been a major and country-specific challenge to the rule of law in Germany. Exploring this challenge allows us to assess to what extent the West German *Rechtsstaatlichkeit* was appropriately implemented during this process and able to fulfil the expectations of the relevant civil society actors and the general public (II).

I. RULE OF LAW EXPERIENCE IN THE GDR – '*UNRECHTSSTAAT*'?

Retrospectively, the rule of law experience in the GDR is often portrayed as rather bleak. In the political discourse after reunification, the GDR has been labelled as '*Unrechtsstaat*'. This is a notion that is used as an antonym to *Rechtsstaat* and that, in a controversial manner, aims at categorising the GDR as a regime in which the rule of law is completely absent.[1] This section outlines the rule of law practice in the GDR (A) before tracing the discourse around the notion of '*Unrechtsstaat*'. (B).

A. The Rule of Law Practice in the GDR

The discussion about, and development of, the notion of a 'socialist rule of law' is insightful in understanding how the GDR approaches the question of the rule

[1] See on the notion's origin in contrasting the FRG to the Nazi regime ch 1, section I.C.

of law.[2] This notion is at the core of the rule of law debate and development that took place in the GDR's foundational phase in the second half of the 1940s as well as during the development of its constitutional practice in the following decades.

To start with, during the process of negotiating and drafting the first Constitution of the GDR of 1949, the notion of *Rechtsstaat* was controversially debated.[3] On the one hand, the representative of the conservative parties in the tradition of the Weimar Republic argued for a formal rule of law understanding with a classical separation of powers in the sense of Montesquieu.[4] On the other hand, socialist politicians initially supported a substantive rule of law understanding (*materieller Rechtsstaat*) – a term that they equated with 'real, substantive democracy'.[5] The notion of separation of powers was rejected and replaced by the idea of sovereign power of the people, akin to the approach by Rousseau.[6] This soon led to a full rejection of the notion of *Rechtsstaat* by the SED (*Sozialistische Einheitspartei Deutschlands*), the later to be leading party of the GDR.[7] This also raised the question what role law should have for the state. From a socialist perspective, it is the state and its structure of 'democratic centralism' that is seen as a key guarantee against an arbitrary exercise of public power rather than the rule of law.[8] As a result, the notion of *Rechtsstaat* was only rarely used during the first decade of the GDR, and if so, primarily in opposition to the Nazi regime.[9]

Since the 1960s, the notion of *Rechtsstaat* regained relevance in the political and constitutional discourse of the GDR. It was not only used to criticise certain legal practices in the FRG (see also below at B) but used constructively to reshape the relationship between law and the socialist state. Law was seen more and more as a tool for shaping social reality. The SED referred to the notion of *Rechtsstaat* in its party programme, and a number of legal reforms were initiated.[10] The GDR was even characterised as the 'only true German *Rechtsstaat*' by the president of the GDR High Court and later also by the state council (*Staatsrat*) of the GDR.[11] The notion of *Rechtsstaat* was thus reshaped as containing elements such as a just legal and social order, law as a tool for social progress, the administration of justice as the responsibility of the entire population, and a system

[2] On the development of this notion, K Sieveking, *Die Entwicklung des sozialistischen Rechtsstaatsbegriffs in der DDR: eine Studie zur Auseinandersetzung mit dem Rechtsstaat in der SBZ-DDR zwischen 1945 und 1968* (Nomos, 1975).

[3] The GDR had, during its existence, three consecutive constitutions: the 1949 Constitution, the 1968 Constitution and the 1974 Constitution.

[4] Sieveking (n 2) 26.

[5] ibid 37.

[6] ibid 39.

[7] ibid 42.

[8] ibid 50.

[9] ibid 54.

[10] ibid 63–64.

[11] ibid 65–66.

of rights and obligations of the citizens.[12] However, in the 1970s, the fate of the notion of *Rechtsstaat* changed again. The political leadership returned to a critical stance towards this notion.[13] This shift was influenced by the political developments in Czechoslovakia in the late 1960s where high-ranking politicians were reproached with revisionism, a reproach that also migrated to the GDR and other countries of the soviet bloc.[14] In this changed political climate, the notion of *Rechtsstaat* was critically conceived as a bourgeois notion that did not have a place in the socialist framework. The notion thus once more lost its relevance. It only became important again in the late 1980s on the path to reforming the GDR and to reunification.

Measured against generally recognised rule of law standards as understood today, there were significant rule of law deficits in the GDR. This includes inter alia a deficient separation of powers and judicial independence, a deficient rights protection regarding both substantive and procedural rights, and lacking media pluralism and freedom.[15] For most of these aspects, the formal legal situation differed greatly from the actual practice. While, if taken at face value, the law of the GDR contained a number of rule of law elements, the legal and social practice looked differently.

To start with, the GDR governance structure was, for the most part, not characterised by a sufficient separation of powers. Initially, however, constitutional law still appeared to be based on this principle, at least to some extent. According to the Constitution of the GDR of 1949, the state power was exercised by a legislative, executive, and judicial branch of government. The legislative power was held by the *Volkskammer*, the 'highest organ of the Republic' (Article 50 GDR Constitution). According to Article 51 of the GDR Constitution, this parliamentary body was to be elected based on a 'general, equal, direct and secret election'. The executive power was to be exercised by the government in particular (Article 91 et seq.) and the judicial power by the ordinary judiciary (Article 126) as well as by administrative courts (Article 138) and labour courts (Article 18). The second Constitution of 1968 which, in contrast to the previous Constitution, was strongly framed around socialist notions, contained much fewer elements of the classical three-prong power structure. The judicial power was still exercised by courts (Articles 90 et seq.), but the Constitution established its function as 'serv[ing] to implement socialist legality, to protect and develop the German Democratic Republic and its state and social order'. This points to the political orientation with which judicial functions were exercised.

[12] ibid 72–83.

[13] ibid 124.

[14] ibid 125.

[15] See, eg, report of the Enquete Commission of the German Bundestag 'Aufarbeitung von Geschichte und Folgen der SED-Diktatur in Deutschland', doc 12/7820, 31 May 1994. On the judicial system: GM Kraut, *Rechtsbeugung? Die Justiz der DDR auf dem Prüfstand des Rechtsstaates* (CH Beck, 1997).

Further, the *Volkskammer* remained the legislative body, but it was expected to work according to a 'principle of unity of decision-making and implementation' (Article 48 (2)). This indicated the close intertwinement of legislative and executive powers in this state structure, especially between the *Volkskammer* and the ministerial council (*Ministerrat*). This lack of separation of powers became even more preeminent after the constitutional reform of 1974. Article 76(1) of the 1974 Constitution stipulated that the ministerial council constitutes 'as organ of the *Volkskammer* the government of the German Democratic Republic'. The 1974 constitutional amendment also introduced the term 'uniform socialist state power' (*einheitliche sozialistische Staatsmacht*) into the Constitution – a term that embodies and consolidates the merging of the branches of power.

In practice, it is uncontroversial that the three branches were closely interlinked and that both legislature and judiciary were controlled, to varying degrees, by the executive branch. As an expression of the lacking 'checks' against the executive branch's power, there was no judicial review of administrative acts for the longest part of the GDR's existence: already in 1952, administrative courts were eliminated.[16] Judicial review of administrative acts was seen as contrary to the idea of 'democratic centralism' which was central to the GDR's understanding of its state structure.[17] Even the body of administrative law was limited and the notion as such contested.[18] Administrative law was seen to be an element of a bourgeois society that had no place in a state order based on the unity of legislation and application of norms.[19] Alternatives such as the GDR petition system were not sufficient to compensate for this lack of executive control.[20]

Further, judicial independence was also not guaranteed in practice. Although Article 127 of the 1949 Constitution and Article 96 of the 1968 Constitution proclaimed that judges are independent and only bound by the constitution and the statutory law, the GDR regime rejected the notion of judicial independence as understood in relation to a separation of powers.[21] The judiciary was characterised by a system of 'political guidance' ensuring that judges and prosecutors 'acted within the political guidelines' established by the political

[16] H Roggemann, 'Gerichtlicher Verwaltungsrechtsschutz in der DDR' (1989) 44 *JuristenZeitung* 579. See also M Stolleis, 'Rechtsstaat und Unrechtsstaat im 20. Jahrhundert' in C Starck (ed), *Recht und Willkür* (CH Beck, 2012) 47, 61.

[17] Roggemann (n 16) 579.

[18] See generally, J Hoeck, *Verwaltung, Verwaltungsrecht und Verwaltungsrechtsschutz in der Deutschen Demokratischen Republik* (Duncker & Humblot, 2003); M Stolleis, *Sozialistische Gesetzlichkeit – Staats- und Verwaltungsrechtswissenschaft in der DDR* (CH Beck, 2009).

[19] Citing a statement by Walter Ulbricht in 1958, Hoeck (n 18) 186–187.

[20] Roggemann (n 16) 579.

[21] H Rottleuthner, 'Steuerung der Justiz in der DDR' (1992) 75 *Kritische Vierteljahresschrift für Gesetzgebung und Rechtswissenschaft* 237, 242–245. See generally, Deutscher Bundestag (ed), *Materialien der Enquete-Kommission 'Aufarbeitung von Geschichte und Folgen der SED-Diktatur in Deutschland'*, vol 4: Recht, Justiz und Polizei im SED–Staat (Nomos, 1995); L Immisch, *Der sozialistische Richter in der DDR und seine Unabhängigkeit* (Peter Lang, 1997).

leadership in Berlin.[22] Through this system that was formally tied to the hierarchy of courts of different instances, significant pressure has been exercised on these actors.[23] Judges had to follow the orders issued by the High Court and could be removed from office as a political sanction.[24]

As to the binding nature of law as a core element of the rule of law, constitutional text and practice also diverged. According to Article 49(1) of the 1968 Constitution, the legislative acts of the *Volkskammer* were 'binding for everyone' ('*für jedermann verbindlich*'). The courts were charged with implementing this 'socialist legality' (Article 90(1) 1968 Constitution). In practice, however, law was not in general binding on all actors that exercised public authority. The SED, the governing political party of the GDR, governed based on political considerations without being bound by law.[25] This was due to the socialist understanding of law, according to which law is seen as an instrument of the ruling classes and thus can be disregarded by the party in the interest of socialist governance.[26] In particular, the constitutional law of the GDR had a low normative power and was changed through political practice to be de facto disregarded.[27] Further, from the perspective of socialist legal theory as practiced in the GDR, socialist legal norms had to be interpreted based on the guidelines of the Marxist-Leninist Party.[28]

Although fundamental and human rights were part of the legal framework of the regime, the practice in this regard was characterised by major structural deficiencies. Formally, the 1949 Constitution contained a range of 'citizen rights' such as, inter alia, equality rights (Articles 6 and 7), the right to personal freedom, inviolability of the home and postal privacy (Article 8), freedom of opinion and of assembly (Article 9), the right to leave the country (Article 10(2)), freedom of association (Article 12) and the right to work (Article 15). Similarly, the 1968 Constitution contained a section on the 'fundamental rights and duties of the citizens'. This section included, inter alia, dignity and personal freedom (Article 19(2)), equality rights (Article 20(1) and (2)), freedom of religion and of conscience (Article 20(1)), the right to participate in elections (Article 22), the

[22] E Blankenburg, 'Changes in Political Regimes and Continuity of the Rule of Law in Germany' in H Jacob (ed), *Courts, law, and politics in comparative perspective* (Yale University Press, 1996) 249, 288.

[23] See generally, H Rottleuthner and A Baer (eds), *Steuerung der Justiz in der DDR – Einflussnahme der Politik auf Richter, Staatsanwälte und Rechtsanwälte* (Bundesanzeiger, 1994).

[24] D Willoweit, *Deutsche Verfassungsgeschichte*, 7th edn (CH Beck, 2013) 221.

[25] On this aspect, D Willoweit, 'Unrechtsstaat, Rechtsstaat – eine richtige Alternative?' in HG Hockerts (ed), *Koordinaten deutscher Geschichte in der Epoche des Ost-West-Konflikts* (Oldenbourg Wissenschaftsverlag, 2004) 245, 250.

[26] Willoweit, Unrechtsstaat (n 25) 253.

[27] G Brunner, *Einführung in das Recht der DDR*, 2nd edn (CH Beck, 1979) 7; Willoweit, Verfassungsgeschichte (n 24) 411.

[28] C Starck, 'Der Rechtsstaat und die Aufarbeitung der vor-rechtsstaatlichen Vergangenheit' (1992) 51 VVDStRL 9, 17. On the notion of 'socialist legality' (sozialistische Gesetzlichkeit), see also Willoweit, Verfassungsgeschichte (n 24) 413.

right to work (Article 24), freedom of opinion (Article 27(1)), freedom of the press (Article 27(2)), freedom of assembly (Article 28), freedom of association (Article 29), privacy of postal and telecommunication (Article 31), freedom of movement (Article 32) and freedom of religion (Article 39). The GDR had even signed and ratified the International Covenant on Civil and Political Rights (see also below at II.A) as well as the International Covenant on Economic, Social and Cultural Rights.

However, the GDR did not guarantee sufficient protection for both substantive and procedural rights. The following is a brief summary of the widespread and structurally enshrined human rights violations that took place in the GDR.

The right to life and physical integrity – a right that, as is worth noting, was not guaranteed formally by the GDR constitutions – has been systematically disregarded in a manner contrary to the rule of law when military or executive agents inflicted severe physical injury on persons in prisons or other forms of detention or even killed these persons.[29] The latter has most prominently been the case when border guards shot persons who attempted to flee from the GDR by crossing the German/German border illegally (see also below at II).

Further, the right to liberty has been structurally violated when prison sentences were disproportionally long, when evidence in criminal cases had been manufactured in view of politically determined judgements, and when persons were imprisoned merely as a result of the exercise of human rights such as the right to freedom of expression.[30] As part of the political suppression, there was a large number of political prisoners. Between 250,000 and 300,000 individuals were sentenced as political prisoners during the existence of the GDR.[31] This was an expression of the repressive state apparatus that aimed not only at suppressing opposition but also very much at deterring opposition in an extensive manner. For the GDR, this practice did not only pay out politically but there was even a financial incentive: the FRG 'bought free' political prisoners at a rate of about DM 100,000.[32]

The state security apparatus of the GDR, the *Staatssicherheit*, commonly abbreviated as *Stasi*, structurally undermined personality rights through its surveillance practice. The *Stasi* had compiled surveillance files for 6 million GDR citizens, which is about a third of its population.[33] These files contained information about all aspects of a person's private and professional life, including their personal relationships with other individuals. The *Stasi* obtained this information from informants, by opening mail, and wiretapping apartments.

[29] Starck (n 28) 20.
[30] Starck (n 28) 20.
[31] C Offe and U Poppe, 'Transitional Justice in the German Democratic Republic and in Unified Germany' in A Czarnota, M Krygier and W Sadurski (eds), *Rething the Rule of Law after Communism* (CEU Press, 2005) 239, 255.
[32] ibid 256.
[33] Starck (n 28) 38.

These latter practices also affected the privacy of postal and telecommunication. To implement this widespread surveillance, the GDR used about 91,000 full-time and 174,000 'unofficial' employees and collaborators.[34]

Further, the freedom of profession has been violated in a widespread manner.[35] For suppressing already young citizens, educational discrimination was an important tool. Whether or not a person was admitted to higher education was based on political considerations such as whether this person had behaved, during their secondary school education, in line with the party guidelines and whether the person was a member of the youth organisations of the state.[36] Access to higher education could, inter alia, also be refused when persons had close relatives in a western state, when they were actively religious or when they did not agree to do military service for the full three years that were expected.[37] In addition to educational discrimination, banning persons from their profession was also a widely used tool. Although this did not happen as a formal ban, people were removed from their positions as a sanction for politically unwanted behaviour.

Furthermore, one of the rule of law violations that took effect on the broader social level was the absence of media pluralism and media freedom in the GDR. The political leadership directed and determined the media content. An office for agitation and propaganda managed the day-to-day input for the state journals, radio, and television programmes. Further, literature, movies and other art forms were subjected to censorship. Both these aspects highlight again the extent to which the constitutional law of the GDR and the lived practice diverged. This practice could develop although the 1949 Constitution declared in its Article 9(2) that censorship will not take place and although Article 27(2) of the 1968 Constitution guaranteed the freedom of the press, the radio, and the television.

As a final example, procedural rights such as the right to a fair trial and its elements have also been violated in a significant manner in different contexts. Probably the most infamous example is the 'Waldheim Proceedings'. These were a series of judgments by the Chemnitz District Court of 1950 that concerned war crimes and crimes of the Nazi regime and that were particularly contrary to rule of law standards. Within a very brief period of time, more than 3,000 persons accused of Nazi crimes were tried and convicted in show trials that lacked basic fair trial standards and in which the outcome was dictated by the political leadership.[38]

[34] Offe and Poppe (n 31) 256.

[35] Starck (n 28) 20.

[36] 'Antwort der Bundesregierung auf die Kleine Anfrage der Abgeordneten Dr. Willfried Penner u.a.', 3 September 1991, Drs 12/1101.

[37] ibid.

[38] S Laskowski, 'Unrecht-Strafrecht-Gerechtigkeit: Die Probleme des Rechtsstaats mit dem DDR-Unrecht' (1994) *Juristische Arbeitsblätter* 151.

Despite these deficits, it bears mentioning that rule of law standards were implemented in certain fields of the legal system of the GDR. For example, during court proceedings in private law cases, procedural rights were guaranteed, and courts were, in ordinary private law matters, bound by law in the sense of the rule of law.[39] With regard to human rights, an aspect in which the GDR was fairly well developed was gender equality – in fact, gender equality was, on many accounts, more advanced in the GDR than in the FRG during the same time period. The constitutions did not only include a general guarantee of gender equality but also a specific provision regarding equal pay for men and women as well as, in the case of the 1968 Constitution, a duty of the state and society to promote women (Article 20(29)). In practice, the integration of women into the workforce was indeed exceptionally high. A gender pay gap did, however, exist, in particular due to different levels of education that men and women still had. And women only held very few of the high political positions within the SED party.

In sum, the rule of law practice in the GDR is characterised by an ambivalent and changing relationship to the notion of '*Rechtsstaat*' as well as by a practice regarding the individual rule of law elements that has shown structural deficiencies in many areas. Not only did the GDR conceive of classical rule of law elements differently, it also did not live up to several of the legal standards that were enshrined in its own constitutions.

B. '*Unrechtsstaat*' in Discourse

Against the backdrop of this rule of law experience in the GDR, this section takes a closer look at the discourse surrounding the notion of '*Unrechtsstaat*' to describe the GDR. This notion has been used and criticised in an emotional manner due to its divisive effect in the German political discourse.[40] We outline how this notion has been employed, by which actors, and in which contexts.

At the outset, it bears mentioning that there is no consensus as to the concrete meaning of the notion of '*Unrechtsstaat*'. It can be understood not only as antonym to '*Rechtsstaat*', that is, as a state that is not based on the rule of law, but also as an unlawful regime, that is related to the '*Unrecht*' as the antonym of law, or as amoral governance structure, that is related to '*Unrecht*' as antonym of morality.[41] However, often, the term '*Unrechtsstaat*' is used without conceptual

[39] Willoweit, Unrechtsstaat (n 25) 250; R Schröder (ed), *Zivilrechtskultur der DDR*, vol 14 (Duncker & Humblot, 1999–2008).

[40] R Hansack, *Unrechtsstaat DDR – Zur Genesis des Terminus politicus Unrechtsstaates nach der Transformation 1989* (Peter Lang, 2015) 11.

[41] On the different connotations from a political science and law perspective, Hansack (n 40) 21–48. On the origin of the word see ch 1. The difference in meanings is partly related to the ambiguity of the antonym of '*Unrecht*', namely the German word '*Recht*', which can be translated as both law and, in the context of Kant, also as right, which has a connotation of moral justice.

reflection about its exact meaning. In general discourse in Germany, it is nonetheless most closely linked to the notion of *Rechtsstaat*,[42] and sometimes seen as part of the trias *Rechtsstaat – Nicht-Rechtsstaat – Unrechtsstaat*.[43] In the discourse about the GDR, the notion is used with different intentions. It can be used as an analytical category for a certain state order, especially in contrast to the rule of law-based order of the FRG and the unified Germany.[44] But it can also be used as a polemical term, without analytical intention and differentiation, but rather as a moral judgement about a political regime.[45]

The notion of '*Unrechtsstaat*' pre-existed the GDR and German reunification. Already in the nineteenth and early twentieth century, this notion has been occasionally used, in particular in political discourse.[46] At this time however, the historical antonym to *Rechtsstaat* was *Polizeistaat* or *Machtstaat* rather than *Unrechtsstaat*. The latter however became prominent after the end of the Second World War, as a means to characterise the Nazi regime.[47] An '*Unrechtsstaat*' is thus by some defined in relation to the Nazi experience, for example as 'a state that misuses the form or medium of the law or – in other words – by means of legal "*Un-Recht*" in the sense of anti-law negates and violates the human dignity of people' due to an 'existential discrimination through exclusion, persecution up to and including psychological, social and physical destruction'.[48]

The notion of '*Unrechtsstaat*' was used occasionally during partition both in relation to the GDR and the FRG. For example, in 1963, the then Federal President of the FRG, Heinrich Lübke, qualified the GDR as '*Unrechtsstaat*' in his proclamation with which he declared the 17 June as national day of remembrance (*Nationaler Gedenktag des deutschen Volkes*).[49] This refers to the 17 June 1953, a major uprising against the government in East Germany which was ended militarily by the soviet army and the GDR police forces. The use of the notion '*Unrechtsstaat*' was thus a moral condemnation of the way in which the GDR supressed its citizens. In contrast, actors within the GDR used the notion of *Unrechtsstaat* with a different connotation. For them, the FRG was an *Unrechtsstaat* because it continued to apply legislation put in place by the Nazi

[42] See also D Johst, 'Die Entdeckung des Unrechtsstaates' in W Konitzer (ed), *Moralisierung des Rechts. Kontinuitäten und Diskontinuitäten nationalsozialistischer Normativität* (Campus, 2014) 127, 128.

[43] Eg, U Lohmann, 'Sozialistischer Rechtsstaat, Unrechtsstaat oder …? Versuch einer Charakterisierung von Staat und Recht in der DDR' in U Lohmann (ed), *Zur Staats- und Rechtsordnung der DDR – Juristische und sozialwissenschaftliche Beiträge 1977-1996* (VS Verlag für Sozialwissenschaften, 2015) 405, 408.

[44] Johst (n 42) 129.

[45] ibid.

[46] Wissenschaftlicher Dienst Deutscher Bundestag, 'Rechtsstaat und Unrechtsstaat: Begriffsdefinition, Begriffsgenese, aktuelle politische Debatten und Umfragen', WD 1 – 3000 – 022/18, p 7, available at www.bundestag.de/resource/blob/575580/dddea7babdd1088b2e1e85b97f408ce2/WD-1-022-18-pdf-data.pdf.

[47] On the development of this notion in relation to the Nazi regime, Johst (n 42). See also ch 1.

[48] Lohmann (n 43) 408.

[49] BGBl I 1963, 397.

regime and it reinstated judges and civil servants that had been employed by this regime.[50] The reference point for the *Recht/Unrecht* dichotomy was thus the Nazi laws and actors. Further, in reaction to the prohibition of the communist party in the FRG (*KPD*) in 1956, observers in the GDR considered this prohibition as in violation of the rule of law and characterised the FRG as a state that cannot be qualified as *Rechtsstaat*.[51]

However, for the pan-German discourse, the notion has gained particular prominence in the context of reunification. It was intentionally used after the end of the GDR to shape its historical image. The notion has created controversies not only among historians but also in the political and social discourse of the past 30 years.

This narrative was already present – and controversially received – in the Unification Treaty (*Einigungsvertrag*) of 1990 between the GDR and the FRG. Article 17 of this treaty qualifies the GDR as '*SED-Unrechts-Regime*'. This qualification was at the time opposed by many citizens of the GDR.[52] However, as the GDR as such ceased to exist in 1990, there were no institutional representatives left to counter the narrative of an '*Unrechtsstaat*' in the further reunification period.[53]

The notion of '*Unrechtsstaat*' has been used both in the 1990s and later with the aim of delegitimising the GDR. Such delegitimation was an explicit aim of post-reunification politics. In 1991, the then-Minister of Justice Klaus Kinkel explicitly requested the German judiciary to contribute to this delegitimation, especially through criminal proceedings against GDR actors.[54] This conferred to the judiciary a specific delegitimation function.[55] This delegitimation agenda has also been implemented by the first parliamentary commission of inquiry (*Enquête-Kommission*) set up by the German *Bundestag* after reunification in 1992 (see also below at II.A). Due to the sole focus on this agenda, there was for example no room for engaging with the reforms that took place in the GDR in certain periods of its existence.[56] The notion of '*Unrechtsstaat*', which has been used in the motions for the establishment of this commission by all the political parties except the Party of Democratic Socialism (PDS), the successor to the GDR's Socialist Unity Party (SED),[57] has shaped the work of this commission.

[50] Sieveking (n 2) 51.
[51] Sieveking (n 2) 53.
[52] Hansack (n 40) 94.
[53] See also Hansack (n 40) 97.
[54] See for the explicit formulation 'Es muß gelingen, das SED-System zu delegitimieren …', statement by Klaus Kinkel of 23 September 1991 at the *Deutscher Richtertag* in Cologne, (1992) *Deutsche Richterzeitung* 4, 5.
[55] U-J Heuer and G Riege, *Der Rechtsstaat – eine Legende? Erfahrungen zweier Rechtswissenschaftler 1990/91 in Volkskammer und Bundestag* (Nomos, 1992) 23.
[56] Critisising this lacking engagement with reforms and reformers, U-J Heuer, 'Vorwort' in U-J Heuer (ed), *Die Rechtsordnung der DDR. Anspruch und Wirklichkeit* (Nomos, 1995) 11, 18.
[57] Hansack (n 40) 114.

A key criticism against using this notion in the context of the commission of inquiry has been that it implicitly equates the GDR with the Nazi regime of the Third Reich. Such an equation has also been criticised more generally in relation to using the term '*Unrechtsstaat*'.[58] The equation – and, for that matter, already the mere comparison – of these two regimes has been controversially discussed.[59] The term '*Unrechtsstaat*' has been used for both regimes, thus creating the allegation that both regimes are comparable. This is an approach that many observers reject in light of the different governance types, the fact that the GDR regime did not result in genocide and world war, and that it was the result of the occupation by a foreign power rather than of a failed democracy as in the case of the Third Reich.[60] In fact, observers stated that the majority of former GDR citizens perceived this equation as a 'personal insult'.[61]

In addition, qualifying the GDR as '*Unrechtsstaat*' emphasises the 'criminal' nature of the GDR regime.[62] This is a perspective that is in line with the primarily criminal law-based approach to transitional justice adopted after reunification (see below at II.A). But presenting the GDR merely as 'criminal regime' and through a criminal lens faces similar criticisms as concerning the delegitimation and Nazi equation agendas.[63]

The academic debate revolved around the definition of the notion of '*Unrechtsstaat*' as well as a differentiated assessment of the rule of law elements. To start with, the use of this notion has been criticised because it led to assessing the rule of law situation in the GDR against the yardstick of the West German rule of law understanding. Several scholars have argued that when assessing the rule of law practice in the GDR, this should be done based on universal or at least common European rule of law standards rather than against the specific understanding of *Rechtstaatlichkeit* as developed in the FRG.[64] Moreover, the implied binary nature of states being either a *Rechtsstaat* or an *Unrechtsstaat* has been criticised. Even the former President of the German Federal Administrative Court (*Bundesverwaltungsgericht*), Horst Sendler, who stated that the GDR might have been 'at its core' an *Unrechtsstaat* and thus triggered the first wave of the academic debate about this notion,[65] qualified his earlier statement. He emphasised that even in such a state, there are areas that live up to the standards of a *Rechtsstaat*.[66] According to him, not everything in the GDR would qualify

[58] Eg, V Schöneburg, 'Recht im nazifaschistischen und im "realsozialistischen" deutschen Staat – Diskontinuitäten und Kontinuitäten' (1992) *Neue Justiz* 49.

[59] H Möller and J Kocka, in Deutscher Bundestag (ed), *Materialien der Enquete-Kommission "Aufarbeitung von Geschichte und Folgen der SED-Diktatur in Deutschland"*, vol 9 (1995) 576–597.

[60] Hansack (n 40) 52.

[61] Heuer (n 56) 19.

[62] Hansack (n 40) 92.

[63] ibid.

[64] Willoweit, Unrechtsstaat (n 25) 252; Starck (n 28) 14.

[65] H Sendler, 'Editorial' (1991) *Neue Justiz* 137.

[66] H Sendler, 'Über Rechtsstaat, Unrechtsstaat und anderes – Das Editorial der Herausgeber im Meinungsstreit' (1991) *Neue Justiz* 379, 380.

as '*Unrecht*', which, for him, underlines the fact that no state is entirely in conformity with rule of law standards as much as no state is entirely in violation of these standards.[67] This ties into the criticism that the notions of *Rechtsstaat* and *Unrechtsstaat* are used in a manner that is too categorical and binary.[68] As there is neither a pure *Rechtsstaat* nor a pure *Unrechtsstaat*, one should analyse the features of a regime individually.[69]

In the broader discourse, political parties, individual political actors and other participants have been divided over whether this is an appropriate characterisation of the GDR or whether it amounts to denying a 'legitimate existence' of the GDR as a state.[70] This issue has been prominent in various contexts. For example, the then-head of the government of the East German state of Saxony-Anhalt, Reinhard Höppner, declared in 1997 that the GDR cannot be characterised merely as '*Unrechtsstaat*'. He said the GDR was 'more than an *Unrechtsstaat*' as it was for many people in East Germany also 'an attempt to build a just society' and the fact that this attempt has failed 'does not discredit those who were looking in this way for a just society'.[71] This triggered a public debate on this notion.[72] Further, in the context of the election of the Federal President (*Bundespräsident*) in 2009, candidate Gesine Schwan rejected the characterisation of the GDR as *Unrechtsstaat* in a newspaper interview. She said that using this notion would imply that everything that happened in the GDR was '*unrecht*', a term that, as mentioned above, can be translated as both illegal and immoral.[73] This led to a renewed public debate about this characterisation and the subsequently elected Federal President Horst Köhler felt compelled to state that, for him, the GDR qualifies as an *Unrechtsstaat*.[74] Other instances include various debates as to whether certain political parties would be willing to form a coalition with the left-wing party *Die Linke* that has opposed the characterisation of the GDR as '*Unrechtsstaat*'. For example, in 2014, the Social Democrats and the Greens in the Parliament of the state of Thuringia declared that they would only enter into a coalition with *Die Linke* if the latter

[67] ibid.

[68] I Müller, 'Die DDR – ein Unrechtsstaat?' (1992) *Neue Justiz* 281. See also Schöneburg (n 58).

[69] ibid.

[70] Eg, statement of a member of the Enquete Commission of the German Bundestag 'Aufarbeitung von Geschichte und Folgen der SED-Diktatur in Deutschland', doc 12/7820, 31 May 1994, p 270.

[71] Speech by Reinhard Höppner, 20 April 1997, 'Gemeinsame Werte als Voraussetzung für Gemeinschaft – Erfahrungen aus dem Prozeß der deutschen Vereinigung', at the conference 'Rechtspolitischer Kongreß' of the Friedrich-Ebert-Stiftung, 18-20 April 1997 in Mainz. For the quote, see Wissenschaftlicher Dienst Bundestag, WD 1 – 3000 – 022/18.

[72] On this debate, R Wassermann, 'Wieviel Unrecht macht einen Staat zum Unrechtstaat?' (1997) *Neue Juristische Wochenschrift* 2152.

[73] 'Gesine Schwan, "Vorsicht! Ich bin die andere!" SPD-Präsidentschaftskandidatin Gesine Schwan sprach mit dem Tagesspiegel über ihre Bewerbung fürs Schloss Bellevue', *Tagesspiegel*, 17 May 2009, available at www.tagesspiegel.de/politik/vorsicht-ich-bin-die-andere-1759957.html.

[74] 'Köhler sieht DDR als Unrechtsstaat. Bundespräsident geht nach Wiederwahl auf Distanz zu Schwan', *Leipziger Volkszeitung* 25 May 2009.

recognised that the GDR was an '*Unrechtsstaat*'.[75] Subsequently, the notion of *Unrechtsstaat* has also been discussed controversially on a more general level, for example in a series of newspaper articles in 2015.[76] Finally, in one of the most recent manifestations of the debate, the German Minister of Justice, Marco Buschmann, engaged with the notion of '*Unrechtsstaat*' at the occasion of the 70th anniversary of the 17 June 1953, the above-mentioned uprising against the government in East Germany. According to him, there is consensus that the GDR was no *Rechtsstaat*.[77] He deduces from that that it must have been an '*Unrechtsstaat*' because:

> Lawyers think in terms of a dichotomy of *Recht und Unrecht*. This leads to the conclusion that a state that has not been a *Rechtsstaat* must be an *Unrechtsstaat*. *Tertium non datur*![78]

He argues that this term is appropriate because it does not disqualify the citizens of such a state, as the term is not *Unrechtsgesellschaft*, a society based on *Unrecht*. And, in his view, the use of the term is not barred by the implicit comparison to the Nazi regime because 'merely because there is always a greater *Unrecht*, this does not turn the *Unrecht* into *Recht* and it thus does not turn the *Unrechtsstaat* to something else than what it is'.[79]

This overview shows that the qualification of the GDR as an '*Unrechtsstaat*' continues to be controversially debated. The emotional reactions that it still triggers among defenders and opponents of this qualification point to Germany's ambivalent experience during the reunification process. The next section takes a closer look at this process and the rule of law experiences linked to it.

II. RULE OF LAW EXPERIENCE IN THE REUNIFICATION CONTEXT

After having outlined in the previous section the rule of law experience in the GDR and related controversies, this section turns to the rule of law experience in the context of German reunification. This includes transitional justice which, in the context of German reunification, has been primarily focussed on criminal

[75] S Prinz, 'Die Linkspartei und der Unrechtsstaat DDR. Der Preis der Macht. Die Koalition "frisst ihre Kinder"' (2015) 464 *Politische Studien* 44.

[76] E-W Böckenförde, 'Rechtsstaat oder Unrechtsstaat?', *Frankfurter Allgemeine Zeitung*, 12 May 2015, available at www.faz.net/aktuell/feuilleton/debatten/war-die-ddr-ein-unrechtsstaat-13587574.html; E Bahr, 'Die DDR war nicht der einzige Unrechtsstaat im Ostblock', *Frankfurter Allgemeine Zeitung*, 16 May 2015; R Scholz, 'Wider die Relativierung: Die DDR war ein Unrechtsstaat', *Frankfurter Allgemeine Zeitung*, 1 June 2015.

[77] M Buschmann, 'Wenn das Recht bloßes Herrschaftsinstrument ist – Noch immer löst der Begriff "Unrechtsstaat" bei einigen ein Störgefühl aus – aber was war die DDR sonst?', *Frankfurter Allgemeine Zeitung*, 14 June 2023, availabe at www.faz.net/aktuell/politik/staat-und-recht/wenn-das-recht-blosses-herrschaftsinstrument-ist-18963690.html.

[78] ibid (authors' translation).

[79] ibid (authors' translation).

liability of GDR actors (A). Second, it relates to the experience and expectations of former GDR citizens after reunification and the perceived juxtaposition of justice and the rule of law (B).

A. A Specific Transitional Justice Experience: Focus on Criminal Liability

Reunification was an occasion for transitional justice, for letting the reunified *Rechtsstaat* process the rule of law deficiencies in the GDR. As the then-Minister of Justice Klaus Kinkel said in 1991, a crucial question is

> whether the Rechtsstaat is capable, in the eyes of the population, to deal with the things with which the forty years of 'Unrechtsregime' in the former GDR has left us.[80]

The German transitional justice experience was characterised by 'a more activist strategy concerning the pre-1989 regime of the GDR and its actors than in any of the other post-Communist countries'.[81] And it focussed strongly on criminal liability.[82] This approach was facilitated by several factors. First, East Germany was integrated into a West German legal order whose legal apparatus could be used *tel quel* rather than having to be created anew after the end of the socialist regime. In contrast to a perpetuation of social elites as in many other transitional justice contexts that are limited to the same society, there were, after the exchange of elites (see below), West German elites at the ready to prosecute and replace East German perpetrators.[83] Further, supporters of the GDR regime 'were expected to be incapable of playing any significant role in the future of unified Germany' so that there 'was no perceived need to extend any leniency to them out of political prudence'.[84] For the actors of the opposition that, in contrast, had a strong standing during and after the reunification process, prosecuting the perpetrators of the GDR regime was a priority. Thus, not to engage in a judicial approach to transitional justice would have 'grossly frustrated the internal opposition forces in the GDR and their allies within the emerging party system'.[85] Moreover, criminal prosecutions were considerably facilitated by the fact that a wealth of documentation and evidence was available in the form of

[80] Translation of the following quote in German: '… ob der Rechtsstaat in den Augen der Bevölkerung in der Lage ist, mit dem fertig zu werden, was uns das vierzigjährige Unrechtsregime in der früheren DDR hinterlassen hat'. Statement by Klaus Kinkel of 23 September 1991 at the *Deutscher Richtertag* in Cologne, see (1992) *Deutsche Richterzeitung* 4, 5.

[81] Offe and Poppe (n 31) 251–252.

[82] B Schlink, 'Rechtsstaat und revolutionäre Gerechtigkeit', Lecture at Humboldt University Berlin 1994, available at edoc.hu-berlin.de/handle/18452/2273.

[83] ibid. See also G Sälter, 'Der Rechtsstaat und das Grenzregime der DDR – Die strafrechtliche Verfolgung der Grenzdelikte in der Bundesrepublik' in J Ganzenmüller (ed) *Recht und Gerechtigkeit – Die strafrechtliche Aufarbeitung von Diktaturen in Europa* (Böhlau, 2017) 115, 116.

[84] Offe and Poppe (n 31) 253.

[85] ibid.

the *Stasi* files – this was not the case to this extent for any other post-Communist state. And finally, the criminal liability approach was already initiated by the GDR regime in 1989 und 1990 before reunification, with some investigations and arrests even of high-ranking officials. After reunification, it thus seemed impossible to 'pursue a more lenient line' than that taken by the post-1989 GDR leadership itself.[86]

To implement the criminal liability approach, a special investigation agency was created, the *Zentrale polizeiliche Ermittlungsstelle für Regierungs- und Vereinigungskriminalität*. This agency was competent for white-collar crimes as well as governmental crimes committed in the GDR. Based on this agency's investigations, a specially created prosecutor's office in Berlin opened criminal proceedings in relation to these acts.

The most salient example of this criminal dimension of transitional justice are the border guard trials.[87] These were criminal proceedings against the members of the GDR military stationed at the German/German border who shot at people attempting to escape to West Germany.[88] At the border of Berlin alone, 122 individuals had been killed; at the entire GDR border, there had been at least 270 reported deaths.[89] Border guards had the order to prevent any individual attempting to escape from the GDR, including by shooting at them with automatic weapons. Of the 275 persons accused of criminal acts in the border regime that were convicted, 223 were simple border guards.[90]

These trials have been broadly discussed both domestically and internationally as they have raised a number of fundamental rule of law questions related to the non-retroactivity of criminal law as well as to the positive vs natural law relationship.[91]

The principle of non-retroactivity of criminal law – an important element of the rule of law – is enshrined in Article 103(2) of the German Basic Law. As a consequence, it was not possible for the German legislator to create retroactively a law based on which citizens of the former GDR could be tried by a criminal court of the reunified Germany. Moreover, the Unification Treaty had also not

[86] ibid 260.

[87] For an overview of criminal prosecutions in relation to the GDR, see K Marxen and G Werle, *Die strafrechtliche Aufarbeitung von DDR-Unrecht – Eine Bilanz* (de Gruyter, 1999).

[88] On the constitutional questions involved in these cases: FCC, decision of 24 October 1996, 2 BvR 1851, 1853, 1875, 1852/94.

[89] Sälter (n 83) 117–118.

[90] Sälter (n 83) 126.

[91] Eg, KA Adams, 'What Is Just: The Rule of Law and Natural Law in the Trials of Former East German Border Guards' (1992–1993) 29 *Stanford Journal of International Law* 271; A Künzler, 'Judicial Legitimacy and the Role of Courts: Explaining the Transitional Context of the German Border Guard Cases' (2012) 32 *Oxford Journal of Legal Studies* 349–381; M Goodman, 'After the Wall The Legal Ramifications of the East German Border' (1996) 29 *Cornell International Law Journal* 727–765; PE Quint, 'Judging the Past: The Prosecution of East German Border Guards and the GDR Chain of Command' (1999) 61 *The Review of Politics* 303–329; Sälter (n 83); I Keller, *Strafrechtliche Aufarbeitung von DDR-Justizunrecht* (Peter Lang, 2013).

regulated this issue. As a result, it was for the courts to decide whether and in what way such trials could take place.[92]

In the border guard trials, the border guards – often still very young at the time of the acts – argued that their actions were legal under the law of the GDR and that, according to this legal order, they were not only allowed but even required to shoot persons trying to cross the border illegally. They even received praise and rewards from the regime after such incidents. Applying a different standard retroactively would, so the resulting argument went, be in violation of Article 103(2) of the Basic Law. However, the Federal Court of Justice (*Bundesgerichtshof*) decided that Article 103(2) was ultimately not applicable to the border guard trials.[93] It upheld a conviction of the border guards for manslaughter. This jurisprudence was motivated by the intention to provide transitional justice – and to do so more swiftly and extensively than had been done in the FRG after the Second World War with regard to the Nazi regime.[94] Moreover, in order to criminally charge members of the political elite of the GDR for crimes committed as part of the border regime, a criminal liability that could only be established in an indirect manner (*mittelbare Täterschaft*) and of the military officials for aiding and abetting, it was necessary to establish the criminal liability of the border guards first.[95]

How did the Court come to the controversial conclusion that Article 103(2) did not hinder the border guards' conviction? The Court held that the norms of substantive criminal law that it had to apply were those of the GDR law of the time. As a consequence, the Court did not consider this to be a case of retroactive application of the law. According to the Court, even under GDR law, the killings at the border were criminal offences. Not only was manslaughter an offence under the GDR Criminal Code, but – crucially – the legal norms that, if applied, would lead to the justification of such killings and thus of the impunity of the border guards were not applicable. To reach this latter conclusion, the Court adopted a controversial reasoning. It held that a legal provision in force at the time of the committed act is only applicable if it does not amount to 'an obvious gross violation of basic principles of justice and humanity'. The Court referred to a concept from legal philosophy that concerns the relationship between positive law and natural law: the so-called Radbruch formula (*Radbruch'sche Formel*). According to this formula that had been postulated by the German legal philosopher Gustav Radbruch in 1946 in relation to prosecutions concerning the Nazi regime, judges can, in exceptional cases, disregard

[92] The then-Minister of Justice Klaus Kinkel explicitly encouraged the judiciary to address this issue. See statement by Klaus Kinkel of 23 September 1991 at the *Deutscher Richtertag* in Cologne, (1992) *Deutsche Richterzeitung* 4, 5.

[93] *Bundesgerichtshof*, decision of 3 November 1992, 5 StR 370/92. See also *Bundesgerichtshof*, decision of 25 March 1993, 5 StR 418/92.

[94] Willoweit, Unrechtsstaat (n 25) 252.

[95] On this motivation for the border guard trials, Sälter (n 83) 126.

the positive law applicable to a case if applying the relevant norm would appear 'unbearably unjust' to them.[96] Considering its rather abstract formulation, this formula was not applied directly by the Court (the Court also explicitly stated that the killings at the German border could not be equated with the atrocities committed by the Nazi regime). Instead, it referred to international human rights standards as a concretised expression of this philosophical formula.

Under this approach, the legal norm of GDR law justifying the killing of persons who crossed the border illegally was not applicable. For the Court, the GDR law had to be interpreted in conformity with international human rights standards.[97] It held that applying the provision justifying border killings would have amounted, already at the time of the act, to a violation of international human rights – to which the GDR was bound. The GDR had signed and ratified the International Covenant on Civil and Political Rights (however not transposed it into domestic law, with the effect that the Covenant was not applicable within the domestic legal order[98]). According to the Court, applying a justification norm for the border killings would have amounted to a violation of Articles 6 and 12 of the Covenant. As a result, the Court decided that, even under GDR law, the border guards were not justified in killing unarmed persons who did not present any danger for life or limb of others. The Court further held:

> the judge is not bound in the sense of pure factuality to the interpretation that was expressed in state practice at the time of the crime .... A ground of justification that would have justified the defendant's behavior was indeed accepted in state practice ...; but even then, such a justification could not be inferred from the correctly interpreted law.[99]

This reasoning has been criticised both before and after the judgment of the *Bundesgerichtshof* as undermining the *Rechtsstaatsprinzip*.[100] As the constitutional lawyer Bernhard Schlink argued in 1994, it amounts to depriving law

[96] The full formulation in German is as follows: 'Der Konflikt zwischen Gerechtigkeit und der Rechtssicherheit dürfte dahin zu lösen sein, daß das positive, durch Satzung und Macht gesicherte Recht auch dann den Vorrang hat, wenn es inhaltlich ungerecht und unzweckmäßig ist, es sei denn, daß der Widerspruch des positiven Gesetzes zur Gerechtigkeit ein so unerträgliches Maß erreicht, daß das Gesetz als "unrichtiges Recht" der Gerechtigkeit zu weichen hat.' ('The conflict between justice and legal security should be solved as follows: the positive law, secured through its statutory form and power, prevails even if its content is unjust and unfit for purpose, unless the contradiction between the positive law and material justice is unbearable to the point that the positive law, as "false law", needs to give way to justice.').

[97] Arguing that justification under criminal law is not possible if this would be contrary to the legal principles accepted by 'civilised nations', Starck (n 28) 27.

[98] See the requirement of transposition in Art 51 of the Constitutions of 1968 and 1974. On this issue, see also H Dreier, 'Gustav Radbruch und die Mauerschützen' (1997) 52 *JuristenZeitung* 421, 425.

[99] *Bundesgerichtshof*, decision of 3 November 1992, 5 StR 370/92 (authors' translation).

[100] For an overview of the critique, see also H Rosenau, *Tödliche Schüsse im staatlichen Auftrag: Die strafrechtliche Verantwortung von Grenzsoldaten für den Schußwaffengebrauch an der deutsch-deutschen Grenze* (Nomos, 1998).

of its dimension of reality.[101] The Court applied the criminal law of the GDR not as it was practiced and recognised at the time but as it *should have been applied*.[102] He argues that the law as addressed in Article 103(2) is indeed the law as recognised and practised and not as retroactively constructed by a court for the purpose of a specific trial. Moreover, according to Schlink, the Court misconstrued the trust of the subjects of law in a continued legal framework as a precondition of Article 103(2) rather than as the rationale of this article.

A further line of criticism relates to how the legal order of the GDR is portrayed in this judgment. It takes GDR legal norms at face value and disregards the fact that certain norms including in the constitution served a propaganda purpose for having the GDR appear among the international community as more rule of law based und human rights abiding than it was in practice.[103] According to this criticism, this amounts to adopting a fiction of the bindingness of these norms and to falsely portraying the GDR as a state that is based on the rule of law.[104] In the same vein, it has been criticised how the court interprets GDR law in light of human rights provisions. Silke Laskowski argued that the GDR 'would have had to change its identity' to be in line with the interpretation that the *Bundesgerichtshof* has given to the law of the GDR – which means that this interpretation must be characterised as an 'ex-post facto re-interpretation' of GDR law.[105] Additionally, Laskowski criticised that this interpretation amounts to constructing an international law liability of the border guards.[106] As the killings at the border were not covered by international criminal law, however, this approach is in her view unconvincing from an international law perspective.

Further, it is also seen as questionable whether the killings constitute extreme or blatant '*Unrecht*' as the Radbruch formula requires, considering that this is a moral question and one that has been controversially debated for the border regime.[107] More generally, critiques of the natural law approach have argued that it is both legally impractical and necessarily rouses the suspicion of being applied in an ideological manner.[108] For those critiques, the only viable solution would have been to change the Basic Law and add an exception to Article 103(2).[109] Josef Isensee, for example, argued that one cannot solve 'the rule of law related dilemma with criminal law means' and should thus forgo the criminal law approach.[110]

[101] Schlink (n 82).
[102] ibid.
[103] Sälter (n 83) 123.
[104] ibid.
[105] Laskowski (n 38) 161.
[106] ibid 161.
[107] ibid 162.
[108] B Pieroth, 'Der Rechtsstaat und die Aufarbeitung der vor-rechtsstaatlichen Vergangenheit' (1992) 51 VVDStRL 91, 103. See also J Isensee, 'Aussprache' (1992) 51 VVDStRL 134, 136.
[109] Pieroth (n 108) 104; Isensee (n 108) 136. Critically, Schlink (n 82).
[110] Isensee (n 108) 136.

Despite the many critical observations in relation to the reasoning of the *Bundesgerichtshof*, the FCC upheld the judgment.[111] The FCC held:

> The strict prohibition of retroactivity in Article 103 Paragraph 2 of the Basic Law finds … its constitutional justification in the special basis of trust that criminal laws carry when they are enacted by a democratic legislature that is bound to fundamental rights. This special basis of trust is no longer applicable if the other state has established criminal offenses in the area of the most serious criminal injustice but has nevertheless excluded criminal liability for certain areas through justification reasons, by encouraging such injustice beyond the written norms, promoting it and thus disregarding in a serious manner the human rights that are generally recognised in the international legal community.
>
> In this very special situation, the requirement of substantive justice, which also includes respect for human rights recognised under international law, prohibits the use of such a justification. The strict protection of trust by Article 103 Paragraph 2 of the Basic Law must then give way to this. Otherwise, the Federal Republic's criminal justice system would contradict its rule of law principles.[112]

The FCC also mentioned the Radbruch formula, which it had already referred to in previous decisions.[113] It had acknowledged that 'in cases of an intolerable contradiction between positive law and justice, the principle of legal certainty can be valued less than that of substantive justice'.[114] It confirms the approach of the *Bundesgerichtshof* to link this formula to international human rights standards and to concretise it in this manner.

Finally, in 2001, the ECtHR also upheld the convictions.[115] The Court ruled the jurisprudence of the German courts to be in line with the principle of the rule of law as well as with the prohibition of non-retroactive criminal law under Article 7 ECHR. It stated:

> The Court considers that it is legitimate for a State governed by the rule of law to bring criminal proceedings against persons who have committed crimes under a former regime; similarly, the courts of such a State, having taken the place of those which existed previously, cannot be criticised for applying and interpreting the legal provisions in force at the material time in the light of the principles governing a State subject to the rule of law. …
>
> The Court considers that a State practice such as the GDR's border-policing policy, which flagrantly infringes human rights and above all the right to life, the supreme value in the international hierarchy of human rights, cannot be covered by the protection of Article 7 § 1 of the Convention. That practice, which emptied of its substance

[111] FCC, decision of 24 October 1996, 2 BvR 1851, 1853, 1875 und 1852/94.

[112] Paras 136, 137 (authors' translation).

[113] Previous decisions include: FCC, decision of 18 December 1953, 1 BvL 106/53; FCC, decision of 19 February 1957, 1 BvR 357/52; FCC decision of 10 May 1957, 1 BvR 550/52.

[114] FCC, decision of 24 October 1996, 2 BvR 1851, 1853, 1875 und 1852/94, para 140 (authors' translation).

[115] ECtHR, *Streletz, Kessler and Krenz v Germany* [GC] – 35532/97, 34044/96 and 44801/98, decision of 22 March 2001.

> the legislation on which it was supposed to be based, and which was imposed on all organs of the GDR, including its judicial bodies, cannot be described as "law" within the meaning of Article 7 of the Convention.[116]

Finally, an additional issue in the border guard trials was the statute of limitations. To overcome this issue, the regulation on the statute of limitations was adjusted. For criminal offices that were formally time-barred under GDR law, but which had not been prosecuted in the GDR because of political considerations, the legislator had created a law according to which the starting time for the statute of limitations was the date of German reunification. This legislation was also criticised as circumventing the non-retroactivity principle in Article 103(2) Basic Law.[117]

Beyond the border guards, other persons responsible for the border regime were criminally charged as part of the criminal liability approach to transitional justice. Among the political elite of the GDR, a number of persons received a prison sentence of several years. This includes, inter alia, the Minister of Defence Heinz Keßler (7.5 years), member of the National Defence Council and last leader of the SED Egon Krenz (6.5 years), the secretary of the National Defence Council General Fritz Streletz (5.5 years), and leader of the border troops General Klaus-Dieter Baumgarten (6.5 years).[118] These individuals were directly responsible for the border regime. Further, members of the military who did not have a direct influence on the regime but, due to their military function, such as head of one of the individual border troops, essentially contributed to the implementation of the regime were convicted as well. These persons received prison sentences of about three years. Both these groups of individuals thus received harsher sentences than the simple border guards, who generally received sentences of one to two years which were set out on probation. The reason for the probation was that the border guards executed orders, they were under pressure, they were misused by the regime, and there was no risk of repetition of such acts.[119]

Further, persons that had formally worked as spies for the *Stasi* (as opposed to persons who collaborated with the *Stasi* 'informally') were also prosecuted. These trials again raised the question of whether they violated Article 103(2) of the *Grundgesetz*. The *Bundesgerichtshof* decided that there was no constitutional law barrier to these prosecutions.[120] The FFC, however, took a different approach. Although it agreed that Article 103(2) did not hinder the criminal prosecution of GDR spies, it held that such a prosecution was barred by the *Rechtsstaatsprinzip* according to Articles 20(3) and 28(1).[121] For the Court, the

[116] Paras 81, 87.
[117] Marxen and Werle (n 87) 5–7, 248–249.
[118] Sälter (n 83) 119.
[119] ibid 120.
[120] *Bundesgerichtshof*, decision of 30 July 1993, 3 StR 347/92.
[121] FCC, decision of 15 May 1996, 2 BvL 19/91.

German reunification created a unique situation in which it would not be in line with the rule of law to prosecute persons who lived at the time of the offences in question in the GDR and acted only from within the GDR territory.

A field of action that was not addressed in terms of criminal liability were the measures of the *Stasi* that purposefully interfered with people's lives. This involved interferences with education and work life as well as family and social life. According to the internal instructions of the *Stasi*, *Stasi* employees and collaborators should adopt practices such as 'finding out about personal weaknesses of persons and fabricating compromising materials' and 'undermining the self-esteem of persons by organizing failures in their professional and social life'.[122] These aspects were not addressed in terms of criminal liability.

As a further part of the legal approach to transitional justice, in addition to criminal liability, reunified Germany reversed the (legal) effects of certain acts of the GDR judiciary and administration. To start with, the Unification Treaty and the Rehabilitation Act (*Rehabilitationsgesetz*) of 1992 addressed certain cases of miscarriage of justice, even though not all cases. The Rehabilitation Act enables the rehabilitation of persons who were the subject of criminal proceedings that were contrary to the principles of a rule of law-based order. Judgements or other decisions against these persons can be nullified, and they can receive financial compensation. There are a number of criminal offences under GDR law that fall in this category as such (section 1(1) Rehabilitation Act). These include, inter alia, 'anti-state agitation' (*staatsfeindliche Hetze*, section 106 GDR Criminal Code), illegal border crossing (*ungesetzliche Grenzüberquerung*, section 213 GDR Criminal Code), evasion from military service (*Wehrdienstentziehung*, section 256 GDR Criminal Code), and treasonous transfer of messages (*Landesverräterische Nachrichtenübermittlung*, section 99 GDR Criminal Code). The act is also applicable to all decisions of the so-called 'Waldheim Proceedings' (see above at I.A).

In addition to the Rehabilitation Act, a parallel legal act in relation to administrative decisions was adopted in 1994. This act makes it possible to repeal administrative acts of the GDR executive branch that were taken contrary to rule of law standards and that resulted in a physical injury, affected property rights, or created professional disadvantages and – cumulatively – that have ongoing effects (section 1(1) *Verwaltungsrechtliches Rehabilitierungsgesetz*).

Furthermore, in 1990, GDR judges had to undergo a screening to determine whether they could continue to exercise a judicial function.[123] Judges who had contributed to GDR judicial injustice were removed from the judiciary. This was seen as especially important considering the fact that it was very difficult to charge GDR judges criminally with perversion of justice.[124]

[122] As cited by Offe and Poppe (n 31) 263–264.

[123] Starck (n 28) 37.

[124] Starck (n 28) 38. See also Kraut (n 15); U Homann, *Herausforderungen an den Rechtsstaat durch Justizunrecht: die Urteile bundesdeutscher Gerichte zur strafrechtlichen Aufarbeitung von NS- und DDR-Justizverbrechen* (Berliner Wissenschafts-Verlag, 2003) 105–183.

A further key dimension of transitional justice are non-legal tools such as truth-finding, remembrance and reconciliation. After German reunification, however, these aims were only addressed in part, with controversial outcomes. With regard to these aims, there had initially been the idea of a tribunal that would investigate the activities of the GDR regime which then developed into the approach of a parliamentary commission of inquiry (*Enquête-Kommission*).[125] The first of two of these commissions was established from 1992 to 1994 (titled 'Dealing with the history and consequences of the SED dictatorship in Germany'[126]). This commission centred its work on the topics of repression by the GDR regime, opposition, and resistance against this repression and German/German political interaction. In contrast, other dimensions of transitional justice such as social, cultural and economic aspects remained unaddressed.[127] But even in the fields that the commission dealt with, it had only a limited outcome. Due to the different political convictions of the members of the commission, it did not result in objective historic research or in concrete suggestions as to how to proceed.[128] Among the general public of former GDR citizens, the work of the commission contributed to the perception that the truth-finding and remembrance activities were one-sided and dominated by West German actors.[129] As a counter-reaction, positive and nostalgic images of the GDR became more prominent – an effect that has repercussions until today.

In light of the shortcomings of the first commission, a second commission was established in order to take a broader approach. It worked from 1995 to 1998 (under the title 'Overcoming the consequences of the SED dictatorship in the process of German unity'[130]) on issues including, inter alia, the social and cultural perspective on GDR history and the question as to how to design a future remembrance culture in Germany. Together, these commissions have produced 17 volumes with almost 30,000 pages of documents. However, the second commission perpetuated the narratives of the first commission such as regarding the notion of '*Unrechtsregime*' and the delegitimisation approach.[131]

More generally, remembrance as a crucial part of transitional justice has been a very controversial aspect of German reunification. Both in the political and academic discourse, there was disagreement as to the right form, extent, and content of GDR remembrance.[132] Different groups of actors competed for control over the remembrance process and the shaping of a historical narrative about the GDR. An important group were the former East German civil rights activists. They advocated for viewing GDR history through the lens of the

[125] Hansack (n 40) 112.
[126] '*Aufarbeitung von Geschichte und Folgen der SED-Diktatur in Deutschland*'.
[127] Hansack (n 40) 117.
[128] ibid 119.
[129] ibid 121.
[130] '*Überwindung der Folgen der SED-Diktatur im Prozess der deutschen Einheit*'.
[131] Hansack (n 40) 121.
[132] ibid 103.

1989 resistance movement. This perspective was opposed, first, to the approach put forward by the PDS: to put an end to investigating into GDR history and to move on; and to advocate an idealised image of the GDR. Second, it was opposed to the position of West German actors that, as outlined above, focused on delegitimising the GDR.[133]

Initially, the *Stasi* and its mass surveillance were at the centre of remembrance activities in the reunified Germany. This is in line with the above-mentioned focus on delegitimising the GDR. However, it soon became apparent that this dimension was not regarded as sufficient by the East German population. Consequently, remembrance was conceived more broadly. Tools for remembrance beyond the two commissions of inquiry included the creation of entities such as the Federal Foundation for the Study of the Communist Dictatorship in Eastern Germany in 1998. The purpose of this foundation is to preserve existing remembrance efforts and to investigate further into 'the causes, history and impact of the dictatorship in the Soviet occupation zone in Germany, the GDR and East Central Europe'.[134] It also included erecting several memorials concerning the German/German border, the remembrance of opposition, resistance, and persecution in the GDR as well as museums with a focus on GDR history.[135]

A final challenge for the rule of law during the reunification process was how to deal with the about 111 km of *Stasi* files that had been preserved as the result of the *Stasi*'s mass surveillance. Dealing with these files involved competing interests: on the one hand, to protect the personality rights of the individuals whose information is contained in the files; and, on the other hand, to obtain evidence for criminal proceedings against perpetrators, to gather knowledge about disappearances and deaths that had remained unclear until then, or to enable persons to obtain rehabilitation.[136] A specific legal act regulates how to balance these interests: the *Stasi* Records Act of 1991 (*Stasi-Unterlagen-Gesetz*). According to section 1 of this act, the purpose of the act is

1. to give individuals access to the information stored about them by the state security service [*Stasi*] so that they can clarify the influence of the state security service on their personal fate,
2. to protect the individual from having their personal rights impaired by the handling of the information stored about them by the state security service,
3. to ensure and promote the historical, political and legal analysis of the activities of the state security service,
4. to provide public and non-public bodies with the necessary information for the purposes specified in this law.

[133] ibid 113.

[134] See the self-description of the foundation available at www.bundesstiftung-aufarbeitung.de/de/foundation.

[135] A list of institutions is available at www.bundesstiftung-aufarbeitung.de/de/erinnern/museen-und-gedenkstaetten/linkliste.

[136] Starck (n 28) 40.

For the individuals concerned as victims, this legal act provides an important element of transitional justice. Under section 13 of the Act, every person can obtain access to their file if there is one. This access possibility has allowed former GDR citizens to gain knowledge about whether, to what extent, and by whom they have been the victim of surveillance. More than 1.7 million people have accessed their respective file.[137]

However, for the individuals who figured in these files as a *Stasi* employee or collaborator, the information policy based on these files was perceived as problematic from a rule of law point of view. The agency in charge of managing the *Stasi* files had a mandate to investigate and to make information available to a range of actors, including, for example, the employers of former *Stasi* employees or collaborators. This often resulted in these persons losing their jobs or not being employed by potential employers, especially when they were holding or seeking a position in public service. The dissemination of information about the files thus entailed de facto sanctions for these persons. Yet, there were no or few procedural rights guarantees for these persons to contest the content of investigations or dissemination. As a result, some saw this as 'violating one of the most fundamental principles the new regime is supposedly based on, namely, the rule of law with its implications of nonretroactivity, the presumption of innocence, and guaranteed access to the court system'.[138]

The files are stored and managed by the *Stasi* Records Archive (*Stasi-Unterlagen-Archiv*) which has venues in Berlin and in the East German states. Since 2021, it is part of the Federal Archive. Previously, the files were independently managed by a specific public agency, the *Bundesbeauftragte für die Unterlagen des Staatssicherheitsdienstes der ehemaligen Deutschen Demokratischen Republik* (BStU). The transfer into the Federal Archive was a controversial matter for many years. One of the issues was that the particularly high standard of data protection required for the *Stasi* files differed from the data protection generally implemented by the Federal Archive. Further, critics feared that the smaller regional offices of the agency that facilitated both general information and access to the files for concerned individuals would be closed. In 2014, the *Bundestag* created an independent expert commission tasked to assess the options for the future of the BStU. The expert commission proposed to include the files into the Federal Archive – a proposal that was criticised in view of the above implications as well as from a symbolic point of view. The BStU had been perceived for 30 years as a symbol of the peaceful revolution and as a unique opportunity to access and research the files of the security agency of a dictatorial regime.[139]

[137] Information according to the Stasi Record Archive, available at www.stasi-unterlagen-archiv.de/en/access-to-records/access-for-private-individuals/.

[138] Offe and Poppe (n 31) 269; M Brandenburger, 'Stasi-Unterlagen-Gesetz und Rechtsstaat' (1995) 28 *Kritische Justiz* 351, 355–358.

[139] See interview with Hildigund Neubert, dissenting member of the expert committee, *Welt Online* 31 March 2016, available at www.welt.de/geschichte/article153847135/Flaggschiff-der-DDR-Aufarbeitung-wird-versenkt.html.

This symbolic function could not be fulfilled by the Federal Archive. In fact, the *Stasiunterlagengesetz* and the independence of the former BStU is a feature that, on the international level and, in comparison to other states, has been regarded as exemplary for transitional justice processes regarding autocratic regimes. As a result, it has been perceived as counterintuitive why Germany would do away with this well-regarded feature.[140]

Concerning the result of the truth-finding, remembrance, and reconciliation tools, it has been observed that the outcome of these tools encountered only a limited interest of the public in the reunified Germany. This might be explained by the fact that the unified German public was composed of more than three quarters of former West German citizens who were not directly affected by this regime. As a result, these dimensions of transitional justice 'ha[ve] played a somewhat marginal role in Germany, at least a much smaller one than it would have played in a separate and permanent democratic successor state of the GDR'.[141]

B. Rule of Law vs Justice: Expectations and Experiences of Former GDR Citizens

German reunification has put a spotlight on the relationship between the rule of law and justice. In the public perception, especially among former GDR citizens, the tension between these two notions was prominent. This has been expressed in a much-cited phrase, attributed to the GDR civil rights activist Bärbel Bohley, which might be loosely translated as follows: 'We expected justice, yet we got the rule of law.'[142]

To engage with this claim, it is useful to briefly look at how the relationship between justice and the rule of law is conceptualised in German legal discourse.[143] For Ingo von Münch, who engaged with this relationship in the context of German reunification, it is impossible to disconnect justice and the rule of law.[144] He argues that a *Rechtsstaat* without justice would merely be an empty shell.[145] For him, justice is inherently linked to the substantive rule of law notion (*materielle Rechtsstaatlichkeit* – see also chapter one).[146] Despite this close interlinkage, it can happen that justice and a specific element of the

[140] ibid.

[141] Offe and Poppe (n 31) 265.

[142] On this statement, I von Münch, 'Rechtsstaat versus Gerechtigkeit?' (1994) 33 *Der Staat* 165; K Löw, '"Gerechtigkeit haben wir erwartet, den Rechtsstaat haben wir bekommen" (Bärbel Bohley)' in K Löw (ed), *10 Jahre Deutsche Einheit* (Duncker & Humblot, 2001) 25.

[143] Eg, von Münch (n 142); C Bäcker, *Gerechtigkeit im Rechtsstaat – Das Bundesverfassungsgericht an der Grenze des Grundgesetzes* (Mohr Siebeck, 2015).

[144] Von Münch (n 142) 174.

[145] ibid.

[146] ibid 175.

rule of law are in conflict/contradiction with each other. For example, the FCC has acknowledged that although *Rechtsstaatlichkeit* includes both substantive justice and legal certainty, both elements cannot always be optimised to the same extent.[147] The relationship between justice and the rule of law is thus multilayered and prone to diverging perceptions as to how justice interests and the rule of law ought to be balanced in specific contexts.

Against this backdrop, we can engage with the expectations and experiences of former GDR citizens after reunification. This relates to how both agents and victims of the GDR regime have been treated in a unified Germany, to the adverse effects of how the economic transition was handled, to the replacement of much of the judicial and administrative 'elite' by people of West German origin, and to persisting inequalities.

The original phrase by Bärbel Bohley relates primarily to how the reunified Germany engages with the victims and perpetrators of the GDR regime. Bohley criticised, for example, that sanctions against members of certain professions were not carried out. According to her, doctors, teachers or lawyers that had breached their professional confidence by providing information to the *Stasi* should have been barred from their profession for a few years.[148] Moreover, victims of the regime saw it as a great injustice that the trial against Erich Honecker, who had been General Secretary of the SED central committee and thus the political leader of the GDR until 1989, failed.[149] The Constitutional Court of the state of Berlin had decided that criminal proceedings against a person with a terminal illness would constitute a breach of the right to human dignity as guaranteed by the Constitution of Berlin.[150] In relation to this issue, Arnold Vaatz, a former minister of the East German state of Saxony has been cited with the observation that 'the *Rechtsstaat* was overwhelmed by the legacy of the peaceful revolution in East Germany'.[151] Some observers stated that former victims of the GDR are likely to have had the impression that the protection of the *Rechtsstaat* primarily benefits the perpetrators rather than the victims.[152] Accordingly, it has been argued that the *Rechtsstaat* 'is blind for legal and moral questions that did not arise in its framework and cannot be defined within this framework'.[153] Moreover, the failure of the Honecker trial also created a perception of injustice from another point of view: the high-ranking

[147] FCC, decision of 26 February 1969, 2 BvL 15, 23/68.

[148] Von Münch (n 142) 167.

[149] ibid. Generally on this trial, AJ McAdams, 'The Honecker Trial: The East German Past and the German Future' (1996) 58 *Review of Politics* 53.

[150] Constitutional Court of the State of Berlin, decision of 12 January 1993, VerfGH 55/92.

[151] As cited by von Münch (n 142) 167 ('daß der Rechtsstaat vom Erbe des friedlichen Umbruchs in Ostdeutschland überfordert werde').

[152] Isensee (n 108) 134.

[153] A Zielke, 'Der Kälteschock des Rechtsstaats', *Frankfurter Allgemeine Zeitung*, 9 November 1991, as cited by von Münch (n 142) 176: 'Der Rechtsstaat … ist blind für rechtliche und moralische Fragestellungen, die nicht seines Rahmens entstanden und definierbar sind.'

officials got away while the lower-level actors, such as border guards or *Stasi* employees, were convicted.[154]

This injustice perception is linked more broadly to the outcome of the trials in relation to the border regime of the GDR. Only ten members of the political elite of the GDR and 42 officers of the military leadership have been convicted for the deaths at the border – as compared to the abovementioned 223 low-rank border guards.[155] Most of the members of the political elite could not be criminally persecuted due to age or illness. But the border trials also have further dimensions of (perceived) injustice. Considering the questionable way in which the judiciary had circumvented the principle of non-retroactivity in the border guard trials, it has been argued that these trials can in themselves be perceived as a contribution to the impression of injustice.[156] Finally, justice in the sense of retribution seemed limited as the border guards who were convicted received relatively mild sentences which were suspended on probation.[157]

In addition to the features of criminal liability that were criticised as unjust, the focus on criminal liability as such can appear as an element of injustice. This is the case because transitional justice, due to this focus, did not or did not sufficiently engage with other negative effects of the regime. In general, this approach 'deemphasizes those deprivations that largely cannot thus be attributed, namely, the "systemic" ills of the apparatuses of ideological control and economic (mis)management'.[158]

Moreover, an aspect that is questionable both with regard to justice and the rule of law relates to the consequences former *Stasi* employers and collaborators had to face in the reunified Germany. Although the initial policy had been not to employ such persons within the public service of the reunified Germany, this policy was not implemented consistently. For example, 12 per cent of the police officers employed in the 1990s as civil servants by the state of Berlin and by the five new *Länder* were known to have worked for the *Stasi* and were employed nonetheless.[159] This can be perceived as unjust both from the perspective of the victims of the *Stasi* and by the persons whose employment was ended due to their *Stasi* involvement. Moreover, this practice has been seen as affecting the rule of law. Claus Offe and Ulrike Poppe consider the rule of law as 'severely violated when – even in the highly sensitive field of police services – the rule that *Stasi* involvement must be sanctioned is frequently, arbitrarily, and opportunistically suspended'.[160]

[154] This criticism was commonly phrased in the form of the then-popular saying: 'Die Kleinen hängt man, die Großen lässt man laufen.' See von Münch (n 142) 182–183.
[155] Sälter (n 83) 126.
[156] Schlink (n 82).
[157] Sälter (n 83) 128.
[158] Offe and Poppe (n 31) 258.
[159] ibid 271.
[160] ibid 271.

An important issue that, from the perspective of many GDR citizens, has led to injustice is the way in which property claims were handled after reunification.[161] This includes the 'Act Relating to Open Property Questions' (*Gesetz über die offenen Vermögensfragen*), a legal act that addressed expropriations and similar actions vis-à-vis West German citizens by the GDR. According to this act, persons whose property had been expropriated by the GDR without compensation or with a compensation that was lower than that received by expropriated GDR citizens, or whose property was put under public management, received their property back. In comparison to similar situations concerning nationals from other states, West German property owners were thus not merely compensated for their loss but benefited from a re-transfer of property. This was perceived as unjust because it was the citizens of the GDR who had risked their life and their freedom when opposing and finally overturning the regime, but it was West Germans who benefited from this by property restitution.[162] Moreover, the restitution also appeared unjust from a constitutional law point of view. As clarified by the FCC, there is no constitutional law requirement stemming from the Basic Law that the compensation in relation to acts of a former state has to be in the form of restitution.[163] Constitutional lawyers have thus argued that the existential impact on the property rights of former GDR citizens was not convincingly balanced against the merely commercial interests of the former property owners from West Germany.[164] It would have been a constitutional obligation of the legislator to ensure that the rights of the former citizens of the GDR were realised, which would have amounted to a 'primacy' of enabling these persons to acquire property rather than a restitution of the property to West Germans.[165] Finally, in addition to this substantive injustice, there has been an element of procedural injustice: the legal act prescribing this property transfer has only been deliberated in the *Bundestag* of the FRG but not in the – then still existing – *Volkskammer*, the legislative body of the GDR.

A further very controversially perceived aspect of reunification and its just or unjust effects concerns the way in which the planning economy of the GDR has been restructured into a market economy. At the core of this restructuring was the so-called *Treuhand*, a trusteeship agency created in 1990 for this restructuring purpose (*Anstalt zur treuhänderischen Verwaltung des Volkseigentums*). This agency took over the management of the state-owned companies of the GDR to gradually privatise or shut down these companies. The government of the reunified Germany instructed this agency to privatise these companies as quickly as possible. This occurred at a time when the East German companies

[161] Hansack (n 40) 91; von Münch (n 142) 179.
[162] Von Münch (n 142) 180.
[163] FCC, decision of 3 April 1991, 1 BvR 1170, 1174, 1175/90.
[164] Von Münch (n 142) 181. See also W Berg, 'Der Rechtsstaat und die Aufarbeitung der vor-rechtsstaatlichen Vergangenheit' (1992) 51 VVDStRL 46, 70–72, 85.
[165] Berg (n 164) 95.

faced a severe economic crisis due to the transition from GDR currency to FRG currency, the collapsing demand for GDR products, and the sudden competition from the West. During the agency's existence between 1990 and 1994, it privatised more than 12,000 East German companies and shut down about 3,700.[166] This led to a massive loss of jobs in the region: of the initially 4.1 million jobs in state-owned companies, only 1.5 million were left in the remaining privatised companies.[167]

Most East Germans are very critical of the *Treuhand*'s practice. The rapid and costly privatisation has been perceived as selling out of the East German economy. Indeed, in no other post-communist country did the economic transformation happen at this pace.[168] This practice has weakened the economy in this region with a long-lasting effect.[169] Many observers argue that it has led the East German population to mistrust the functioning of the market economy of which they had become a part.[170] There was also a legitimacy issue: in 1993, all the directors of this agency, as well as 81 per cent of its heads of department, were from West Germany.[171] Moreover, some of the *Treuhand* managers who decided on whether to invest in rebuilding a certain company came from competing companies in the West and were thus biased against supporting a competing East German company.[172] A legal construction made it possible not to allow for representative bodies, which actively circumvented (indirect) participation in the privatisation decision and process by staff representatives.[173] Moreover, the governments of the newly created East German *Länder* also lacked genuine influence on the privatisation process, an additional aspect of the weak legitimacy of the *Treuhand* practice.[174] As a result, and as the only way of action available, employees of the companies that the *Treuhand* wanted to shut down protested fiercely against such decisions, including by strikes, protest marches, the occupation of parliamentary buildings, and even hunger strikes – mostly without success.[175] In general, the *Treuhand* has been seen as

[166] See the numbers provided by the *Bundeszentrale für Politische Bildung*, available at www.bpb.de/kurz-knapp/hintergrund-aktuell/201919/die-geburtsstunde-der-treuhand/.

[167] ibid.

[168] See J Roesler, 'Nur den Anforderungen des Marktes verpflichtet? Autokratische Züge und demokratische Ansätze der Treuhandprivatisierung', available at www.bpb.de/themen/deutschlandarchiv/54068/nur-den-anforderungen-des-marktes-verpflichtet/.

[169] K Steinitz, 'Die Treuhandanstalt und der wirtschaftliche Absturz Ostdeutschlands' in U Plener (ed), *Die Treuhand – der Widerstand in Betrieben der DDR – die Gewerkschaften (1990–1994). Tagung vom 2. April 2011 in Berlin* (NORA, 2011) 15.

[170] See overview of the *Bundeszentrale für Politische Bildung*, available at www.bpb.de/kurz-knapp/hintergrund-aktuell/201919/die-geburtsstunde-der-treuhand/.

[171] Roesler (n 168).

[172] ibid.

[173] ibid.

[174] ibid.

[175] ibid. See also U Plener (ed), *Die Treuhand – der Widerstand in Betrieben der DDR – die Gewerkschaften (1990–1994). Tagung vom 2. April 2011 in Berlin* (NORA, 2011).

having worked in the interest of the West German industry rather than in the interest of the people.[176]

The practice of the *Treuhand* is prone to raise tempers and to be politically instrumentalised until today. For example, in 2019, the left-wing party *Die Linke* and the right-wing party AFD ('Alternative for Germany' – *Alternative für Deutschland*) put forward an initiative to set up a parliamentary commission of inquiry regarding this agency. The *Linke* politician Dietmar Bartsch labelled the practice of the *Treuhand* as a 'disaster' and as one of the main reasons for the frustration of many East Germans until today.[177]

A final aspect that has led to injustice perceptions on a more long-term scale was the replacement of much of the judicial, administrative and political elite by people of West German origin. To start with, after reunification, the judges and prosecutors of the former GDR (as well as law professors) had to reapply for their positions.[178] In the re-application process, they were screened, inter alia, as to whether they were members of the party (SED) or even collaborators of the *Stasi* and whether they had participated in political trials.[179] This procedure was perceived by the judges and prosecutors as 'prejudgment of their entire professional practice'.[180] Only about two thirds of the former judges and prosecutors attempted to regain their position and of those, only about half succeeded.[181] Against this backdrop and considering that the per capita number of judges and prosecutors in the GDR was four times lower than in the FRG,[182] there was a considerable demand for judicial staff in the new East German states. These several thousands of vacant positions were filled by West German lawyers. Many of them were young graduates who saw career opportunities that they might not have had if they had stayed in the West German states.[183] As judicial appointments are typically lifetime appointments as public servants, these positions were filled for many decades with persons of West German origin. Moreover, almost all the judges in higher courts came from West Germany.[184]

Similarly to this replacement of elites within the judiciary, high-ranking administrative positions have been filled after reunification with West German staff.[185] The administration of the FRG served as an 'elite reservoir for staffing the

[176] Eg, Steinitz (n 169) 17.

[177] See parliamentary debate as reported here: www.bundestag.de/dokumente/textarchiv/2019/kw26-de-treuhandanstalt-646326.

[178] D Majer, 'Die Überprüfung von Richtern und Staatsanwälten in der ehemaligen DDR' (1991) 24 *Zeitschrift für Rechtspolitik* 171.

[179] Majer (n 178) 173.

[180] ibid 178.

[181] Blankenburg (n 22) 275.

[182] Majer (n 178).

[183] Blankenburg (n 22) 276.

[184] HU Derlien, 'German Unification and Bureaucratic Transformation' (1993) 14 *International Political Science Review* 319, 328.

[185] Derlien (n 184) 319.

bureaucracy [of East Germany] after unification'.[186] The 'personnel policy' was used 'as a means to politically control and professionally integrate the inherited eastern bureaucratic apparatuses'.[187] For the administration, however, the initial staffing requirements were inversed as compared to the judiciary. The GDR administration had a large number of personnel which made it necessary to reduce these numbers after reunification. Administrative staff 'could be let go for lack of qualification or lack of demand if agencies were abolished' and 'collaboration with the *Stasi* or past offences against principles of humanity and legality meant unconditional dismissal'.[188] This created some demand for importing administrative staff from West Germany. Although the overall percentage of West German staff was less high than in the judiciary, the percentage differed greatly depending on the rank. In general, 'the higher the position, the larger the proportion of West German imports', with, for example, 52 per cent of higher civil servants in the state of Brandenburg in the early 1990s being from West Germany and with 'almost every state secretary in the Lander ministries [being] a West German'.[189]

Finally, elites were also 'imported' on the political level. In the early 1990s, 'three out of five East German prime ministers were recruited from the western part of the country, as were four of the five justice ministers and the majority of the economics and finance ministers'.[190]

However, (perceived) justice issues have not only existed in the immediate aftermath of reunification. Rather, there are many issues and inequalities that continue to exist until this date. This includes underrepresentation of East Germans among the country's holders of elite position and inequalities among the East and the West as to aspects such as wages and pensions.

To start with, a recent study (that has been supported by the *Ostbeauftragter*, the Federal Representative for East Germany) has traced the extent to which the underrepresentation of East Germans among the elite in Germany persists today. For the period between 2018 and 2023, the study outlines this underrepresentation for different sectors of society.[191] Overall, East Germans hold 12.2 per cent of elite positions as compared to their constituting 20 per cent of the German population. The underrepresentation is most pronounced in the military, the judiciary, academia, and the economy. It seems to have decreased in the administration (from 9.9 per cent in 2018 to 14 per cent in 2022). Politics is the only field without nominal underrepresentation but only when considering political positions on the level of the *Länder*. The study also points to the dynamics of

[186] ibid 324.
[187] ibid 320.
[188] ibid 326.
[189] ibid 328.
[190] ibid 327.
[191] See overview document available at www.ostbeauftragter.de/resource/blob/2044590/2224378/59b5ce5f9b473cfd77688e8c94f3ebfd/elitenmonitor-data.pdf?download=1.

the underrepresentation. It highlights the fact that it did not naturally decrease due to a generational change. In fact, of the vacant positions that were still held by West Germans in 2018, only 8.1 per cent were filled with East Germans after the West Germans retired. But inversely, of positions held by East Germans in 2018, 53.9 per cent were filled with West Germans. It is also worth noting that even within the East German states, East Germans are still underrepresented in elite positions.

As to further inequalities, a salient example is that there continues to be a significant pay gap between the East and West. For example, in 2019, there was still a gap of 17 per cent between the average income in East and West Germany, and in 2022, a gap of more than €12,000 per year was reported.[192] Moreover, the pensions in East Germany have been lower than pensions in West Germany for more than three decades. Only since mid-2023 has the pension level been unified.[193] Initially, East German pensioners received only about 40 per cent of the West German pension level. Such inequalities have arguably contributed to the perception of many East Germans that in the German society after reunification, they are treated in an unjust manner, are valued less than West Germans and seen as some sort of second-class citizens.[194] In recent years, the right-wing party AFD has played to these feelings. At least initially, it was particularly successful in eastern German states (while its polls have meanwhile increased all over Germany). This shows how the injustice perceptions continue to shape both the social and political reality in Germany today.

III. CONCLUSION

The chapter has shown that the rule of law experience in the GDR and in the reunification process was multilayered and has often been controversially discussed. In the GDR, rule of law standards codified in the law and the experience in practice diverged greatly and led to major rule of law deficiencies. Both these facts tie into the controversy about the characterisation of the GDR as '*Unrechtsstaat*' that continues to be debated until today. Further, the reunification process has been a true challenge to the rule of law, both legally and in terms of the experience of the persons concerned. Its ambivalent legacy shapes the rule of law and justice experience of East Germans until today.

[192] See the analysis provided by the *Hans-Böckler-Stiftung*, available at www.lohnspiegel.de/thematische-analysen-20014-14943.htm; as well as the media report on the 2022 pay gap available at www.tagesschau.de/wirtschaft/finanzen/gehalt-differenz-ost-west-lohngefaelle-101.html.

[193] See information provided by the Federal Government at www.bundesregierung.de/breg-de/aktuelles/rente-ost-west-angleichung-2172482.

[194] According to a representative survey of August 2023, 43% of East Germans feel like 'second class citizens'. See survey by Infratest Dimap conducted between 28 and 30 August 2023, available at www.infratest-dimap.de/umfragen-analysen/bundesweit/umfragen/aktuell/33-jahre-wiedervereinigung/.

4

The German Rule of Law Experience in Times of Crisis

RULE OF LAW requirements are often tested in times of (perceived or real) crisis, and Germany is no exception in this regard. Issues of emergency powers, especially in the context of anti-terrorism, have been discussed in various countries and legal orders.[1] This chapter provides insights into the German public and legal debates on emergency measures and how they relate to the rule of law. In a first section, we discuss the challenge of terrorism and the impact of anti-terrorism measures on the rule of law (I). The second section turns to two recent crises during which state measures were criticised as detrimental to the rule of law: the so-called 'refugee crisis' of 2015 and the 2020 COVID-19 pandemic (II).

I. TERRORISM AND COUNTERTERRORISM MEASURES AS A RULE OF LAW CHALLENGE OVER TIME

A. Challenges to Fair Trial and Substantive Human Rights Protection

Terrorism and counterterrorism measures have challenged both substantive human rights and procedural rights, the latter especially in the criminal law context. In Germany, several historical events have caused controversial debates on appropriate limitations of fundamental rights due to terrorist attacks, namely extreme left-wing terrorism by the Red Army Faction (*Rote Armee Fraktion*, RAF) throughout the 1970s, counterterrorism measures after the 9/11 terrorist attacks and reactions to ongoing issues of right-wing and religiously motivated terrorism in Germany.

[1] In the US, there has been a protracted debate on the rule of law in the wake of the 9/11 attacks, with international spillover; in France, emergency powers have been newly discussed in reaction to the 2015 terrorist attacks; a similar discussion has taken place in Belgium and the UK, to name just a few examples. The Minerva Center for the Rule of Law under Extreme Conditions is a whole research centre devoted to the issue. See on the German emergency powers discourse, A-B Kaiser, *Ausnahmeverfassungsrecht* (Mohr-Siebeck, 2020); and T Barczak, *Der nervöse Staat* (Mohr-Siebeck, 2020); E-W Böckenförde, 'Der verdrängte Ausnahmezustand' (1978) *Neue Juristische Wochenschrift* 1881.

These instances of terrorism and counterterrorism measures have challenged the rule of law to diverging extents. On the one end of the spectrum are the actions of the RAF that have caused an unequalled crisis within the FRG and the reunified Germany. The RAF conducted terrorist attacks and kidnappings which caused more than 30 deaths of high-ranking individuals from politics, administration, businesses etc, as well as several hundred injured persons. These activities lasted from 1970 to the early 1990s but peaked in 1977 with what has come to be known as '*Deutscher Herbst*' (German Autumn).[2] It includes the kidnapping and killing of Hanns Martin Schleyer, the abduction of the Lufthansa aircraft *Landshut*, and the suicide of several members of the RAF who were in prison at the time. This period and the reactions by state authorities led to a major crisis of the rule of law in Germany. In comparison, the instances of terrorism and counterterrorism measures since the beginning of the twenty-first century were significant but did not lead to such major crises.

First, as a response to RAF terrorist attacks, a series of limitations to defence rights in criminal procedure were introduced[3] and explicitly criticised as limiting and potentially abridging the liberal rule of law ideal.[4] A first issue in this regard was the exclusion of defence lawyers. In the *Schily* case of 1972/73, the *Bundesgerichtshof* had excluded the defence lawyer Otto Schily from the defence of his client, the RAF terrorist Gudrun Ensslin, because he was suspected of having transmitted a note from Ensslin to another member of the RAF outside of prison. The FCC declared this measure unconstitutional.[5] According to the court, such an exclusion infringes upon the lawyer's freedom of profession under Article 12(1) of the Basic Law which is justified neither by legislation nor by a pre-constitutional norm of customary law. For the court, the regulation at the time fell short of the requirements of the *Rechtsstaatsprinzip* because the statutory legal basis was lacking in clarity and completeness. It further stressed that for criminal proceedings that fulfil rule of law standards, it is crucial that the accused can choose a defence lawyer whom they trust. This was necessary, according to the court, so that the accused did not become a mere object of state action but could use, as a subject of the proceedings, his or her procedural rights. This reasoning implicitly related the *Rechtsstaatsprinzip* to the protection of human dignity as enshrined in Article 1(1) of the Basic Law, and explicitly invoked the *Rechtsstaatsprinzip* with regard to the values of legal

[2] Incidentally, 1977 is the year in which the use of the term '*Rechtsstaat*' in parliamentary speech peaks for the first time: www.zeit.de/politik/deutschland/2019-09/bundestag-jubilaeum-70-jahre-parlament-reden-woerter-sprache-wandel#s=rechtsstaat%2Crechtsstaatlichkeit%2Crechtsstaatlichen.

[3] For an overview and critical assessment see I Müller, 'Neuestes und allerneustes Strafprozeßrecht' (1978) *Kritische Justiz* 301. An accessible introduction to the broader context and history of the Red Army Faction is S Aust, *Der Baader-Meinhoff-Komplex* (Goldmann Verlag, 1998).

[4] H Dahs, 'Das "Anti-Terroristen-Gesetz"- eine Niederlage des Rechtsstaats' (1976) *Neue Juristische Wochenschrift* 2145.

[5] FCC, decision of 14 February 1973, 2 BvR 667/72.

clarity and completeness of the statutory basis. As a result of this decision, the legislator amended the Code of Criminal Procedure and included detailed provisions creating the possibility to exclude defence lawyers.[6]

In subsequent cases relating to the exclusion of defence lawyers in the proceedings against RAF members (the so-called *Stammheim* Proceedings, named after the prison where several high-ranking RAF leaders were detained and eventually committed suicide), the FCC took a more reluctant approach.[7] It did not review in detail the constitutionality of the novel provisions in the Code of Criminal Procedure despite several scholars questioning its constitutionality.[8] Instead, the court left a wide leeway to the legislator to regulate the exclusion of defence lawyers.[9]

A further issue of procedural rights during the RAF proceedings of the 1970s was the trial in absentia, a practice that is very problematic under rule of law standards. Several defendants during the *Stammheim* Proceedings had been declared unfit to stand for trial for a certain period of time. The defendants were in poor health due to being held in solitary confinement and sensory deprivation as well as due to a hunger strike. In order for the proceedings to continue, the court decided to conduct the trial in absentia based on legal provisions that had been included in the Code of Criminal Procedure shortly before the beginning of these trials.[10] When the defendants challenged these measures, the *Bundesgerichtshof* upheld them based on the reasoning that the defendants had caused the health issues themselves, including by 'forcing' the authorities to keep them under the above-mentioned draconian prison conditions.[11] The court stated that a trial in absentia is necessary to ensure the administration of criminal justice as an expression of the rule of law. The rationale was to avoid that defendants could 'sabotage' their proceedings by putting themselves into a state in which they would be unfit for trial. This decision has been criticised for several reasons, including for not engaging with the human dignity dimension of conducting a trial in absentia and for accepting that defendants are permanently excluded from the hearings even if their health situation improves.[12] However, despite these issues, when the FCC subsequently came to decide the matter, it rejected the complaints by the defendants for procedural reasons and did not see any violation of fair trial rights in relation to such trials in absentia.[13]

[6] Sections 138a to 138d Code of Criminal Procedure.

[7] FCC, decision of 8 April 1975, 2 BvR 207/75.

[8] See M Putzer, *Gerichte, Terror und Verfahren* (Mohr Siebeck, 2015) 90.

[9] FCC, decision of 8 April 1975, 2 BvR 207/75: 'The Federal Constitutional Court is not required to examine whether the legislature has found the most appropriate, reasonable and fair solution' (authors' translation).

[10] Sections 231a and 231b Code of Criminal Procedure.

[11] *Bundesgerichtshof*, decision of 22 October 1975, 1 STE 1/74 – StB 60-63/75.

[12] Putzer (n 8) 101. Critical on the concerned procedural law provisions, H-J Rudolphi, 'Strafprozeß im Umbruch' (1976) 9 *Zeitschrift für Rechtspolitik* 165, 172–173; P Rieß, 'Die Durchführung der Hauptverhandlung ohne Angeklagten' (1975) *Juristenzeitung* 265.

[13] FCC, decision of 21 January 1976, 2BvR 941/75.

Another very controversial measure that affected procedural rights during criminal proceedings was the Communication Ban Act (*Kontaktsperregesetz*) of 1977. With this Act, the legislator had made it possible to ban any communication of prisoners with each other, with persons outside of prison, and even with their defence lawyers.[14] The conditions for such bans are, inter alia, that life, limb, or freedom of a person is in imminent danger and that the danger appears to emanate from a terrorist organisation. Both before this Act came into force and after, such a communication ban had been imposed on imprisoned RAF members. This gave rise to several decisions of the *Bundesgerichtshof* and the FCC on the matter.

In a decision of September 1977, the *Bundesgerichtshof* held that such a communication ban in the context of the kidnapping of Hanns Martin Schleyer, the then-President of the German Employers' Association, was justified.[15] The aim to protect the life of Schleyer and thus the right to life as one of the most important values of the legal order was, according to the Court, a sufficient reason to ban even the communication between the prisoners and their defence lawyers. For the Court, there was at the time a plausible danger that such communication might have increased the risk for Schleyer's life. This decision has been criticised for demonstrating a general mistrust against the defence lawyers in the terrorist cases of the 1970s who were under a general suspicion of collaborating with the terrorists.[16] As a result, the Court considered a weak factual basis as sufficient for establishing the danger required for the measure.[17] This has been criticised as undermining fundamental rights and rule of law elements such as the legality principle.[18] More generally, this jurisprudence has been seen as opening the gates for restricting constitutional guarantees for the sake of public security interests, with commentators warning that this would lead to a structural erosion of the rule of law under the pretext of state emergency measures.[19]

In a subsequent decision of October 1977, the *Bundesgerichtshof* reigned in this approach somewhat.[20] It adopted a restrictive interpretation of the Communication Ban Act that had just come into force before this second decision. It however sustained the extraordinary nature of these provisions and addressed once again the factual basis of the ban in an insufficient manner – which raises the question of whether the procedure could be qualified as an effective remedy as required by the right to a fair trial.[21]

[14] The relevant provisions are Sections 31 to 38 Introductory Act to the Courts Constitution Act (EGGVG).

[15] *Bundesgerichtshof*, decision of 23 September 1977, StB 215/77.

[16] Putzer (n 8) 111–112.

[17] ibid.

[18] Putzer (n 8) 113.

[19] G Lübbe-Wolff, 'Rechtsstaat und Ausnahmerecht' (1980) 11 *Zeitschrift für Parlamentsfragen* 110; K Amelung, 'Nochmals: § 34 StGB als öffentlichrechtliche Eingriffsnorm?' (1978) *Neue Juristische Woschenschrift* 623.

[20] *Bundesgerichtshof*, decision of 13 October 1977, 3 ARs 27/77.

[21] Putzer (n 8) 116–117.

In 1978, the FCC decided that the Communication Ban Act was in line with constitutional law.[22] Its reasoning was based on the then recently developed notion of the state's obligation to protect the right to life, to physical integrity, and to liberty (see also below). In this context, the *Rechtsstaatsprinzip* can be affected when communication bans aim at preventing terrorists from obtaining the release of prisoners by way of extorsion. The Court held, however, that communication bans were proportional measures. It stressed in particular that the security of the state and its population are as valuable as the fundamental rights of the individuals concerned and that security is crucial for the legitimacy of the institution of the state as such. To limit the impact on individual rights, the Court adopted, as did the *Bundesgerichthof*, a restrictive interpretation of the preconditions for such bans. However, the Court's reasoning has been criticised for deficits regarding a tendentious weighing of the involved rights and interests as well as deficits regarding the factual basis of the decision.[23]

Taken together, these procedural counter-terrorism measures have reduced the level of fair trial guarantees to a significant extent. Although they originate from the extraordinary circumstances of the RAF terrorism period, their legislative basis has remained in place since this time. Moreover, the outlined Court decisions show that during the time of the '*Deutscher Herbst*', the judiciary gave broad leeway to state authorities in their fight against RAF terrorism, which led to procedural rights being significantly impacted.

Second, in addition to challenging procedural rights guarantees, terrorist kidnappings and hijackings have led to the question of whether there is a state duty to protect the life of a person, even if possibly to the detriment of the life of others.[24] This question came to the fore both in the context of the RAF kidnappings during the 1970s and in the aftermath of the 9/11 attacks in the US.

To start with, the kidnapping and eventual killing of Hanns Martin Schleyer in 1977 by the RAF was not only a major crisis in post-war German history but also the occasion for an important decision of the FCC on the duty to protect the life of a person. In the *Schleyer* case of 1977, Schleyer's son had requested a preliminary injunction from the FCC against the government of the FRG and of several *Länder* to fulfil the demands of the kidnappers in order to save his father's life. The kidnappers had demanded to release and grant clear passage out of the FRG for a number of prisoners named by them. The case was about whether the state has an obligation under constitutional law to fulfil demands addressed by way of blackmailing if otherwise there is a risk for the life of an

[22] FCC, decision of 1 August 1978, 2 BvR 1013, 1019, 1034/77.

[23] Putzer (n 8) 125–131.

[24] For the debate following RAF kidnappings in the 1970s see M Schröder, 'Staatsrecht an den Grenzen des Rechtsstaates: Überlegungen zur Verteidigung des Rechtsstaates in außergewöhnlichen Lagen' (1978) *Archiv des öffentlichen Rechts* 121.

abducted person or other individuals other than the blackmailers. The FCC held in its decision[25] that

> [t]he state has a duty, deriving from Art. 2(2) first sentence in conjunction with Art. 1(1) second sentence of the Basic Law to protect every human life. This duty of protection is comprehensive. It requires the state to protect and nurture each life, an obligation which includes, above all, safeguarding it from unlawful interference by third parties ….[26]

However, according to the Court, the state has discretion to choose how to protect life in specific circumstances. When exercising this discretion, the state must also take into account the rights and interests of the German population in general. The Court stated:

> The Basic Law not only gives rise to a duty to protect individuals, but also to protect all citizens as a group. To discharge this duty effectively, the competent state organs must be in a position to respond appropriately to the circumstances of the specific case; this alone precludes any advance determination of the means available. Furthermore, such determination cannot be made under constitutional law, because it would mean, in particular, that terrorists would be able to predict the state's response. That would make it impossible for the state to protect its citizens.[27]

In this decision, the FCC thus granted broad leeway to state authorities for fulfilling their duty to protect the lives of its citizens. At the same time, by establishing the notion of a duty to protect, it created, for the counter-terrorism context, a constitutional basis for state measures with the potential to affect the fundamental rights of other individuals.

After these rule of law challenges posed by left-wing terrorism, the next significant phase in which terrorism and counterterrorism affected the rule of law began with the counterterrorism legislation in reaction to the 9/11 attacks in the US. It was followed by a series of right-wing terrorism from 2000 to 2007 by the so-called 'National-Socialist Underground' (*Nationalsozialistischer Untergrund*, NSU), which we mentioned briefly in chapter two and which included, inter alia, nine murders of persons with Turkish and Greek roots and more than 40 further attempted murders based on racist motives. Last, Germany has been the target of fundamentalist Islamist terrorism such as in Berlin in 2016 with 13 deaths.

To start with, the notion of the duty to protect established by the FCC was important for the counter-terrorism legislation after the 9/11 attacks. As a reaction to these attacks and to a small incident in 2003 in Frankfurt (Main) during which a person in a small private plane threatened to direct the plane into one of the city's Skyscrapers, the German legislator enacted the Aviation

[25] FCC, decision of 16 October 1977, 1 BvQ 5/77, English translation provided by the court at www.bundesverfassungsgericht.de/SharedDocs/Entscheidungen/EN/1977/10/qs19771016_1bvq000577en.html.
[26] Para 14.
[27] Para 16.

Security Act (*Luftsicherheitsgesetz*) in 2005. According to this act in its original version, the armed forces were authorised to shoot down an aircraft intended to be used as a weapon in crimes against human lives and under the condition that such a measure would be the only possible manner to prevent this danger (Section 14(3)). This provision would have also made it possible to shoot down an aircraft in which would not only be terrorists but also innocent passengers and crew members.

The act was challenged before the FCC. In its decision of 2006, it addressed the issue that the state can have conflicting constitutional obligations vis-à-vis two different groups of persons at the same time.[28] The Court decided that the provision of Section 14(3) violated the right to life enshrined in Article 2(2) and the right to human dignity under Article 1(1) of the Basic Law, to the extent that it affects persons on board the aircraft who are not participants in the crime.[29] It declared the provision void. The Court stressed that human dignity is the supreme value of German constitutional law,[30] and that it absolutely prohibits 'any treatment of a human being by public authority which fundamentally calls into question his or her quality of a subject, his or her status as a legal entity'.[31] In relation to the right to life, human dignity prohibits that the state encroaches upon the right to life by its own actions and it also requires the state to protect human life in the sense of a duty to protect:

> This duty of protection demands of the state and its bodies to shield and to promote the life of every individual, which means above all to also protect it from unlawful attacks, and interference, by third parties ....[32]

In a situation in which a kidnapped plane is used as a weapon, the state has a duty to protect towards the persons on the ground who might die if the plane is led by the terrorist to crash into a building. At the same time, it has an obligation not to violate the right to life of the passengers and crew members in the plane. The Court resolves this issue by referring to the right to human dignity of the latter group of persons. The Court held that when the state shoots down an aircraft, the state treats the passengers and crew 'as mere objects of its rescue operation for the protection of others'.[33] It stated that

> the crew and the passengers of the plane cannot escape this state action but are helpless and defenceless in the face of it with the consequence that they are shot down in

[28] FCC, decision of 15 February 2006, 1 BvR 357/05. English translation provided by the court at www.bundesverfassungsgericht.de/SharedDocs/Entscheidungen/EN/2006/02/rs20060215_1bvr035705en.html.

[29] It is only mentioned here for completeness that the Court held the Aviation Security Act unconstitutional also for formal legal reasons. The federal legislator lacked the competence to enact this legislation (see paras 89 et seq.). This concerns the question whether the use of military force within the territory of the German state and outside of times of war is admissible under constitutional law.

[30] Para 119.

[31] Para 121.

[32] Para 120.

[33] Para 124.

> a targeted manner together with the aircraft and as result of this will be killed with near certainty. Such a treatment ignores the status of the persons affected as subjects endowed with dignity and inalienable rights. By their killing being used as a means to save others, they are treated as objects and at the same time deprived of their rights; with their lives being disposed of unilaterally by the state, the persons on board the aircraft, who, as victims, are themselves in need of protection, are denied the value which is due to a human being for his or her own sake.[34]

As a result, shooting down aircrafts 'cannot be justified by invoking the state's duty to protect those against whose lives the aircraft that is abused as a weapon … is intended to be used'.[35] Although the Court recognises that the state has a 'broad margin of assessment, valuation and organisation' as to its obligation to protect, such protective actions can only be based on 'means the use of which is in harmony with the constitution'.[36] For the Court, the discussed measure does not fulfil this condition due to its violation of the human dignity and right to life of the passengers and crew members.

This judgment of the FCC has been broadly discussed. While some observers agreed with the outcome of the decision,[37] others criticised it both from a legal and political perspective.[38] This includes arguments such as that the right to human dignity was not violated and that this judgment would de facto paralyse the state in situations such as 9/11 because it would not allow for any legal defence against this kind of attack.[39] Some observers even suggested that it would be impossible to regulate the reaction of the state to such attacks and that this reaction should only remain in the political realm.[40] However, the legislator reacted to this decision by amending the aviation security law. Section 14(3) in its amended version now only allows to force an aircraft into another direction, to force it to land, to threaten it with the use of weapons, or to fire off warning shootings.

In contrast to the above instances in which the state has reacted to terrorism or the threat of terrorist attacks with legislation and other measures that were a challenge to the rule of law in Germany, the reaction of the state to the

[34] Para 124.

[35] Para 137.

[36] Para 138.

[37] Eg, D Winkler, 'Verfassungsmäßigkeit des Luftsicherheitsgesetzes' (2006) *Neue Zeitschrift für Verwaltungsrecht* 536; K Baumann, 'Das Urteil des BVerfG zum Luftsicherheitseinsatz der Streitkräfte' (2006) *Juristische Ausbildung* 447. See also W Hecker, 'Die Entscheidung des Bundesverfassungsgerichts zum Luftsicherheitsgesetz' (2006) 39 *Kritische Justiz* 179.

[38] Critical, eg, M Baldus, 'Gefahrenabwehr in Ausnahmelagen – Das Luftsicherheitsgesetz auf dem Prüfstand' (2006) *Neue Zeitschrift für Verwaltungsrecht* 532; C Gramm, 'Der wehrlose Verfassungsstaat?' (2006) *Deutsches Verwaltungsblatt* 653; G Spendel, 'Luftsicherheitsgesetz und Bundesverfassungsgericht – Eine notwendige Kritik' (2006) *Recht und Politik* 131; C Hillgruber, 'Der Staat des Grundgesetzes – nur "bedingt abwehrbereit"?' (2007) *JuristenZeitung* 209.

[39] Hillgruber (n 38); Gramm (n 38); T Linke, 'BVerfGE 115, 118' in J Menzel and R Müller-Terpitz (eds), *Verfassungsrechtsprechung*, 3rd edn (Mohr Siebeck, 2017) 766, 771.

[40] O Lepsius, 'Das Luftsicherheitsgesetz und das Grundgesetz' in F Roggan (ed), *Mit Recht für Menschenwürde und Verfassungsstaat* (Berliner Wissenschaftsverlag, 2006) 47, 69–71.

right-wing terrorism by the NSU in the early 2000s has been seen by many as a failure of the *Rechtsstaat*. To start with, the various state authorities charged with the criminal investigation into the individual murders and other crimes of this terrorist group have, for many years, failed to recognise the link between these crimes as well as the ideological motivation for them. The reasons for this failure included the inefficient cooperation among the agencies involved due to, inter alia, the federalist structures and the multitude of security-related agencies.[41] As a further reason, there are structural deficiencies in these agencies when it comes to understanding how right-wing extremist groups function in Germany today.[42] Moreover, after the NSU was discovered – rather by chance than by effective investigations – the criminal proceedings against the persons involved have raised the question whether they lived up to the expectations of a *Rechtsstaat*. On the one hand, one of the members of the core group, Beate Zschäpe, has been convicted, inter alia, for murder and participation in a terrorist organisation, and was sentenced to lifelong imprisonment.[43] On the other hand, several persons who were involved with the group were only convicted for supporting a terrorist organisation rather than for aiding and abetting the murders, and have thus received only relatively short sentences. This has been criticised as demonstrating to right-wing extremists in Germany that they have not much to fear from the side of the *Rechtsstaat*.[44]

Moreover, the state has taken the NSU terrorism as an occasion to limit fundamental rights for security purposes. This is the case for the database on right-wing extremists (*Rechtsextremistendatei*). This database was created to provide a centralised source of information that can be accessed by security authorities on the federal and the *Länder* level. However, the Federal Ombudsman for Data Protection has disapproved of this database because it uses sensitive personal data even of persons who only have a coincidental connection with potential terrorists. Further, the database has been criticised for undermining the separation between police and intelligence service, a separation deemed necessary in a *Rechtsstaat* to avoid an abuse of powers as it had happened during the Nazi regime with the *Gestapo* that had both intelligence and police powers.[45]

A similar issue exists for the Counter-Terrorism Database Act (*Antiterrordateigesetz*). This Act has established a common database for the police and intelligence service in relation to the fight against international

[41] R Will, 'Der deutsche Rechtsstaat in Zeiten des rechtsextremen Terrors' in Institut für Friedensforschung und Sicherheitspolitik an der Universität Hamburg (ed), *OSZE Jahrbuch 2012* (Nomos, 2013) 183, 191.

[42] Will (n 41) 192.

[43] *Oberlandesgericht* München, decision of 11 July 2018, 6 St 3/12; *Bundesgerichtshof*, decisions of 12 August 2021, 3 StR 441/20; FCC, decision of 30 September 2022, 2 BvR 2222/21.

[44] A Ramelsberger, 'Der wehrhafte Rechtsstaat? Da lachen ja die braunen Brüder', *Süddeutsche Zeitung*, 15 December 2021.

[45] MA Zöller, 'Diskussion um neue Rechtsextremisten-Datei: Wer alles weiß, soll nicht alles dürfen', *LTO*, 21 November 2011, available at www.lto.de/recht/hintergruende/h/diskussion-um-neue-rechtsextremisten-datei-wer-alles-weiss-soll-nicht-alles-duerfen/.

terrorism. The FCC assessed the constitutionality of this act in its decision of April 2013.[46] It held that the Act was, in general, in line with constitutional requirements. The Court allowed the exception to the division between police and intelligence services.[47] It decided, however, that not all provisions in the law were sufficiently concrete and limited to what is necessary for pursuing the act's goal. It also held that the unrestricted provisions on data obtained through interferences with the privacy of correspondence and telecommunications violated fundamental rights.

Another important decision that restricted state powers in the counter-terrorism context is the decision of the FFC of 2016 on the investigatory powers of the Federal Criminal Police Office (FCPO).[48] The legal act regulating these powers (*BKA-Gesetz*) authorised the FCPO to carry out covert surveillance measures in order to avert dangers posed by international terrorism. In the view of the Court, these regulations were, in their extent at the time, incompatible with the Basic Law. Although the Court found that covert surveillance measures as such do not violate constitutional law, the specific rules of the legal act in question did not satisfy the principle of proportionality. The Court outlined in detail to what extent each measure contained in the Act had to be adjusted by the legislator. This concerned, inter alia, the means of surveillance for which the scope of application needed to be limited; the insufficient protection of the core of private life with regard to remote searches of information technology systems; the lack of specific provisions to ensure respect for the principle of proportionality; and the unconstitutionality of the FCPO's powers to share data with other authorities.

Further legislative acts reviewed by the FCC that have affected fair trial and substantive human rights standards can only be briefly mentioned here. They include, inter alia, the decision on the provisions of the North Rhine-Westphalia Constitution Protection Act regarding remote searches and Internet surveillance measures,[49] and the precautionary retention of telecommunications traffic data by private service providers without specific grounds.[50]

These examples highlight that the role of the judiciary and especially of the FCC in limiting risks to the rule of law in the counter-terrorism context has changed over the decades. While during the peak of the RAF terrorist activities, the judiciary set only rather few limits to the counter-terrorism measures that affected rule of law guarantees, the jurisprudence has been more restrictive since the turn of the millennium. Nonetheless, in the counter-terrorism context, legislative attempts to encroach upon certain rule of law standards continue to exist.

[46] FCC, decision of 24 April 2013, 1 BvR 1215/07.
[47] See also a subsequent decision on data-mining in the context of the Counter-terrorism Database Act, FCC, decision of 10 November 2020, 1 BvR 3214/15.
[48] FCC, decision of 20 April 2016, 1 BvR 966/09.
[49] FCC, decision of 27 February 2008, 1 BvR 370/07, 1 BvR 595/07.
[50] FCC, decision of 2 March 2010, 1 BvR 256/08.

B. 'Self-affirmation' or Transgression of the *Rechtsstaat*?

As shown in the previous section, the risk for rule of law guarantees and fundamental rights is particularly high during times of crises, where the state needs to assert itself against what it perceives as important threats. To the extent that such threats are labelled as 'existential' to the state, the term *Rechtsstaat* has not only been used to draw limits to state action. Rather, it has also, and increasingly, been used to justify 'tough' state action and, therefore, lend a veneer of legitimacy to the very measures that threaten rule of law guarantees through an understanding of the rule of law as 'law and order'.[51] This regularly ushers in debates on whether the *Rechtsstaat* is threatened by actors outside of the state, such as terrorists, or whether the threat to the *Rechtsstaat* rather lies in state action undermining procedural guarantees. We discuss this ambivalence with regard to the crises addressed in the previous section.

After the RAF attacked the German embassy in Stockholm, Sweden, in 1975, social democratic Chancellor Helmut Schmidt said: 'Those who want to safeguard the *Rechtsstaat* must be ready to go to the very limits of what the *Rechtsstaat* allows.' While this quote itself stays true to the liberal origins of the *Rechtsstaat* and requests only that the limits of what is allowed under the rule of law be carefully determined,[52] the *Rechtsstaat* was used to justify measures that might be considered going beyond those limits. During the parliamentary debate on the Communication Bans Act, several parliamentarians expressed the view that this Act was necessary in order to 'protect the *Rechtsstaat*'. Similarly, Minister of Justice Vogel described the tightening of procedural guarantees for political inmates as a 'victory of the *Rechtsstaat*'.[53] To be sure, and as mentioned, these measures were heavily criticised by several legal scholars as eroding the liberal basis of the *Rechtsstaat*.[54] Yet, others argued that the primary danger to the *Rechtsstaat* did not emanate from the state measures against the RAF terrorists but rather from the actions of the terrorists in the first place.[55] These were some of the first steps towards a redefinition of the *Rechtsstaat* to a principle that is more closely associated with law and order politics than with liberal ideas of the state that protects due process guarantees and fundamental freedoms.[56]

A prominent scholarly discussion taking place in the 1970s and onwards as a reaction to the anti-terrorist legislation in criminal procedural law revolved around the notion of a state of emergency and the question to what extent

[51] This is not a new phenomenon. See for a similar development in rule of law assistance, S Humphreys, *Theatre of the Rule of Law. Transnational Legal Intervention in Theory and Practice* (Cambridge University Press, 2010).

[52] For the quote and a doctrinal analysis of these limits see Schröder (n 24).

[53] Quoted after A Söllner, 'Jürgen Habermas und die kritische Theorie des gegenwärtigen Rechtsstaates – Versuch einer wissenschaftsgeschichtlichen Einordnung' (1982) 10 *Leviathan* 97.

[54] Dahs (n 4).

[55] C Starck, 'Der Rechtsstaat in der politischen Kontroverse' (1978) *JuristenZeitung* 746.

[56] M Pichl, *Law statt Order. Der Kampf um den Rechtsstaat* (Suhrkamp, 2024) 47–49.

specific rules for emergency situations relating to terrorism should apply. Among others, Achim von Winterfeld observed an exceptional character of many of the provisions introduced into procedural law as part of the anti-RAF legislation.[57] He argued for a 'law of state self-defense for the preservation of the *Rechtsstaat*' ('*Staatsnotwehr zur Erhaltung des Rechtsstaates*').[58] This suggestion is closely related to the idea of an 'enemy law' as advocated subsequently by Günther Jakobs, a part of the law that applies to state enemies, stands outside of the ordinary *Rechtsstaat*, and is not subjected to the generally applicable rule of law guarantees.[59] Jakobs argued for a clear distinction between the body of law that regulates the state of normalcy and the body of law applicable during the state of emergency. This distinction aims at excluding any elements of non-rule of law regulation from the body of law that reflects rule of law standards. For Jakobs, a clearly defined 'enemy law' is less dangerous for the *Rechtsstaat* than intermingling elements of 'enemy law' with the ordinary procedural law.[60] This approach has been strongly criticised in legal scholarship for its underlying distinction between citizens and enemies.[61]

The notion of the *Rechtsstaat* as a state that is attacked from the outside and needs to be protected against external threats was brought to the fore again in the wake of 9/11 and the discussions surrounding the 2005 Aviation Security Act. We have seen in the preceding section that the FCC developed a stricter jurisprudence and declared unconstitutional those provisions of the Aviation Security Act that allowed for shooting down aircrafts with suspected terrorists on board. This decision was harshly criticised from the conservative spectrum, again invoking the defence of the *Rechtsstaat* from outside attacks as the main argument as to why such measures should have been declared permissible. The most prominent voice in this regard was legal scholar Otto Depenheuer, who published his views in a short book titled 'Self-affirmation of the *Rechtsstaat*'.[62] This book rose to prominence after then-Minister of the Interior Wolfgang Schäuble, who respected, yet disagreed with, the FCC's decision, recommended Depenheuer's book in an important German weekly newspaper, *Die Zeit*.[63]

In this book, Depenheuer designates Islamist terrorists as the absolute 'negation of the secular *Rechtsstaat*' and asserts a 'legal asymmetry' between the *Rechtsstaat*, which is bound by constitutional guarantees including human dignity, and the 'terrorists', who only use brute force and do not respect any

[57] A von Winterfeld, 'Terrorismus – "Reform" ohne Ende?' (1977) *Zeitschrift für Rechtspolitik* 265.

[58] ibid.

[59] G Jakobs, 'Kriminalisierung im Vorfeld einer Rechtsgutsverletzung' (1985) 97 *Zeitschrift für die gesamte Strafrechtswissenschaft* 751, 784; see also G Jakobs, 'Bürgerstrafrecht und Feindstrafrecht' (2004) *Onlinezeitschrift für Höchstrichterliche Rechtsprechung zum Strafrecht* 88.

[60] Jakobs, Bürgerstrafrecht (n 59) 95.

[61] For an overview of the debate, see Putzer (n 8) 199–202.

[62] O Depenheuer, *Selbstbehauptung des Rechtsstaats* (Schöningh, 2007).

[63] G Hofmann, 'Schäubles Nachtlektüre' (2007) 33 *Die Zeit* 7.

limits.[64] He then relies on Carl Schmitt's friend-enemy distinction to argue that the *Rechtsstaat* should free itself from self-imposed shackles and impose a specific legal regime on those 'enemies' that purportedly negate the very essence of the *Rechtsstaat*. Such a specific regime should be free of rule of law guarantees, because the people ('enemies') to which it applies deny the very essence of the *Rechtsstaat*. Therefore, Depenheuer argues, they should not be entitled to benefit from its guarantees.[65] As a last consequence, and in direct response to the FCC's decision regarding the Aviation Security Act, Depenheuer introduces the idea of the 'citizen's sacrifice'.[66] He asks: 'Might the *Rechtsstaat* be allowed, as a last resort, to sacrifice innocent citizens to secure its own existence if this is the only way to fend off a terrorist attack?'[67] He then answers the question in the affirmative: the citizens guarantee the existence of the *Rechtsstaat* with their life; through their sacrifice, so the argument goes, the citizens guarantee the *Rechtsstaat*; the *Rechtsstaat* can only assert itself if its citizens are willing to die for it.[68]

Many observers have pointed out how Depenheuer's argument is incompatible with the rule of law understanding in German constitutional law. Similar to Jakobs, he adopts the much-criticised idea of an 'enemy law'. It has also been pointed out how his approach is dangerously close to the prerogative state observed by Ernst Fraenkel (see chapter one), because it is of course the state who declares individuals as 'enemies'.[69] His idea of the 'citizen's sacrifice' had already been declared unconstitutional by the FCC.[70] Heiner Bielefeldt, at the time Director of the German National Human Rights Institution, vehemently argued that the very essence of the *Rechtsstaat* consisted in its being bound to fundamental values of the Constitution, including human dignity, and that Depenheuer's position led to a complete abridging of rule of law guarantees under the German Basic Law.[71]

Although Depenheuer's position was certainly the most extreme, it did not come out of a vacuum. The German debate on the *Rechtsstaat* had long been shaped by an ambiguous understanding of the notion.[72] Public law scholarship as early as 1950 developed an understanding of the *Rechtsstaat* as the law-based, protective state, and has traditionally been sceptical of the rule of law's liberal dimension.[73] Depenheuer's use of the term *Rechtsstaat*, while incompatible

[64] Depenheuer (n 62) ch I.
[65] ibid ch III.
[66] ibid ch IV.
[67] ibid 76.
[68] ibid ch IV, especially 100, 104.
[69] M Hawel, 'Dämmerung des demokratischen Rechtsstaats?' (2009) *Kritische Justiz* 64.
[70] FCC, decision of 15 February 2006, 1 BvR 357/05.
[71] H Bielefeldt, *Gefahrenabwehr im demokratischen Rechtsstaat. Zur Debatte um ein "Feindrecht"* (German Institute for Human Rights, 2008).
[72] See for historical origins of the term and its use in constitutional doctrine, ch 1.
[73] M Stolleis, *Geschichte des öffentlichen Rechts in Deutschland*, vol 4 (CH Beck, 2012) 215.

with any jurisprudential understanding of the notion, leads to a discursive shift, where the term is used to mask a tension between rule of law guarantees and security considerations.[74] This case is a case where a generally respected public law professor uses the term *Rechtsstaat* to defend measures that undermine the very guarantees the *Rechtsstaat* affords. This was taken up by a senior member of the Federal Government. Such developments clearly impact the rule of law culture in a country.[75] And it ushered in considerable discursive disputes around the notion of the *Rechtsstaat*, which at times masked genuine rule of law issues. We will discuss two such examples in the following section.

II. RULE OF LAW DEBATE AND PRACTICE DURING THE REFUGEE AND COVID CRISES

The ambiguity of the *Rechtsstaat* in public discourse has increased in recent years, even if its constitutional foundations, as discussed in chapter one, are relatively clear. Yet, German public discourse is increasingly facing situations where those who defend abridging fair trial and other procedural rights in emergency situations might do so in the name of the *Rechtsstaat*. At the same time, criticism of such measures can also be dressed in those exact same terms. This is perhaps best visible in juxtaposing the rhetoric and measures that were taken during two moments that are largely regarded as two of the main societal crises that the German Federal Republic has had to face over the past decade: the so-called 'refugee crisis' in 2015/16 and the COVID-19 pandemic in 2020. In this section, we will address what legal measures were taken during the two crises and to what extent these measures challenge rule of law principles and guarantees under German constitutional law. We will contrast this with the *Rechtsstaat* rhetoric during these crises.

A. Rule of Law Standards and Discursive (Mis)use of the *Rechtsstaat* During the 'Refugee Crisis'

In 2015, the Office of the UN High Commissioner for Refugees noted an all-time high of forcibly displaced people, with a record number of 4.9 million refugees from Syria as a result of the Syrian civil war.[76] It also noted in the same report that specifically in the second half of 2015, over one million people, mostly from Syria, but also other countries including Afghanistan and Kosovo, sought asylum and protection in Europe (even though Turkey remained the country to

[74] On this tension, see C Calliess, 'Sicherheit im freiheitlichen Rechtsstaat' (2002) *Zeitschrift für Rechtspolitik* 1.

[75] Bielefeldt (n 71) 6.

[76] UNHCR, *Global Trends 2015*, available at www.unhcr.org/media/unhcr-global-trends-2015.

host most Syrian refugees, with close to one million people).[77] Over one million people crossed the Mediterranean Sea (only about 3 per cent entered the EU via land), often in unfit ships and dangerous circumstances risking their lives, with the vast majority of refugees arriving in Greece, followed by Italy.[78] Due to the dire circumstances on several Greek islands, many refugees sought to continue their journey to other countries, typically via the Balkans, re-entering the EU in Hungary or Croatia. Hungary implemented increasingly strict measures against the refugees and several incidents of police violence against refugees were recorded. Many refugees had heard that Germany was not sending back refugees even if they had entered the EU in a different country; this prompted many refugees to leave Hungary and travel on to Austria and Germany. German chancellor Angela Merkel and Austrian chancellor Werner Faymann decided in an emergency session not to refuse entry to refugees at the borders, which led to over one million refugees entering Germany between September 2015 and the summer of 2016.[79] It is this decision not to refuse entry to refugees at the border that evolved into a contentious discursive point regarding the *Rechtsstaat*, even if, from the point of view of positive law, the German Government was not under an obligation to close its borders.[80] Interestingly, the public debate thus revolved around a perceived 'lack of the rule of law' due to a situation that was claimed as unlawful, whereas other issues which arguably raise considerable rule of law challenges were not framed as such. We first address some rule of law challenges that were not discussed in these terms before turning to the discursive (mis)use of the term *Rechtsstaat* in public discourse.

The unprecedented number of refugees brought with it several rule of law challenges, both at the German and European levels.[81] First, the German Federal Office for Migration and Refugees, which is the main executive entity to handle asylum procedures in Germany, was completely overwhelmed with the high number of newly arriving refugees. The Office already faced an enormous backlog in 2015 and simply did not manage to even register roughly half a million asylum seekers in 2015, only catching up on registrations in 2016.[82] It sped up proceedings in 2016, but often at the expense of quality. The Office used field offices and employed many people ad hoc, often with insufficient training. As

[77] ibid 7.

[78] International Organisation for Migration, 'Irregular Migrant, Refugee Arrivals in Europe Top One Million in 2015: IOM', available at www.iom.int/news/irregular-migrant-refugee-arrivals-europe-top-one-million-2015-iom.

[79] U Herbert and J Schönhage, 'Vor dem 5. September. Die "Flüchtlingskrise" 2015 im historischen Kontext' (2020) 30–32 *Aus Politik und Zeitgeschichte* 27.

[80] See K Hailbronner and D Thym, 'Grenzenloses Asylrecht? Die Flüchtlingskrise als Problem europäischer Rechtsintegration' (2016) *Juristenzeitung* 753.

[81] See DV Kochenov and B Grabowska-Moroz, 'The Loss of Face for Everyone Concerned. EU Rule of Law in the Context of the "Migration Crisis"' in V Stoyanova and S Smet (eds), *Migrants' Rights, Populism and Legal Resilience in Europe* (Cambridge University Press, 2022) 115.

[82] D Thränhardt, 'Die Asylkrise 2015 als Verwaltungsproblem' (2020) 30–32 *Aus Politik und Zeitgeschichte* 37.

a result, the chances of receiving protection in Germany varied significantly according to where exactly in Germany a request was filed. Similarly, there is a relatively high success rate where asylum seekers whose request for protection was denied went to court: in 2019, German courts reversed almost half of the negative decisions concerning Afghanis, and over a third of the rejections concerning Syrians.[83] While this is not generally considered a structural challenge to the rule of law in Germany, the high reversal rates point to a systematic issue at the Federal Office for Migration and Refugees, which in turn has led to a decrease of trust in the Office's proceedings. In 2019, 75 per cent of negative decisions were challenged in court, whereas in 2015, only 32 per cent of negative decisions underwent judicial review.[84] This is notwithstanding the fact that in many cases, access to courts is not an obvious choice for refugees whose requests were denied.

A second set of issues relating to the rule of law concerned the impact of the migration crisis on the German judiciary. The high number of refugees meant a stark increase in asylum cases.[85] This situation was a considerable challenge for the administrative courts. As a result of the additional workload, the length of procedures both for asylum cases and for other cases pending before these courts increased. To cope with this situation, the legislator created the possibility for the state to employ temporary administrative court judges (*Richter auf Zeit*). These temporary judges were recruited from the administration by way of secondment and served as judges for a few years before later returning to the administration. As this construction is not unproblematic from the point of view of judicial independence and the separation of powers,[86] the law enabling such temporary judges was challenged before the FCC. However, the FCC upheld the legislation in a controversial decision in 2018.[87]

A third rule of law issue concerned the question whether the way in which the EU Member States dealt with the movement of migrants across the EU undermined the rule of law. During the peak of the so-called refugee crisis, states systematically disregarded the EU migration regulation enshrined in the Dublin III Regulation.[88] According to this regulation, migrants were supposed to stay in

[83] Thränhardt (n 82) 41.

[84] ibid 40.

[85] From 58,974 pending cases at the end of 2015, to 159,965 at the end of 2016 and 372,443 at the end of 2017. See statistic of the Ministry for Asylum, Migration and Integration, 'Das Bundesamt in Zahlen 2017', p 62, available at www.bamf.de/SharedDocs/Anlagen/DE/Statistik/BundesamtinZahlen/bundesamt-in-zahlen-2017.pdf?__blob=publicationFile&v=17.

[86] See also the statement of the association of judges 'Neue Richtervereinigung' of 9 October 2015, Ausschuss-Drs 18 (4)414, 2.

[87] FCC, order of 22 March 2018, 2 BvR 780/16. Critically on this decision: separate opinion by FCC Judge Hermanns; D Burchardt, 'Der Grundsatz richterlicher Unabhängigkeit: eine verhaltensbezogene Perspektive' (2022) 70 *Jahrbuch des Öffentlichen Rechts* 453.

[88] Regulation (EU) No 604/2013 of the European Parliament and of the Council of 26 June 2013 establishing the criteria and mechanisms for determining the Member State responsible for examining an application for international protection lodged in one of the Member States by a third-country national or a stateless person.

the Member State through which they first entered the EU. The Member State of first entry was responsible for conducting the asylum procedure. Yet, due to the high number of refugees, the states of first entry were not able to conduct asylum procedures for all incoming refugees and allowed them to migrate further to other Member States such as Germany which then conducted the asylum procedures for these persons. This practice was criticised across Europe as blatantly disregarding applicable law.[89] It led to a systematic collapse of the Dublin system which not only undermined the authority of European migration law but also resulted in rule of law issues within the Member States. For Germany, the legal discussion was centred around Section 18 of the Asylum Act (*Asylgesetz*). In relation to entry at the border, this provision stipulates that a 'foreigner shall be refused entry if … there are indications that another country is responsible for processing the asylum application based on European Community law or an international treaty and proceedings to admit or re-admit have been initiated'. Based on this provision, several political actors and scholars argued that the German border authorities were required to refuse entry to the refugees that came to Germany via Austria and other EU Member States (see below). However, this argumentation did not sufficiently take into account the interplay between the Dublin III Regulation and the German Asylum Act.[90] According to this legal framework, Germany becomes indeed responsible for conducting an asylum procedure when a person cannot be retransferred to the original Member State, and the Dublin III Regulation prevails over Section 18 of the Asylum Act.[91] While the collapse of the Dublin system has indeed been a challenge for the rule of law, the claim that domestic law was disregarded during the migration crisis is less convincing.

While a majority of the German public was at first supportive of the refugees, welcoming them in the fall of 2015 at train stations and providing volunteer work at shelters, this changed over the following months. In July 2016, only 27 per cent of the German public was supportive of Merkel's policy towards refugees (encapsulated by her statement 'We can do it' – '*Wir schaffen das*') and believed that Germany could, in fact, manage the high number of arrivals. This stands in contrast to an initial 43 per cent who had been supportive of the statement in September 2015, according to a YouGov poll.[92] Several factors might have contributed to the turn in public opinion. Initial enthusiasm ebbed away as local communes were increasingly overburdened, long lines at local agencies of the

[89] For a summary of the problematic features of this regulation and its failure during the crisis, see European Parliament Report A9-0245/2020 on the implementation of the Dublin III Regulation, 2 December 2020 – (2019/2206(INI)), available at www.europarl.europa.eu/doceo/document/A-9-2020-0245_EN.html.

[90] For the latter, in particular Section 26a Asylum Act.

[91] D Thym, 'Der Rechtsstaat und die deutsche Staatsgrenze', *Verfassungsblog*, 22 January 2016, verfassungsblog.de/der-rechtsstaat-und-die-deutsche-staatsgrenze/; Hailbronner/Thym (n 80) 756.

[92] YouGov, 'Nur noch 27 Prozent sagen: "Wir schaffen das"', 30 July 2016, yougov.de/politics/articles/16067-nur-noch-27-prozent-sagen-wir-schaffen-das.

Federal Office for Migration and Refugees and at social services were common, and various politicians from across the political spectrum were quick to link a series of sexual assaults during New Year's Eve 2015/16 in different German cities that involved a group of Northern African migrants with the arrival of refugees over the previous months. This was a watershed moment in shifting public perception and in its wake led to high polling numbers for the right-wing populist party 'Alternative for Germany' (*Alternative für Deutschland*, AfD).[93] It was also coupled with calls for a harsher posture against migrants found guilty of criminal offences.

In this climate, the discourse between supporters and critics of migration policies not only became rather heated but also revolved around the notion of the *Rechtsstaat*. The main controversy concerned the question of whether Chancellor Angela Merkel and the Federal Government should have closed the borders in the fall of 2015, when Germany was faced with the highest number of refugees in its history. The doctrinal discussion first centred around whether closing the borders would have been lawful under EU and German constitutional law,[94] but soon moved to whether Germany had an obligation to close the border, as asserted by former FCC Judge Udo Di Fabio in a controversial expert opinion rendered to the state of Bavaria, whose government openly opposed Merkel's decision to welcome the refugees.[95] While the expert opinion's main claims were debated amongst legal scholars,[96] the then-Minister President of the state of Bavaria, Horst Seehofer, gave an interview in a newspaper in which he labelled the high number of arrivals of refugees as a 'rule of injustice [*Herrschaft des Unrechts*]', thus using the very term coined by Gustav Radbruch to describe the Nazi regime.[97] This came only a few weeks after another former FCC Judge, Hans-Jürgen Papier, had given an interview to another major newspaper, in which he had stated: 'Never before has the rule of law-based order of the Federal Republic of Germany [*rechtsstaatliche Ordnung*] experienced a gap between law and reality as wide as it does today. This is unacceptable in the long term.'[98]

[93] J Hörner, 'The rise of the AfD after Cologne poses a serious challenge for Merkel's policy on refugees', 27 January 2016, blogs.lse.ac.uk/europpblog/2016/01/27/the-rise-of-the-afd-after-cologne-may-force-merkel-to-change-course-on-refugees.

[94] Thym (n 91).

[95] U Di Fabio, 'Migrationskrise als föderales Verfassungsproblem – Gutachten im Auftrag des Freistaates Bayern', 8 January 2016, available at img.welt.de/bin/di-fabio-gutachten-150937063.pdf.

[96] See, eg, the criticism voiced by J Bast and C Möllers, 'Dem Freistaat zum Gefallen: über Udo Di Fabios Gutachten zur staatsrechtlichen Beurteilung der Flüchtlingskrise', *Verfassungsblog*, 16 January 2016, verfassungsblog.de/dem-freistaat-zum-gefallen-ueber-udo-di-fabios-gutachten-zur-staatsrechtlichen-beurteilung-der-fluechtlingskrise/.

[97] 'Seehofer: "Es ist eine Herrschaft des Unrechts"', *Süddeutsche Zeitung*, 9 February 2016 (reporting on the original interview given to the newspaper *Passauer Neue Presse*). For an explanation of the term *Unrechts-Staat* and its importance in German rule of law discourse, see chs 1 and 3.

[98] H-J Papier, 'Eklatantes Politikversagen in der Flüchtlingskrise', *Handelsblatt*, 12 January 2016, www.handelsblatt.com/politik/deutschland/ex-verfassungsrichter-papier-eklatantes-politikversa-

Papier was the first to explicitly frame the fact that Germany had *not* closed its borders to the refugees as incompatible with the *Rechtsstaat* – despite the fact that it is relatively undisputed that the Federal Government had no obligation to close the borders in the first place.[99] In addition, it is not clear whether Papier argued for a specific violation of any principle of the *Rechtsstaat* – the statement in the interview rather suggests that it is the mere violation of an unspecified legal or constitutional norm that is considered a threat to the *Rechtsstaat*. The doctrinal principle of the *Rechtsstaat* does not, however, contain a general obligation to abide by the law – this is contained in the very notion of the law and would mean that any violation of the law by the state would amount to a violation of the constitution.[100] Rather, Papier's statement is best thought of as a rhetorical move: by coupling an alleged legal violation with the term *Rechtsstaat*, Papier purports that the decision not to close the border constitutes a fundamental violation of basic principles of the German legal order.

This trope was taken up by Otto Depenheuer, who, as we saw, had already used (or arguably misused) the term *Rechtsstaat* to great effect in his defence of an extraordinary criminal law for terrorists and the obligation of citizens to sacrifice their lives if this was the only way to avert a terrorist attack in the mid-2000s.[101] Jointly with Christoph Grabenwarter, he published an edited volume in 2016 titled 'The State and the Refugee Crisis: Between Good Will and Applicable Law'. In the preface to the volume, the editors state: 'The *Rechtsstaat* is in the process of evaporating in the context of the wave of refugees, with the applicable law being effectively suspended.'[102] This is again an assertion without explicating how exactly the current refugee crisis endangers principles associated with the *Rechtsstaat*. The only sustained engagement with the term *Rechtsstaat* in the volume is by former FCC Judge Peter M. Huber – who, however, does not address the refugee crisis at all, but rather argues in his contribution that EU law and institutions have a decidedly different perspective on judicial review and give less importance to procedural criteria and competence allocation as does German law, which in turn he considers a challenge to the German notion of *Rechtsstaat* with its focus on courts and judicial review.[103] This is also pointed out by a critical review of the edited volume, which further discusses the fact

gen-in-der-fluechtlingskrise/12818088.html: 'Noch nie war in der rechtsstaatlichen Ordnung der Bundesrepublik die Kluft zwischen Recht und Wirklichkeit so tief wie derzeit. Das ist auf Dauer inakzeptabel.'

[99] See, eg, D Thym, 'Der Rechtsbruch-Mythos und wie man ihn widerlegt', *Verfassungsblog*, 2 May 2018, verfassungsblog.de/der-rechtsbruch-mythos-und-wie-man-ihn-widerlegt/; Hailbronner and Thym (n 80).

[100] C Möllers, 'Rechtsstaat' in U Kischel and H Kube (eds), *Handbuch des Staatsrechts. Neuausgabe Band II* (CF Müller, forthcoming) 517, 553.

[101] See section I.B of this chapter.

[102] O Depenheuer and C Grabenwarter, 'Vorwort', in O Depenheuer and C Grabenwarter (eds) *Der Staat in der Flüchtlingskrise: zwischen gutem Willen und geltendem Recht*, 2nd edn (Schöningh, 2017) 7.

[103] PM Huber, 'Der Rechtsstaat unter Druck' in Depenheuer and Grabenwarter (n 102) 42.

that many legal questions remain unanswered, and the edited volume is thus a rather alarmist book without, in most cases, providing the requisite legal or theoretical analyses for sounding the alarm.[104]

It seems that the preface of the edited volume was not shared with the authors prior to publication, according to one of the contributors, Klaus Ferdinand Gärditz.[105] Yet, the book was a further step to discursively elevating the purported violation of law to a violation of the *Rechtsstaat*, which lasted for several years and is arguably still present today. In 2018, a group of around 30 public intellectuals, politicians, and publicists petitioned the German Parliament to 'reinstate legality at the German borders'.[106] The 'Joint Declaration 2018' is short and comprises only two sentences: 'It is with growing dismay that we observe how Germany is being damaged by illegal mass immigration. We show our solidarity with those who are peacefully demonstrating to restore the rule of law-based order [*rechtsstaatliche Ordnung*] at our country's borders.'[107] Daniel Thym, a Professor of migration and refugee law who had explained in various blog posts, articles, and talks why there had been no violation of the law in 2015, suggested that the declaration was mostly intended to 'pursue the strategic goal of delegitimizing politics in general and avoiding a factual dispute by challenging the system as such'.[108]

This might be true, but the declaration, years after the alleged violation of the law and its association with the term *Rechtsstaat*, shows that the terminology sticks. Germany's right-wing populist party, the AFD, filed a dispute between federal organs at the FCC on the grounds that there had not been a sufficient parliamentary debate about whether or not the borders should have been closed in 2015, and that therefore, the party's rights had been violated. The FCC rejected this claim as inadmissible, arguing that the dispute between federal organs was not intended to discuss the objective constitutionality of a policy but rather to invoke an organ's own rights.[109] Yet, party legal advisor Stephan Brandner asserted that 'because the FCC has not found anything to the contrary, it is clear that Merkel's government is responsible for millions of violations of the law and for hollowing out the *Rechtsstaat*'.[110] Former FCC Judge Susanne Baer has warned against this appropriation of the term *Rechtsstaat*: 'populists even claim to be the only true defenders of the rule of law themselves, to in fact destroy it'.[111]

[104] D Schmalz, 'Review of: Der Staat in Der Flüchtlingskrise. Zwischen gutem Willen und geltendem Recht by Otto Depenheuer and Christoph Grabenwarter' (2016) 49 *Kritische Justiz* 260.

[105] Reported by S Detjen and M Steinbeis, *Die Zauberlehrlinge: der Streit um die Flüchtlingspolitik und der Mythos vom Rechtsbruch* (Klett-Cotta, 2019) 96.

[106] Petition 79822, 'Gemeinsame Erklärung 2018' of 17 May 2018, available at epetitionen.bundestag.de/content/petitionen/_2018/_05/_17/Petition_79822.html.

[107] ibid.

[108] Thym (n 99).

[109] FCC, decision of 11 December 2018, 2 BvE 1/18.

[110] Quoted after Detjen and Steinbeis (n 105) 164.

[111] S Baer, 'The Rule of – and Not by Any – Law. On Constitutionalism' (2018) 71 *Current Legal Problems* 335, 339.

B. Rule of Law Standards and Discursive (Mis)use of the *Rechtsstaat* During the COVID-19 Pandemic

The COVID-19 pandemic challenged legal orders and the rule of law in various countries across the world.[112] The EU Parliament declared the pandemic to be a 'stress test' for democracy and the rule of law in Europe.[113] In Germany, the President of the FCC, Stephan Harbarth, also made a similar statement.[114] Germany was amongst those countries that did not formally declare a state of emergency in light of the pandemic – in fact, the German Basic Law does not contain the term 'state of emergency', but rather contains various articles on different emergency situations dispersed throughout the Basic Law, and only since a constitutional reform in 1968. The reluctance to rely on a state of emergency is clearly linked to Germany's history and specifically the fact that emergency decrees in the last days of the Weimar Constitution led to a collapse of executive and legislative powers, ultimately helping to consolidate the power of the Nazi regime.[115]

None of the emergency powers that the Basic Law provides were invoked during the pandemic. Instead, and unlike in other countries, the regular provisions of the Basic Law in terms of procedure and guarantees continued to apply in an unprecedented factual situation.[116] The early days of the pandemic were thus marked by an interplay of the federal and state legislators and executive authorities, especially at a local level. In line with the principle that all public acts need to be grounded in law, the German Federal Parliament and the state Parliaments adopted a multitude of legislative acts and amendments that have led to a convoluted body of 'COVID'-legislation.[117] One of the most important legislative amendments was the overhaul of Section 5 of the little-known

[112] See the symposium convened by Joelle Grogan on *Verfassungsblog*, compiling reports from almost 100 jurisdictions: J Grogan, 'States of Emergency', *Verfassungsblog*, 26 May 2020, verfassungsblog.de/states-of-emergency/, DOI: 10.17176/20200526-133657-0, and the follow-up symposium, J Grogan, 'Power and the COVID-19 Pandemic – Introduction & List of Contributions: #PowerandPandemic', *Verfassungsblog*, 22 February 2021, verfassungsblog.de/power-and-the-covid-19-pandemic/, DOI: 10.17176/20210222-154018-0. Regarding European states, see also Venice Commission, Interim Report on the Measures taken in the EU Member States as a Result of the Covid-19 Crisis and their Impact on Democracy, the Rule of Law and Fundamental Rights, 8–9 October 2020, CDL-AD(2020)018.

[113] European Parliament, resolution of 13 November 2020 on the impact of COVID-19 measures on democracy, the rule of law and fundamental rights, P9_TA(2020)0307.

[114] On this statement, 'Verfassungsrichter: Corona-Regeln sind "Stresstest" für Demokratie', *Berliner Zeitung*, 3 April 2021, www.berliner-zeitung.de/news/verfassungsrichter-corona-regeln-sind-stresstest-fuer-demokratie-li.150311.

[115] See ch 1; for this explanation also S Jürgensen and F Orlowski, 'Critique and Crisis: The German Struggle with Pandemic Control Measures and the State of Emergency', *Verfassungsblog*, 19 April 2020, verfassungsblog.de/critique-and-crisis-the-german-struggle-with-pandemic-control-measures-and-the-state-of-emergency/.

[116] H Dreier, 'Rechtsstaat, Demokratie und Föderalismus in der Corona-Pandemie' (2021) *Die Öffentliche Verwaltung* 229.

[117] For a list, see de.wikipedia.org/wiki/Liste_der_infolge_der_COVID-19-Pandemie_erlassenen_deutschen_Gesetze_und_Verordnungen.

Federal Infection Protection Act (*Infektionsschutzgesetz*), which introduced an 'epidemic state of national concern' as a new legal concept in late March 2020.[118] According to this new provision, the Parliament could declare an 'epidemic state of national concern' under the condition that there was a serious concern for public health. It had to renew this epidemic state every three months. Under the epidemic state of national concern, the executive was authorised to take various measures, including the adoption of executive ordinances and wide-ranging measures, such as school closings, distance rules, restrictions to private and public meetings, curfews, etc.

This first phase, in which the new Section 5 delegated vast power to the executive without specifying its limits, has been criticised as unconstitutional, because Article 80(1) of the Basic Law explicitly requires that authorisations of executive decrees need to specify 'the content, purpose and scope of the authority conferred'.[119] It was only in November 2020 that the Parliament amended the Infection Protection Act to provide a proper legislative basis for executive action, an important feat of the German *Rechtsstaat* and the principle of legality.[120] Between March 2020 and December 2022, the Infection Protection Act was amended no less than 19 times,[121] and was complemented by executive action at the federal and state levels. This led to a convoluted regulation, impenetrable at times even for people with legal training. The resulting lack of legal clarity can be seen as a rule of law deficit during this period.

As the measures authorised by the Infection Protection Act were formulated rather vaguely at first and had to be put into place at the federal level, a practice emerged through which the extent of the measures and their application were discussed in regular meetings convened by the chancellor, joining the Federal Government and the ministers of the *Länder* (*Bund-Länder-Runde*). These meetings became highly anticipated media events, even though the '*Bund-Länder-Runde*' was an informal exchange between the Federal Government and the state prime ministers. This institution is typically charged with the coordination of administrative matters, but during the pandemic, it occupied a de facto legislative position with a wide-ranging impact on the development of Corona policies at the state and federal levels.

This weakened role of the legislator is the first key rule of law issue that Germany, much like many other countries, faced during the pandemic.[122] This

[118] Art 1 of the *Gesetz zum Schutz der Bevölkerung bei einer epidemischen Lage von nationaler Tragweite vom 27.03.2020*, BGBl I S 587.

[119] See for this assessment, T Kingreen, 'Der Demokratische Rechtsstaat in der Corona-Pandemie' (2021) *Neue Juristische Wochenschrift* 2766.

[120] AK Mangold, 'Germany and COVID-19: A Most Eventful Year', *Verfassungsblog*, 7 April 2021, verfassungsblog.de/germany-and-covid-19-a-most-eventful-year/.

[121] J Gallon and AK Mangold, 'Grundrechte und Rechtsstaat in der Krise: Hat sich die Verfassungsordnung während der Corona-Pandemie bewährt?' (2023) 9 *Politikum* 12.

[122] On this issue in European countries, see interim report of the Venice Commission (n 112) and European Parliament, resolution of 13 November 2020 on the impact of COVID-19 measures on democracy, the rule of law and fundamental rights, P9_TA(2020)0307.

is problematic against the backdrop of the separation of powers and democratic legitimacy, as both the *Rechtsstaat* and the principle of democracy require that Parliament ought to regulate all important parts of human life.[123] Already in the first months of the pandemic, various constitutional law scholars published analyses of the constitutional law issues at stake, criticising the takeover by the executive, the lack of clarity in the Infection Protection Act, and the informal coordination mechanism between state governments and the Federal Government replacing parliamentary activity.[124] In particular, they pointed to a considerable change 'in the horizontal balance of powers', affecting fundamental principles of the rule of law.[125] As one of the strongest critics, Oliver Lepsius has been adamant that while formally, the *Rechtsstaat* and its institutions remained intact, the situation as such challenged, if perhaps not the doctrinal formal components of the *Rechtsstaat*, then its very nature as an open and participatory state.[126] He went as far as stating: 'The rule of law is seriously tainted. The rule of law hygiene must urgently be restored, otherwise there is the greatest risk of infection here.'[127]

A second key rule of law issue that was widely discussed not only among constitutional law scholars but also the general public relates to the far-reaching fundamental rights limitations ensuing from the anti-COVID measures and the question of their proportionality. The legal basis for many restrictions was Section 28 of the Federal Infection Protection Act, which during the early days of the pandemic allowed for restrictions on the freedom of movement. This provision was considered to be too vague to serve as a legal basis for wide-ranging rights restrictions and, therefore, to violate the principle of specificity and the requirement that every public act must be grounded in a sufficiently clear formal law – key properties of the German understanding of the *Rechtsstaat*.[128] Scholars emphasised early on that the German Basic Law provides for exceptional situations to still be regulated by the Basic Law and pointed to flaws in the measures taken by the government.[129] Some scholars even argued that there was a systematic absence of the principle of proportionality,[130] while others urged

[123] See for the principle of essentiality ch 1, for this assessment and criticism of the meetings as the main place of policy decisions Kingreen (n 119).

[124] Asserting a key role for constitutional law scholarship during the pandemic HM Heinig, T Kingreen, O Lepsius, C Möllers, U Volkmann and H Wißmann, 'Why Constitution Matters – Verfassungsrechtswissenschaft in Zeiten der Corona-Krise' (2020) *JuristenZeitung* 861.

[125] ibid 868.

[126] O Lepsius, 'Partizipationsprobleme und Abwägungsdefizite im Umgang mit der Corona-Pandemie' (2021) 69 *Jahrbuch des öffentlichen Rechts* 705.

[127] 'Der Rechtsstaat ist schwer beschmutzt. Die rechtsstaatliche Hygiene muss dringend wieder hergestellt werden, sonst droht hier das größte Infektionsrisiko.' O Lepsius, 'Vom Niedergang grundrechtlicher Denkkategorien in der Corona-Pandemie', *Verfassungsblog*, 6 April 2020, verfassungsblog.de/vom-niedergang-grundrechtlicher-denkkategorien-in-der-corona-pandemie/, DOI: 10.17176/20200406-131152-0.

[128] Dreier (n 116) 230–237.

[129] Heinig et al (n 124).

[130] Lepsius (n 126).

state institutions to take the principle of proportionality more seriously.[131] The German Public Law Professors Association dedicated a special session to studying the consequences of the pandemic in early 2021, assessing the extent to which basic rights were protected during the pandemic and discussing key parts of the *Rechtsstaat* such as, inter alia, the principle of essentiality and proportionality, albeit not necessarily under the label of the *Rechtsstaat*.[132] The proportionality of the anti-COVID measures was also a concern at the European level. In 2020, the European Parliament urged EU Member States to ensure that, in the fight against the pandemic, they respect the principle of proportionality and the rule of law.[133]

The issue of rights restrictions and their proportionality led to a large number of cases that applicants brought to the courts to challenge the anti-COVID measures. German courts issued over 2,000 decisions reviewing various measures in different parts of Germany between March 2020 and December 2022.[134] The FCC ultimately confirmed the constitutionality of the measures taken under the Infection Protection Act in a much-criticised decision in November 2021.[135] A large part of these cases were decided based on a proportionality assessment by the courts. This yardstick was, however, not unproblematic in a situation such as the pandemic because, especially at the beginning of the pandemic, courts weighed the right to life and to health *of the entire population* against the freedoms of the individual applicant.[136] In later decisions, however, courts returned to appropriately protecting fundamental freedoms. As a result, the percentage of cases in which applicants successfully challenged measures increased significantly.[137] With regard to this later judicial practice and the active role of the judiciary during the pandemic, many observers applauded the functioning of the judiciary and its role for the rule of law, including the then-Minister of Justice Christine Lambrecht according to whom 'the *Rechtsstaat* had worked marvelously during the pandemic', with citizens being able at all times to challenge measures before the courts.[138] Similarly, former FCC Judge Susanne Baer attested that the *Rechtsstaat* functioned well during the pandemic. Yet, as in the context of the migration crisis, she issued a warning with regard to the critical perception of the rule of law during the pandemic:

[131] Eg, D Murswiek, 'Die Corona-Waage – Kriterien für die Prüfung der Verhältnismäßigkeit von Corona-Maßnahmen' (2021) *Neue Zeitschrift für Verwaltungsrecht* 281.

[132] See contributions in 'Staat und Gesellschaft in der Pandemie' (2021) 80 VVDStRL.

[133] European Parliament, resolution of 13 November 2020 on the impact of COVID-19 measures on democracy, the rule of law and fundamental rights, P9_TA(2020)0307.

[134] Gallon and Mangold (n 121) 16.

[135] FCC, decision of 19 November 2021, 1 BvR 781/21 et al.

[136] A Klafki, 'Kontingenz des Rechts in der Krise – Rechtsempirische Analyse gerichtlicher Argumentationsmuster in der Corona-Pandemie' (2021) 69 *Jahrbuch des öffentlichen Rechts* 593, 596.

[137] ibid 493.

[138] Interview with Christine Lambrecht, BMJV Podcast 'Recht so ?!', episode 10 'Corona – Stresstest für den Rechtsstaat?', 10 February 2021, available at www.bmj.de/SharedDocs/Audio/DE/Rechtso_Podcast_Audio10.html.

> The *Rechtsstaat* has clearly proven itself. But it now has to defend itself against accusations that it has failed in some way. These are very problematic attacks on the *Rechtsstaat*.[139]

This warning addressed the many discursive attacks and claims of failure of the *Rechtsstaat* within the general debate. Not only constitutional law scholars but also politicians and actors within civil society had taken up the narrative of a failing *Rechtsstaat* that stemmed in particular from the debate during the early phase of the pandemic. At the German *Bundestag*, several parties introduced draft declarations that used the narrative of an endangered *Rechtsstaat*.[140] Among the general public, the *Rechtsstaat* narrative was taken up by the many groups of protesters that, more and more vividly – and at times also violently – went to the streets to protest against rights limitations caused by anti-COVID measures and against vaccination requirements. At a time when demonstrations were restricted by health measures, they claimed, for example, that the *Rechtsstaat* must allow for such demonstrations; other measures were declared to be proof of Germany becoming a dictatorship. In turn, those who looked at these protests with concern, taking into account that a considerable part of these protesters seemed to aim at challenging the structures of the state as such, called for the *Rechtsstaat* to counter these attempts.[141] An example of a rather drastic call was the statement by the Prime Minister of the state of Saxony, Michael Kretschmer, who said in reaction to radical protest in his state: 'The *Rechtsstaat* must act before there are deaths.'[142]

In sum, the *Rechtsstaat* was very much at the centre of the societal discourse during all phases of the pandemic. Critics and defenders of anti-COVID measures alike made recourse to this notion, often in a rather excessive manner. In substance, however, while the COVID-19 pandemic ushered in a whole host of questions with regard to the separation of powers, federalism, executive powers, fundamental rights protection, and the interplay of scientific expertise and the law, it is fair to say that the main institutions of the *Rechtsstaat* – with the exception of the early days, where the executive had too extensive powers and proportionality was not appropriately applied – were not fundamentally threatened.[143]

[139] Interview with Susanne Baer, BMJV Podcast 'Recht so ?!', episode 1 'Rechtsstaat 101', 21 September 2021, available at www.bmj.de/SharedDocs/Audio/DE/Rechtso_Podcast_Audio1.html.

[140] See, eg, motion of the party FDP, 6 May 2020, 'Rechtsstaat in der Corona-Krise verteidigen – Bürger- und Freiheitsrechte bewahren', Drs 19/19009; motion of the party Die Grünen, 4 November 2020, 'Rechtsstaat und Demokratie in der Corona-Pandemie', Drs 19/23980.

[141] Eg, R Steinke, 'Die Enthemmten', *Süddeutsche Zeitung*, 12 December 2021, availabe at www.sueddeutsche.de/meinung/coronaleugner-telegram-maske-protest-rechtsstaat-1.5485284.

[142] See 'Kretschmer zu radikalen Corona-Protesten: "Rechtsstaat muss handeln, bevor es Tote gibt"', *Tagesspiegel*, 7 January 2022, available at www.tagesspiegel.de/politik/rechtsstaat-muss-handeln-bevor-es-tote-gibt-8017159.html.

[143] Gallon and Mangold (n 121).

III. CONCLUSION

This chapter has discussed some challenges to the *Rechtsstaat* posed by times of emergency. Overall speaking, German legal institutions have dealt relatively well with exceptional circumstances and have, especially in the past two decades, shown a general resilience against extending executive powers or curtailing fundamental rights in times of crises. Yet, in recent years, there has been a different trend that requires caution: the term *Rechtsstaat* has been appropriated not only by right-wing populists, but also by respected members of public law scholarship to elevate purported violations of the law – decisions that were not unlawful and on some accounts even legally warranted – to fundamental challenges to the German legal order. This bears the risk of overextending the notion of the *Rechtsstaat*, rendering it meaningless. It is therefore important to emphasise the content of the *Rechtsstaat* and highlight why certain measures do not violate this principle, even if the purported legal infraction was true. More so than actual measures taken during times of crises, the discursive use and arguably misuse of the term pose a challenge to its salience in the future.

5

The German Rechtsstaat *in the European and International Context*

THE GERMAN NOTION of *Rechtsstaat* is integrated in a 'European and global discourse about the rule of law'.[1] As a result, it is not insulated in its domestic legal context but influenced by European and international standards. At the same time, Germany and its understanding of *Rechtsstaat* influence the rule of law notion and practice on the European and global levels. This chapter explores this interaction between the rule of law in Germany and the European and international levels. It provides an overview of the normative and political influence of European and international rule of law standards and instruments on Germany; and inversely of the impact that Germany has on the European and international rule of law standards and practice. We first outline the interaction with the European level (I) before turning to the interaction with the international level (II).

I. INTERACTION OF EUROPEAN AND DOMESTIC RULE OF LAW STANDARDS

Germany and its domestic legal order interact with the European rule of law standards in a two-fold manner. The fact that Germany is deeply embedded in the multilayered European legal space influences the German rule of law notion and practice (A). And Germany as a Member State of the EU and of the Council of Europe influences the legal and political rule of law standards of these organisations (B).

A. European Influence on the Rule of Law Notion and Practice in Germany

Rechtsstaatlichkeit as a legal notion and practice in Germany predates, at least in part, the country's participation in the European regional integration project (see chapter one). However, Germany's membership in the EU and the Council of Europe – the two key regional organisations relevant to the rule of law in

[1] K-P Sommermann in H von Mangoldt, F Klein and C Starck (orig eds), *Grundgesetz Kommentar*, vol 2, 7th edn (CH Beck, 2018) Art 20, para 247.

Europe – have contributed to, and continue to contribute to, shaping how the rule of law in Germany is legally implemented and experienced in practice. This section highlights the different dimensions in which this European influence takes place.

i. German Rechtsstaatlichkeit *in the Context of the Council of Europe*

Since the end of the Second World War, rule of law monitoring in the framework of the Council of Europe has been the bedrock of regional rule of law monitoring in Europe. The Council of Europe is a regional organisation that aims at advocating and safeguarding the rule of law, human rights and democracy. According to Article 2 of the Statute of the Council of Europe, all Member States must accept the principle of the rule of law. (West-)Germany has been a member of this organisation since 1951.[2] A key motivational factor for the country to join this organisation was reputational in nature. Germany was one of the states at this time and also during later periods of enlargement of the Council of Europe that wished to demonstrate their transition to a democratic and human-rights-abiding state based on the rule of law after a period of autocratic rule.[3] In 1952, Germany accepted the jurisdiction of the then-Commission and the ECtHR, the legal institutions in charge of monitoring compliance with the European Convention of Human Rights. It has since been subjected to both a political (by the Committee of Ministers of the Council of Europe) and a judicial (by the ECtHR) monitoring of human rights and rule of law standards.

Since the 1990s, a further body has been part of the political prong of this monitoring infrastructure: the European Commission for Democracy through Law, called 'Venice Commission', which is an advisory body to the Council of Europe. Since the 2000s, this Commission has engaged with the rule of law prong of the Council of Europe and issued reports and recommendations. This includes, in particular, its 2010 'Report on the Independence of the Judicial System'[4] and its 2011 'rule of law checklist'.[5] The 'rule of law checklist' has had an impact on how rule of law elements are perceived both in Europe and in Germany. In Germany, the checklist is for example referenced in the information material on the notion of *Rechtsstaat* provided to the public by the Federal

[2] The GDR has not been a member of the Council of Europe.

[3] On this motivation among Member States, E Bates, *The Evolution of the European Convention on Human Rights – From Its Inception to the Creation of a Permanent Court of Human Rights* (Oxford University Press, 2010) 284; A Nussberger, *The European Court of Human Rights* (Oxford University Press, 2020) 12.

[4] Report on the Independence of the Judicial System Part I: The Independence of Judges, adopted by the Venice Commission at its 82nd Plenary Session (Venice, 12–13 March 2010).

[5] The checklist includes detailed questions with regard to the following six topics: 1. Legality (supremacy of the law), 2. Legal certainty, 3. Prohibition of arbitrariness, 4. Access to Justice before independent and impartial courts, 5. Respect for human rights, 6. Non-discrimination and equality before the law.

Agency for Civic Education (*Bundeszentrale für politische Bildung*).[6] The Venice Commission has also issued specific recommendations regarding German rule of law structures. This includes the recommendation regarding the separation of powers between the judiciary and the executive mentioned in chapter two above.

As to the judicial review by the ECtHR, rule of law-related issues play an important role.[7] Germany has regularly been subjected to this review. There have been 363 judgments against Germany from 1959 to 2022, of which 202 have found one or more violations of the Convention or its Protocols.[8] Among the judgments against Germany, many concern rights that are largely important for the rule of law. This includes the length of proceedings (102), the right to fair trial (30), the right to an effective remedy (25) and punishment without law (10). Among the applications that are filed before the ECtHR against Germany, the success rate is 55.6 per cent – this is mid-range in comparison to the other Council of Europe Member States.

Among the ECtHR judgments that have had a significant impact on rule of law elements in Germany is the *König v Germany* decision of 1978.[9] In this case, the applicant who was a medical practitioner whose authorisation to practise had been withdrawn by the administrative authorities, challenged the length of procedure before the administrative jurisdiction against this withdrawal as a breach of Article 6(1) ECHR, although the explicit wording of this provision only includes fair trial rights in the context of 'the determination of his civil rights and obligations or of any criminal charge'. In this case and in related decisions,[10] the Court interpreted the term 'civil rights' extensively in a way that led to applying the fair trial guarantees of Article 6 inter alia to procedures before administrative courts. This had a significant impact on the procedural law of many Member States including Germany as the expanded application of these provisions required states to change their procedural law frameworks substantially. Germany was indeed among the Member States that initially showed strong resistance against this jurisprudence,[11] but came to accept it over time.

This decision also stands at the beginning of the long line of judgments against Germany finding a violation of Article 6 due to lengthy proceedings before the different branches of the German judiciary (see also chapter two). In

[6] Available at www.bpb.de/system/files/dokument_pdf/IzPB_351_Rechtsstaat_barrierefrei.pdf.

[7] See generally on the rule of law aspects of the ECtHR jurisprudence, G Lautenbach, *The Concept of the Rule of Law and the European Court of Human Rights* (Oxford University Press, 2013).

[8] See the ECtHR statistics for 1959–2022 available at www.echr.coe.int/documents/d/echr/stats_violation_1959_2022_eng.

[9] ECtHR, *König v Germany*, judgment of 28 June 1978, application no 6232/73, paras 88–90.

[10] Eg, ECtHR, *Ringeisen v Austria*, judgment of 16 July 1971, application no 2614/65, para 94; *Benthem v the Netherlands*, judgment of 23 October 1985, application no 8848/80.

[11] H Keller and A Stone Sweet, 'Assessing the Impact of the ECHR on National Legal Systems' in H Keller and A Stone Sweet (eds), *A Europe of Rights: The Impact of the ECHR on National Legal Systems* (Oxford University Press, 2008) 677, 696.

its Grand Chamber decision *Sürmeli v Germany* of 2006,[12] the Court stressed that general measures would be needed to remedy this issue. As Germany did not take such measures, the Court addressed this issue more forcefully by way of a pilot judgment in the case *Rumpf v Germany* in 2010.[13] It ordered Germany to 'set up … at the latest within one year … an effective domestic remedy or combination of such remedies capable of securing adequate and sufficient redress for excessively long proceedings'. Germany complied with this decision. This further demonstrates the structural impact of the ECtHR jurisprudence on key rule of law features in German procedural law.

The significant impact on the procedural and legal structures within Member States has been described as the constitutional impact of the ECtHR jurisprudence on the domestic legal orders. Legal scholars from Germany are among the observers that have pointed out this feature of the interrelation between the Convention system and the law of the Member States.[14]

ECtHR judgments have of course not only shaped the procedural law. To further illustrate the Court's impact on Germany, the following examples provide some insights into the practice. They are linked to the thick understanding of the rule of law in Germany (see chapter one) that includes the protection of human rights.

A first important series of decisions concerned the relationship between the Convention system and the German legal order. The landmark decisions in this regard are the two decisions of the ECtHR in the cases *von Hannover v Germany I* (2004) and *II* (2012) as well as the FCC's reaction to the former judgment in its *Görgülü* decision of 2004. This saga concerned the publication of holiday photos of Princess Caroline von Hannover without her consent. In its first decision of 2004, the ECtHR ruled that the way in which the FCC had balanced the freedom of expression of the media outlet and the Princess's right to privacy was not in conformity with the Convention. The FCC reacted to that in *Görgülü*, deciding that there is no obligation for domestic courts to implement the ECtHR judgments 'in a schematic way'.[15] Rather, implementing these judgements in such a manner could 'violate fundamental rights in conjunction with the principle of the rule of law'.[16] In *von Hannover v Germany II*, the ECtHR took a conciliatory stance and did not find a violation of the Convention, considering that, and as long as, the FCC or another domestic court took the

[12] ECtHR, *Sürmeli v Germany*, judgment of 8 June 2006, application no 75529/01.
[13] ECtHR, *Rumpf v Germany*, judgment of 2 September 2010, application no 46344/06.
[14] See, eg, C Tomuschat, 'Europe – a Common Constitutional Space' in B de Witte and C Forder (eds), *The Common law of Europe and the Future of Legal Education* (Kluwer, 1992) 133, speaking of 'far-reaching repercussions on the constitutional systems' (para 135; regarding the impact of the Art 6 jurisprudence, para 143); J Frowein, 'The Transformation of Constitutional Law through the European Convention on Human Rights' (2008) 41 *Israel Law Review* 489.
[15] FCC, decision of 14 October 2004, 2 BvR 1481/04, para 47.
[16] ibid.

ECtHR jurisprudence duly into account.[17] As a result, these cases do not only demonstrate the impact of the ECtHR jurisprudence on German constitutional law but also on the relationship between the domestic and European judiciary.

Other important decisions of the ECtHR that are impactful regarding the rule of law practice in Germany concern the preventive detention regime in German criminal law (*Sicherungsverwahrung*). The ECtHR has shaped this regime significantly. It has inter alia found violations of the Convention concerning a retroactive extension of the preventive detention,[18] an indefinite duration of the detention order[19] and the lack of a timely and thorough judicial review of the offender's preventive detention.[20] A further example is the case *Gäfgen v Germany* of 2010.[21] In this case, the applicant, who had kidnapped (and eventually killed) a child, claimed that, while interrogating him and trying to determine where the child was at the time, the police had threatened him with torture. The ECtHR found indeed a violation of the prohibition of torture.[22] In German criminal law, the question whether torture can be justified in such circumstances has however been controversially debated – including with reference to rule of law arguments.[23]

ii. German Rechtsstaatlichkeit *in the Context of the EU*

Rechtsstaatlichkeit in Germany is embedded in, and under the influence of, EU rule of law standards. This concerns both the legal notion and the practice of the rule of law.

a. Rule of Law Notion

The notion of the rule of law is part of the EU legal framework. It has two dimensions: the rule of law as it concerns the EU itself, and the rule of law within the Member States. The rule of law dimension that is addressed to EU institutions has been developed first. Once it was established, it served as the basis for constructing the second rule of law dimension – the one that addresses

[17] ECtHR, *von Hannover v Germany (No 2)*, judgment of 7 February 2012, applications nos 40660/08 and 60641/08, para 107: 'Where the balancing exercise has been undertaken by the national authorities in conformity with the criteria laid down in the Court's case-law, the Court would require strong reasons to substitute its view for that of the domestic courts.'

[18] ECtHR, *M v Germany*, judgment of 17 December 2009, application no 19359/04.

[19] ECtHR, *Haidn v Germany*, judgment of 13 January 2011, application no 6587/04.

[20] ECtHR, *HW v Germany*, judgment of 19 September 2013, application no 17167/11.

[21] ECtHR, *Gäfgen v Germany*, judgment of 1 June 2010, application no 22978/05.

[22] ibid.

[23] See, eg, RD Herzberg, 'Folter und Menschenwürde' (2005) *Juristenzeitung* 321; V Erb, 'Notwehr als Menschenrecht – Zugleich eine Kritik der Entscheidung des LG Frankfurt am Main im "Fall Daschner"' (2005) *Neue Zeitschrift für Strafrecht* 593; H Götz, 'Das Urteil gegen Daschner im Lichte der Werteordnung des Grundgesetzes' (2005) *Neue Juristische Wochenschrift* 953.

Member States.[24] Both dimensions thus must be understood in close connection with each other.

Regarding the first dimension, Article 2 TEU stipulates that the EU 'is founded on the values of respect for human dignity, freedom, democracy, equality, the *rule of law* and respect for human rights' (emphasis added).[25] The rule of law is thus one of the pillars of the Union. It is shaped as a universal concept, despite its roots in the rule of law understandings of the Member States.[26] As the EU is not a state and many of the languages of EU Member States have state-related notions of the rule of law such as 'Rechts*staat*', a specific notion has been developed to capture its rule of law structure and transform it into a legal concept: a community based on the rule of law – in German translated as '*Rechtsgemeinschaft*'.[27] The CJEU has used this notion as a basis for the judicial review of acts of the EU institutions.[28] Another crucial part of the rule of law in the EU is the protection of fundamental rights. EU fundamental rights were initially developed by the CJEU as part of the general principles of Community law based on a comparative analysis of domestic law[29] and later enshrined in the EU Fundamental Rights Charter, which has been binding law since 2009. Further rule of law elements in EU law have also developed jurisprudentially.[30] This includes, inter alia, the proportionality principle,[31] the principle of legal certainty,[32] and the protection of legitimate expectations.[33] The rule of law

[24] On this two-step development, DH Scheuing, 'Europäische Union und Rechtsstaatlichkeitsgebot' in H Scholler (ed), *Die Sicherung des Rechtsstaatsgebotes im modernen europäischen Recht – anhand von Garantien im Recht der Europäischen Union sowie in Russland und Deutschland* (Duncker & Humblot, 2011) 27, 41.

[25] Such a provision including the reference to the rule of law has been part of the treaty law since the Treaty of Amsterdam of 1999.

[26] On this universal character, S Martini, 'Die Pluralität von Rule-of-Law-Konzeptionen in Europa und das Prinzip einer europäischen Rule of Law' in M Kötter and GF Schuppert (eds), *Normative Pluralität ordnen – Rechtsbegriffe, Normenkollisionen und Rule of Law in Kontexten dies- und jenseits des Staates* (Nomos, 2009) 303, 323.

[27] The CJEU used this notion for the first time in: CJEU, *Les Verts/European Parliament*, decision of 23 April 1986, 294/83, ECLI:EU:C:1986:166, para 23.

[28] See, eg, CJEU, *Associação Sindical dos Juízes Portugueses*, decision of 27 February 2018, C-64/16, ECLI:EU:C:2018:117, paras 31 and 36: 'The European Union is a union based on the rule of law in which individual parties have the right to challenge before the courts the legality of any decision or other national measure relating to the application to them of an EU act. … The very existence of effective judicial review designed to ensure compliance with EU law is of the essence of the rule of law.'

[29] CJEU, *Stauder*, decision of 12 November 1969, 29/69, ECLI:EU:C:1969:57.

[30] See also L Pech, '"A Union Founded on the Rule of Law": Meaning and Reality of the Rule of Law as a Constitutional Principle of EU Law' (2010) 6 *European Constitutional Law Review* 359.

[31] Eg, CJEU, *Schräder*, decision of 11 July 1989, 265/87, ECLI:EU:C:1989:303, para 21; CJEU, *Toeters*, decision of 11 November 2004, C-171/03, ECLI:EU:C:2004:714, para 51.

[32] Eg, CJEU, *Banque Indosuez*, decision of 16 October 1997, C-177/96, ECLI:EU:C:1997:494, para 27; CJEU, *ASM Brescia*, decision of 17 July 2008, C-347/06, ECLI:EU:C:2008:416, para 69.

[33] Eg, CJEU, *von Deetzen*, decision of 28 April 1988, 170/86, ECLI:EU:C:1988:214; CJEU, *Spain/Council*, decision of 7 September 2006, C-310/04, ECLI:EU:C:2006:521, para 81.

notion in EU law is seen as an ongoing obligation for the EU institutions to shape the EU and its law in a rule of law-based manner.[34]

The second dimension of the rule of law in the EU, that is the rule of law obligations of the Member States, is closely linked to the above rule of law elements. The CJEU has required Member States to respect the formal rule of law obligations as well as the fundamental rights when they act within the scope of application of EU law. Member States act in particular within this scope when they implement EU law or limit the common market freedoms.[35] Both domestic and European actors have become more and more aware over the decades that the functioning of the EU requires a well-established rule of law practice in the Member States.[36] The rule of law has thus been emphasised in the EU treaties as a shared value among Member States (Article 2 TEU). Respecting the rule of law is a condition for any state that wishes to accede to the EU (Article 49 TEU) as well as being a requirement for existing Member States such as Germany.

Despite the fact that the rule of law requirements addressed to the EU are strongly influenced by the domestic rule of law notions in the Member States (see also below at B) and that the rule of law requirements of EU law towards the Member States are based on a common rule of law value, the rule of law notions on the domestic and European level are not congruent. In fact, when putting the EU rule of law standards in relation to the domestic standards in German constitutional law, one can observe that these standards correspond in part, that they are in part divergent, and that they tend to converge over time.

Differences exist both conceptually and in substance. Conceptually, the notion of 'community based on the rule of law' is used by the CJEU with a stronger focus on formal rule of law elements. The Court emphasises in particular the principle of legality and the judicial review of all acts of all EU institutions as elements of the rule of law when applied to the EU.[37] Another difference is the fact that the German *Rechtsstaatsprinzip* is conceptualised in a more abstract manner than the rule of law notion in EU law. In the latter, the individual guarantees are explicitly enshrined and referred to as such while in German constitutional law, the *Rechtsstaatsprinzip* is an abstract notion that is applied directly as legal principle. On the one hand, this makes it more broadly justiciable and relevant for decision-making in individual cases. On the other hand, its abstract nature also makes it more difficult for the subjects of law to

[34] Scheuing (n 24) 29.

[35] CJEU, *Wachauf*, decision of 13 July 1989, 5/88, ECLI:EU:C:1989:321, para 19; CJEU, *ERT*, decision of 18 June 1991, C-260/89, ECLI:EU:C:1991:254, paras 42–44.

[36] Scheuing (n 24) 43.

[37] See already CJEU, *Granaria*, decision of 13 February 1979, 101/78, para 5 ('right to challenge the validity of regulations by legal action'). See also CJEU, *Commission/France*, decision of 5 October 2006, C-232/05, para 57: 'the European Community is a community based on the rule of law in which its institutions are subject to judicial review of the compatibility of their acts with the Treaty and with the general principles of law'.

determine what this principle entails, thus creating less legal certainty than the direct approach offers.[38]

In substance, differences exist, amongst others, in relation to fair trial standards and certain other human rights standards. For example, certain rights of defence are part of the EU rule of law understanding but not necessarily of the German one.[39] Further, public liability is guaranteed more extensively in EU law than in German law, in particular with regard to unlawful legislative and judicial acts.[40] In contrast, the specific German notion that a public authority cannot infer competences from a provision that only attributes a certain function is not part of a European rule of law understanding.[41]

Despite these differences, many commonalities exist between the rule of law understanding within EU law and German domestic law. EU law contains most of the guarantees that are clustered under the umbrella of the *Rechtsstaatsprinzip* in German constitutional law (see chapter one above). This is also the case for the separation of powers which is not addressed as such within the EU but has an adapted equivalent with the judicially shaped 'principle of institutional balance'.[42] Although many of these elements are not explicitly linked to the notion of a 'community based on the rule of law', they are part of the legal infrastructure of the EU.

In addition, one can observe a trend towards converging rule of law standards within the European states,[43] a trend that has also influenced the German rule of law understanding. Such converging tendencies are often mediated by transnational effects: rule of law standards and understandings from other Member States shape rule of law-related notions and provisions on the EU level and, from there, migrate to the German domestic legal order. This happens when EU law requires Member States to adapt their domestic law accordingly; and when, based on the primacy of EU law, EU rule of law-related standards directly replace the applicability of domestic norms.

As an expression of such convergence, observers have described a pan-European core understanding of the rule of law.[44] It is composed of overlapping elements of the French '*état de droit*', the common law notion of the rule of law, the German '*Rechtsstaat*', the Spanish '*Estado de derecho*' and many more. Key elements of this common understanding are the separation of powers and

[38] R Ullerich, *Rechtsstaat und Rechtsgemeinschaft im Europarecht* (Nomos, 2011) 212.

[39] E Schmidt-Aßmann, 'Der Rechtsstaat' in J Isensee and P Kirchhof (eds), *Handbuch des Staatsrechts, vol. II: Verfassungsstaat*, 3rd edn (CH Beck, 2004) § 26, para 105.

[40] CD Classen, in H v Mangoldt, F Klein and C Starck (orig eds), *Grundgesetz Kommentar*, 7th edn (2018) Art 23 GG, para 33.

[41] Classen (n 40) para 32a.

[42] CJEU, *EP/Council*, decision of 22 May 1990, C-70/88, ECLI:EU:C:1990:217.

[43] PM Huber, 'Rechtsstaat' in M Herdegen, J Masing, R Poscher and KF Gärditz (eds), *Handbuch des Verfassungsrechts* (CH Beck, 2021) § 6, para 105; Martini (n 26) 340.

[44] Using the German term 'gemein-europäischer Grundbestand', Schmidt-Aßmann (n 39) para 100.

individual rights guarantees.[45] Further rule of law elements that are common to the European legal orders are the principle of legality, the principle of proportionality, the principle of legitimate expectations and the access to justice.[46] In contrast, differences between the rule of law understandings in the domestic legal orders in Europe relate, for example, to whether each understanding focusses on formal rule of law elements or also includes substantive rule of law elements. Further, in comparison to other legal orders, observers have considered the German *Rechtsstaatsprinzip* to be of a particularly detailed and systematic nature.[47]

b. Rule of Law Practice

In addition to shaping legal rule of law content, the EU has – more recently – also taken up a monitoring and enforcement function regarding the rule of law standards within its Member States.[48] The EU has developed a 'rule of law toolbox' to prevent and assess threats to the rule of law in its Member States and resolve breaches thereof. The yearly EU Rule of Law Reports is such a recently created instrument. As a key element of the EU *rule of law mechanism*, these reports have since 2020 monitored the rule of law situation in the Member States.[49] They concern in particular the judicial system, anti-corruption measures, media pluralism and freedom, and separation of powers. For Germany, these reports have enhanced the transparency of the rule of law practice and highlighted existing issues in Germany as, previously, there have been no such regular and publicly available rule of law assessments in the country. For several years now, these reports on Germany have pointed out that, despite the overall good rule of law practice, several issues exist (see also chapter two). One of the recurring issues is threats and attacks against journalists that have increased in recent years, with a slight decrease after the end of the pandemic.[50] Although the overall level of media freedom in the country is rather high, such attacks remain a concern in Germany. Further aspects mentioned in the 2023 Rule of Law Report on Germany are the lack of reform as to the power of Ministers of Justice to give instructions to prosecutors in individual cases (see also chapter two);

[45] Martini (n 26) 319.

[46] Huber (n 43) para 105.

[47] Schmidt-Aßman (n 39) para 101; Sommermann (n 1) para 232.

[48] For an overview of the development of the EU's rule of law policy and practice, see R Coman, *The Politics of the Rule of Law in the EU Polity Actors, Tools and Challenges* (Palgrave, 2022); A Bakardjieva Engelbrekt, A Moberg and J Nergelius (eds), *Rule of Law in the EU – 30 Years After the Fall of the Berlin Wall* (Hart, 2021); C Closa and D Kochenov (eds), *Reinforcing Rule of Law Oversight in the European Union* (CUP, 2016).

[49] The reports are available at commission.europa.eu/strategy-and-policy/policies/justice-and-fundamental-rights/upholding-rule-law/rule-law/rule-law-mechanism_en.

[50] The 2023 Rule of Law Report as well as the country chapter for Germany are available at commission.europa.eu/publications/2023-rule-law-report-communication-and-country-chapters_en.

and the still pending update of Germany's strategic anti-corruption framework (although there are no systemic enforcement issues with regard to anti-corruption rules).[51]

Other tools within the 'rule of law toolbox' have not been used against Germany yet but could be used if a rule of law backsliding should occur in Germany in the future. This is the case for the *rule of law framework*, within which, the EU Commission assesses a (potential) threat to the rule of law situation in a Member State and issues recommendations to the Member State concerned.[52] It then monitors whether these recommendations are implemented. If this is not the case, the EU can eventually trigger the *Article 7 procedure* which allows to suspend the voting rights of the representative of the government of that Member State in the Council. In addition, the *Conditionality Mechanism* has been created in 2021 in order to counter rule of law backsliding with financial sanctions.[53] It allows the EU to take measures such as suspending payments or other economic advantages that Member States would normally receive.[54]

In addition to these mechanisms, the CJEU has developed a jurisprudence to safeguard judicial independence in the Member States, especially in reaction to the rule of law backsliding in Poland.[55] This jurisprudence covers different aspects ranging from the age limit for judges to the appointment of judges and the disciplinary regime for judges.[56] The Court emphasised that the

> requirement that courts be independent, which is inherent in the task of adjudication, forms part of the essence of the right to effective judicial protection and the fundamental right to a fair trial, which is of cardinal importance as a guarantee that all the rights which individuals derive from EU law will be protected and that the values common to the Member States set out in Article 2 TEU, in particular the value of the rule of law, will be safeguarded.[57]

Although the Court developed the jurisprudence in light of the Polish situation, the standards that it established are of course applicable to all Member States, including Germany.

[51] ibid.

[52] COM(2014)158 of 11 March 2014.

[53] Regulation (EU, Euratom) 2020/2092 of the European Parliament and of the Council of 16 December 2020 on a general regime of conditionality for the protection of the Union budget. The CJEU confirmed the legality of the regulation in two decisions of 16 February 2022: *Hungary v Parliament and Council*, C-156/21, ECLI:EU:C:2022:97 and *Poland v Parliament and Council*, C-157/21, ECLI:EU:C:2022:98.

[54] Art 5 of the Regulation 2020/2092.

[55] See for an overview, M Wendel, 'Enforcing the independence of national courts by means of EU law standards, procedures and actors as exemplified by the crisis of the Polish judiciary' in K Meier, A Lorenz and M Wendel (eds), *Rule of Law and the Judiciary* (Nomos, 2023) 123.

[56] Eg, CJEU, *A.K.*, decision of 19 November 2019, C-585/18, ECLI:EU:C:2019:982; *Commission/Poland*, decision of 5 November 2019, C-192/18, ECLI:EU:C:2019:924; *Commission/Poland*, decision of 24 June 2019, C-619/18, ECLI:EU:C:2019:531; *A.B.*, decision of 2 March 2021, C-824/18, ECLI:EU:C:2021:153; *Commission/Poland*, decision of 15 July 2021, C-791/19, ECLI:EU:C:2021:596.

[57] CJEU, *Commission/Poland*, decision of 5 November 2019, C-192/18, ECLI:EU:C:2019:924, para 106.

While Germany's membership in the EU generally has had a positive effect on safeguarding the rule of law in the country, some observers have also argued that such a membership can negatively affect certain elements of the rule of law. As part of the EU with its highly integrated supranational structure, the separation of powers in Germany as well as in other Member States can be affected. This is in particular discussed regarding the role of the domestic Parliament and whether its legislative powers are undermined in the context of the legislative procedure on the EU level during which Member States are primarily represented by actors that belong to the (domestic) executive branch of government.[58] It is the governmental representatives that take part in the EU legislative process as members of the Council. This leads to a situation in which the domestic legislature has, if at all, only a very limited role in the implementation of EU acts. Even when the legislature has to transpose EU directives, the leeway is often rather narrow, with much of the regulatory content being (co-)decided by executive representatives in the Council.[59]

Another aspect that has been seen as a challenge for legal certainty as an element of the rule of law is the fact that domestic and EU law are so densely interwoven that it is at times hard to determine for the subjects of these legal provisions which norm applies in which case.[60] This is in particular due to the primacy of EU law according to which domestic legal provisions are not applicable when they are in conflict with EU law, while however staying in force and also remaining applicable in situations that do not touch upon EU law. Moreover, even if the domestic law is not rendered inapplicable by EU law, it often must be interpreted in light of EU law which leads to an adapted norm content. The complexity of interrelations with norms being applicable differently in different situations thus challenges legal certainty in EU Member States, including in Germany.

B. Germany's Conceptual, Legal and Political Influence on the Rule of Law in Europe

After having highlighted the European embeddedness of, and impact on, Germany, the following section turns to Germany's influence on the rule of law in Europe. This influence has been of a legal and political nature.

i. German Influence on the Rule of Law Notion and Standards in Europe

The notion of *Rechtsstaat* has been described as one of Germany's 'top exports' (*Exportschlager*)[61] and as an element that became part of the European legal

[58] Huber (n 43) para 69.
[59] ibid.
[60] See also Schmidt-Aßmann (n 39) para 106.
[61] Ullerich (n 38) 52.

culture during the second half of the twentieth century.[62] In most European states, the terminology that is used corresponds to a translation of *Rechtsstaat* rather than of the common law term 'rule of law'.[63] Moreover, the notion of the EU as a 'community based on the rule of law'[64] – *Rechtsgemeinschaft* – has been significantly shaped by the German lawyer and first President of the European Commission Walter Hallstein.[65] This notion is also closely linked to the German notion of *Rechtsstaat* rather than to the common law notion of the rule of law.[66] It is not primarily conceived as an expression of parliamentary sovereignty but as a value with a range of guarantees.[67]

Beyond terminology, German constitutional law and the jurisprudence of the Federal Constitutional Court have contributed to shaping certain rule of law standards in European constitutional law. As we have seen, rule of law standards have migrated from the domestic level to the EU and back to the (other) domestic legal orders, a movement that also originated from the German legal order. The most prominent example is the principle of proportionality that has found its way into EU law and from there into the legal orders of other Member States. This is a principle that has been primarily developed in the jurisprudence of the FCC and, from there, has migrated not only to other domestic and regional legal orders in Europe but also beyond – to the extent of having become a universal principle.[68]

Further, for the specific context of the EU, the German Basic Law requires rule of law standards within this organisation. In Article 23(1) as introduced by the constitutional legislator in 1992 after the German reunification, the Basic Law stipulates that

> the Federal Republic of Germany shall participate in the development of the European Union that is committed to democratic, social and federal principles, *to the rule of law* and to the principle of subsidiarity and that guarantees a level of protection of basic rights essentially comparable to that afforded by this Basic Law. (emphasis added)

This provision is termed '*Struktursicherungsklausel*', a norm aimed at securing structural guarantees. The term was introduced by the constitutional legislative commission in charge of designing the constitutional amendments in relation to

[62] P Häberle and M Kotzur, *Europäische Verfassungslehre*, 8th edn (Nomos, 2016) para 1066.
[63] Ullerich (n 38) 53.
[64] See, eg, CJEU, *Les Verts/European Parliament*, decision of 23 April 1986, case 294/83, para 23; *E and F*, decision of 29 June 2010, case C-550/09, para 44; *Inuit Tapiriit Kanatami*, decision of 3 October 2013, case C-583/11 P, para 91.
[65] W Hallstein, *Europäische Reden*, T Oppermann (ed) (Deutsche Verlags-Anstalt, 1979).
[66] See P Cruz Villalón, 'Rule of (German) Law?: On Legal Hegemony in the EU', *Verfassungsblog*, 12 December 2020, verfassungsblog.de/rule-of-german-law/, DOI: 10.17176/20201012-113324-0.
[67] ibid.
[68] J Saurer, 'Die Globalisierung des Verhältnismässigkeitsgrundsatzes' (2012) 51 *Der Staat* 3. See also O Lepsius, 'Die Chancen und Grenzen des Grundsatzes der Verhältnismäßigkeit' in M Jestaedt and O Lepsius (eds), *Verhältnismäßigkeit – Zur Tragfähigkeit eines verfassungsrechtlichen Schlüsselkonzepts* (Mohr Siebeck, 2015) 1, 2.

German reunification.[69] It has been interpreted by constitutional scholars and by the FCC as setting up conditions under which Germany can transfer powers to the EU and be a member of this supranational organisation.[70] One of these conditions is that the EU is, in terms of its structural design, based on the rule of law. The FCC has used Article 23(1) prominently in its *Maastricht* decision of 1993.[71] Although it focused mostly on democracy as 'structural principle' of the EU as enshrined in Article 23, it has positioned this article as a limit for European integration. Article 23(1) of course does not bind the EU directly but rather obliges the constitutional organs of the German state to ensure that any form of the EU of which Germany is a Member State respects the structural guarantees listed in this article. Similar structural principles for the German state are guaranteed as part of the so-called eternity clause (Article 79(3) Basic Law) – and Article 23 transfers these guarantees to the European context.[72]

With regard to *Rechtstaatlichkeit*, Article 23 demands that the EU is organised according to some form of separation of powers, a requirement that is considered to be fulfilled by the European law equivalent of 'institutional balance' (see also above).[73] Further, Article 23 requires the EU to abide by the principle of legality so that the executive and judicial actors are bound by law and that higher ranking law binds the law that is derived from it.[74] In addition, legal certainty[75] as well as access to justice against EU acts[76] must also be guaranteed. Some scholars also include human rights protection and the principle of proportionality into this list of rule of law related requirements,[77] as well as state liability (*Amtshaftung*).[78]

A further landmark judgment of the FFC on the structural guarantees of Article 23 is the *Lisbon* decision of 2009.[79] In this decision, the Court assessed in substance whether the Treaty of Lisbon creating the institutional structure of the EU in place today is in conformity with German constitutional law. It set up competence-related boundaries, subject matters for which Germany cannot transfer its entire competences to the EU. Some of these limits concern rule of

[69] See *Bericht der Gemeinsamen Verfassungskommission* of 5 November 1993, BT-Drs 12/6000, p 20.

[70] R Scholz in G Dürig, R Herzog and R Scholz (orig eds), *Grundgesetz-Kommentar*, 100th EL (CH Beck, 2023) Art 23, paras 70 et seq.

[71] FCC, decision of 12 October 1993, 2 BvR 2134, 2159/92. Critical in the potential implications of this decision, SJ Boom, 'The European Union after the Maastricht Decision: Will Germany Be the "Virginia of Europe?"' (1995) 43 *American Journal of Comparative Law* 177.

[72] Scholz (n 70) para 71.

[73] R Uerpmann-Wittzack in I von Münch and P Kunig (eds), *Grundgesetz-Kommentar*, 7th edn (2021), Art 23, paras 36–37; Classen (n 40) para 32a; HD Jarass in HD Jarass and B Pieroth (eds), *Grundgesetz für die Bundesrepublik Deutschland*, 17th edn (CH Beck, 2022) Art 23, para 16.

[74] Classen (n 40) paras 30, 32; Jarass (n 73) para 16.

[75] Scholz (n 70) para 76.

[76] Jarass (n 73) para 16.

[77] Scholz (n 70) para 76.

[78] Classen (n 40) paras 30, 33.

[79] FCC, decision of 30 June 2009, 2 BvE 2/08.

law related aspects such as fair trial guarantees in criminal procedures. Moreover, in the *OMT* decision of 2016, the Court has linked a tool that it had developed with regard to EU law to the *Rechtsstaatsprinzip*: its ultra vires review.[80] When undertaking this review, the Court assesses whether an act of the EU or one of its institutions is outside of the competences transferred to the EU. The Court describes the rule of law dimension of this review as follows:

> the ultra vires review serves to protect the rule of law. In national law, the principle of the legality of the administration … requires that the task in question have been validly assigned and – for infringements upon the legal sphere of individuals – that there be a limited and specific legal authorisation of the executive branch …. This applies accordingly to the public authority exercised by the European Union ….[81]

It should be noted that this jurisprudence of the FCC has developed a life of its own. It has been used both by domestic actors in Germany and by actors in other EU Member States as a political tool. It has been used by certain EU-critical actors within Germany to bring political conflicts before the Constitutional Court. A much-criticised decision in this regard is the *PSPP* decision (*Weiß*) of 2020 which concerned the politically controversial public sector purchase programme of the ECB within which the ECB and national central banks purchased governmental bonds of Member States to counter the financial and Euro crises. In this decision, the FCC reviewed an act of the ECB and a related judgment of the CJEU and declared the former in violation of the principle of proportionality and the latter to be an ultra vires act on which it is not bound.[82] This decision has triggered a discussion among legal academics as to whether with such FCC decisions, Germany becomes a 'legal hegemon' in Europe.[83]

The discussion about a potential German 'legal hegemony' points to the fact that the jurisprudence of the Constitutional Court does not only concern the relationship between the German legal order and the EU legal order. Rather, it can also impact the rule of law practice in other Member States due to the influential position of the Court in European legal discourse.[84] This is particularly the case when courts in other Member States refer to the jurisprudence of the German Court regarding the application of EU law and CJEU decisions within their domestic legal orders. This can lead to non-compliance with EU law provisions and CJEU decisions that can potentially undermine the rule of law in the EU. Jurisprudential notions that have been prominently shaped by the FCC and that have since been referred to by actors in other European states include the ultra vires review mentioned above as well as the notion of constitutional

[80] FCC, decision of 21 June 2016, 2 BvR 2728/13.

[81] ibid 152.

[82] FCC, decision of 5 May 2020, 2 BvR 859/15.

[83] See the discussion on the *Verfassungsblog*, available at verfassungsblog.de/category/debates/german-legal-hegemony-debates/.

[84] See generally, M Wendel, 'Comparative reasoning and the making of a common constitutional law: EU-related decisions of national constitutional courts in a transnational perspective' (2013) 11 *International Journal of Constitutional Law* 981.

identity. Based on the latter, the FCC can declare EU legal acts non-applicable in Germany if the act violates principles that are considered to be part of the constitutional identity of Germany.[85] This jurisprudence as well as the ultra vires review have been taken up by the constitutional courts in several other EU Member States and even in non-EU states such as Russia.[86] They are used to justify the non-application of EU law, CJEU decisions or – in the case of Russia – ECtHR decisions within the respective domestic legal orders.

Moreover, a similar phenomenon has occurred in relation to the Council of Europe regime. Here, the jurisprudence of the FCC also has influenced judicial actors in other Member States, although to a lesser extent than in the EU context. The *Görgülü* decision of 2004 that shaped the impact of the ECtHR jurisprudence within the German legal order has especially exercised such an influence.[87] As mentioned above, the FCC established in this decision, on the one hand, that the rule of law element that the judge is bound by law includes being bound by the European Convention of Human Rights and the jurisprudence of the ECtHR. On the other hand, however, the Court said that it would violate both fundamental rights and the *Rechtsstaatsprinzip* if an ECtHR decision is enforced 'in a schematic way, in violation of prior-ranking law'.[88] This second prong allows domestic courts not to implement ECtHR decisions in certain cases. This approach has been taken up in certain other Council of Europe Member States explicitly or implicitly. Most prominently, the Russian Constitutional Court has explicitly referenced the *Görgülü* decision to justify its pushback against the ECtHR.[89] Further, in Hungary, the German approach to the relationship of domestic law towards the ECHR and the ECtHR jurisprudence has been referred to by one of the judges of the Hungarian Constitutional Court.[90] Moreover, the UK Supreme Court has adopted a very similar wording to that of the FCC in *Görgülü* when it held that 'the HRA requires our courts to "take into account" EurCtHR decisions, not necessarily to follow them'.[91] Other critical judicial stances such as by the Italian and the Lithuanian Constitutional

[85] See, eg, FCC, decision of 30 June 2009, 2 BvE 2, 5/08, 2 BvR 1010, 1022, 1259/08, 182/09; decision of 14 January 2014, 2 BvR 2728, 2729, 2730, 2731/13, 2 BvE 13/13; decision of 15 December 2015, 2 BvR 2735/14; decision of 21 June 2016, 2 BvR 2728 bis 2731/13, 2 BvE 13/13.

[86] See, eg, Polish Constitutional Court, decision of 11 May 2005, K 18/04 and decision of 24 November 2010, K 32/09, section 3.3; Czech Constitutional Court, decision of 26 November 2008, Pl. US. 19/08, paras 120, 139, 216; Danish Supreme Court, decision of 6 April 1998, I 361/1997; Russian Constitutional Court, decision of 19 April 2016, no 12-П/2016. See also AF Tatham, *Central European constitutional courts in the face of EU membership: The influence of the German model in Hungary and Poland* (Brill, 2013).

[87] FCC, decision of 14 October 2004, 2 BvR 1481/04.

[88] ibid 47.

[89] Russian Constitutional Court, decision of 14 July 2015, no 21-P/2015, translation provided by the Venice Commission in CDL-REF(2016)019.

[90] See E Polgári, 'Hungary: "Gains and Losses" – Changing the Relationship with the European Court of Human Rights' in P Popelier, S Lambrecht and K Lemmens (eds), *Criticism of the European Court of Human Rights* (Intersentia, 2016) 295, 314.

[91] United Kingdom Supreme Court, *Manchester City Council (Respondent) v Pinnock (Appellant)*, judgment of 3 November 2010, [2010] UKSC 45, para 48.

Court are also regarded as inspired by the *Görgülü* rationale.[92] Finally, the *Görgülu* decision has been cited by political actors such as the initiators of the 'Self-Determination Initiative' in Switzerland that aimed at weakening the status of the ECHR in the Swiss legal order.[93]

ii. German Influence on the Rule of Law Politics in Europe

In addition to influencing legal standards for the rule of law, Germany has had political influence on the rule of law practice in Europe. This has been most prominently the case in the context of the EU. To start with, it is due to the German rule of law understanding how actors in Germany approached highly political issues of European governance. In Germany with its strong role of courts and especially of the FCC, it is part of the rule of law practice that even highly political issues are justiciable before courts. The power-limiting function of (public) law is at the forefront of this understanding. In German constitutional legal practice, it is common for the FCC to review acts of the legislature or the government, issuing power-limiting orders or demanding legislative amendments. Notions such as a political question doctrine do not exist (see also above at chapter one). This contrasts with a power-enabling or -shaping function of law that, in the public law context, is emphasised more in other Member States.[94] As a result, virtually all the important developments of EU law and governance of the past decades have been challenged before the FCC. This Court does not only perceive itself as actor in charge of shaping Germany's relationship towards the EU – the actors that bring such cases to the Court also see the judicial route as important way of enforcing their political agenda. This includes, inter alia, treaty amendments, the human rights protection against EU acts, acts of EU institutions such as the ECB or the CJEU, and important EU legal tools such as the European Arrest Warrant.[95] This very salient judicial route has caused legal and political conflicts with the EU. A prominent example are the various decisions of the FCC relating to acts of EU institutions during the financial crisis. One of the rule of law related issues in this regard was whether and to what extent there should be a judicial control of the ECB.[96] While, based on a German constitutional law understanding, such a control is perceived as natural and important (even though not necessarily legally required by Article 23 of the Basic Law[97]), EU actors stemming from other constitutional orders did not always share this approach.[98]

[92] See H Keller and R Walther, 'The Bell of Görgülü Cannot Be Unrung – Can it?' (2020) *Global Community Yearbook of International Law and Jurisprudence* 83.

[93] ibid 95.

[94] Huber (n 43) para 107.

[95] See the decisions cited in n 85 as well as eg, decision of 5 May 2020, 2 BvR 859/15; decision of 22 October 1986, 2 BvR 197/83.

[96] On this conflict as resulting from diverging rule of law understandings, Huber (n 43) paras 91–92.

[97] Classen (n 40) para 32.

[98] On this aspect, Huber (n 43) para 92.

Germany's rule of law-related influence also concerns the political and legal mechanisms against a rule of law backsliding in EU Member States. To start with, the German Government had a role in developing the EU rule of law toolbox. For example, the EU review mechanism based on the Rule of Law Report by the EU Commission (see above) has been introduced under Germany's Presidency of the Council of the EU. The German Foreign Office emphasised its support for the rule of law as a value in the EU as well as for the creation of a preventive mechanism (in addition to the reactive mechanisms within the rule of law toolbox) to ensure that the rule of law standard in all Member States remains high.[99] It took the Rule of Law Report as a basis for institutionalising a dialogue among Member States within the structure of the Council of the EU.

As to German actors within the European Parliament, the impact is more ambivalent. On the one hand, the European Parliament has repeatedly taken resolutions regarding the rule of law backsliding in Poland and Hungary as well as in Slovakia. German members of the European Parliament have supported these resolutions.[100] However, on the other hand, the approach to rule of law backsliding within one of its major European political groups, the European People's Party (EPP) has been less clear. The EPP, which describes itself as a 'centre-right, pro-European political party' and which is composed of members of the different centre-rights parties from the Member States, had to decide what stance to take in relation to parties such as the Hungarian FIDEZ that, although at the time still a member of the EPP, had taken a right-wing turn. Manfred Weber, a German member of the European Parliament and chairman of the EPP fraction since 2014 (and later *Spitzenkandidat* for the EPP), opted for a long time for relativising any critique of the lacking rule of law practice of this party and for keeping FIDEZ within the EPP until its membership was eventually suspended in 2019. This approach has been heavily criticised as it allowed Victor Orbán to keep presenting himself as mainstream European politician as the EPP did not take a clear position against a party whose agenda is to undermine the rule of law.[101]

[99] See statement of 2 October 2020 on the website of the foreign office, available at www.auswaertiges-amt.de/en/aussenpolitik/europe/rule-of-law-europe/2341072.

[100] See, eg, resolution of 12 September 2018 on a proposal calling on the Council to determine, pursuant to Article 7(1) TEU, the existence of a clear risk of a serious breach by Hungary of the values on which the Union is founded, [2019] OJ C433; resolution of 1 March 2018 on the Commission's decision to activate Article 7(1) TEU as regards the situation in Poland, [2019] OJ C129; resolution of 15 September 2022 on the proposal for a Council decision determining, pursuant to Article 7(1) of the Treaty on European Union, the existence of a clear risk of a serious breach by Hungary of the values on which the Union is founded, [2023] OJ C125; resolution of 24 November 2022 on the assessment of Hungary's compliance with the rule of law conditions under the Conditionality Regulation and state of play of the Hungarian RRP, [2023] OJ C167.

[101] See, eg, RD Kelemen, 'The European Union's authoritarian equilibrium' (2020) 27 *Journal of European Public Policy* 481. See also more generally for a critical take on the EU reaction to domestic democratic backsliding: RD Kelemen, 'Europe's Other Democratic Deficit: National Authoritarianism in Europe's Democratic Union' (2020) 52 *Government & Opposition* 211.

Moreover, German right-wing members of the European Parliament, that is members from the German party AFD (*Alternative für Deutschland*, 'Alternative for Germany'), have shaped the right-wing political group of the European Parliament, the Identity and Democracy Group, in a significant manner. The majority of members of the Identity and Democracy Group came from the Italian *Lega* but the German MPs were the third-largest group of MPs within this political group. Although the right-wing MPs at the European Parliament have regrouped differently after the 2024 elections, the number of AFD MPs on the European level has increased with these elections considering the growing support for the AFD in Germany.

In sum, this section has shown that, for the most part, Germany has been an engine for the rule of law in Europe. This includes the notion of the rule of law as well as specific rule of law standards. In some respects, however, German actors have been a brake to the rule of law, politically and arguably also jurisprudentially.

II. INTERACTION OF INTERNATIONAL AND DOMESTIC RULE OF LAW STANDARDS

Unlike in the European context, Germany's interaction with rule of law debates at the global level is more one-directional. Germany considers support for the rule of law at the global level and in other countries as an integral part of its foreign policy and has been an active supporter of the rule of law in the United Nations and other fora. Yet, this is primarily understood as Germany promoting its own rule of law tradition abroad; global debates on the rule of law beyond the European context have little to no influence on the domestic rule of law debate in Germany. Internationally, Germany promotes a rule of law conception that emphasises judicial review, the importance of courts, and a well-functioning administration that adheres to the rule of law, as well as the protection of fundamental rights. This section first addresses Germany's efforts in supporting a rules-based international order multilaterally (A) and then turns to Germany's rule of law assistance as an integral part of Germany's foreign policy and development cooperation (B).

A. Germany's Support for a 'Rules-based International Order' in Multilateral Fora

While the rule of law is an old ideal, it only gained prominence in international debates in the 1990s. Rule of law assistance programmes mushroomed throughout the 1990s, so much so that Thomas Carothers famously diagnosed a 'rule of law revival' in 1998, observing that 'one cannot get through a foreign policy debate these days without someone proposing the rule of law as a solution to the world's troubles'.[102] Carothers was concerned with transnational cooperation to build the rule of law within states, something today best known as 'rule of law assistance activities', and this has been the predominant activity of international organisations such as the World Bank and the United Nations.[103] At the same time, there has been – at least since the Non-Aligned Movement's 1989 Declaration on the Issue of Peace and the Rule of Law in International Affairs – a parallel debate on how to foster the rule of law between states.[104] While Germany has not been a primary driver of rule of law debates in international fora, it has consistently supported the rule of law in multilateral settings. Germany's understanding of the rule of law is closely tied to its traditional rule of law notion, emphasising the importance of judicial review. More broadly, Germany also advocates for the application of liberal values beyond the state, lately labelled as a 'rules-based international order'.[105]

Germany has consistently spoken out in favour of the rule of law at the United Nations and in other multilateral fora. In the Security Council's first-ever thematic debate on the rule of law, Germany's permanent representative to the UN, Gunter Pleuger, stated that 'the rule of law is a main pillar for ensuring enduring peace in the world' and highlighted the importance of rule of law assistance in post-conflict settings.[106] Germany participated in almost all open debates on the rule of law in the Security Council, including at times when it was not an elected Council member.[107] In these debates, Germany generally expressed support for the rule of law.

In line with the traditional understanding of the rule of law as intimately linked to a well-functioning court system and judicial review, Germany has repeatedly emphasised the importance of both international and domestic courts as part and parcel of supporting the rule of law internationally. In the

[102] T Carothers, 'The Rule of Law Revival' (1998) 77 *Foreign Affairs* 95, 95.

[103] For an overview and critique of the rule of law activities in the World Bank see T Krever, 'The Legal Turn in Late Development Theory: The Rule of Law and the World Bank's Development Model' (2011) 52 *Harvard International Law Journal* 287; for an overview of rule of law debates and activities within the United Nations see H Birkenkötter, 'The United Nations and the Rule of Law' in M Sevel (ed), *Handbook on the Rule of Law* (Routledge, forthcoming).

[104] UN Doc A/44/191.

[105] See, eg, Federal Foreign Office, 'Promoting international law and a rules-based order: Foreign Minister Baerbock in Geneva', www.auswaertiges-amt.de/en/aussenpolitik/themen/menschenrechte/foreign-minister-baerbock-at-the-human-rights-council-the-conference-on-disarmament-and-the-donor-conference-for-yemen-in-geneva/2584476; Statement by Germany during the Conference on Disarmament, 3 March 2022, UN Doc CD/2302; Remarks by Secretary Antony J. Blinken, German Foreign Minister Annalena Baerbock, and Indian External Affairs Minister Subrahmanyam Jaishankar at the Munich Security Conference 2024, www.state.gov/secretary-antony-j-blinken-german-foreign-minister-annalena-baerbock-and-indian-external-affairs-minister-subrahmanyam-jaishankar-at-the-munich-security-conference/.

[106] See, eg, the statement of the German representative, Gunther Pleuger, to the Security Council at its first open debate on the rule of law, UN Doc S/PV.4833, pp 15–17.

[107] See, eg, the open debates of 29 June 2010, UN Doc S/PV.6347 (and resumption) and of 19 February 2014, UN Doc S/PV.7113.

2004 UN Security Council Open Debate on the rule of law, Germany highlighted the role of courts in transitional justice, in particular the International Criminal Court, but also domestic judicial systems, as well as the importance of the International Court of Justice.[108] In another open debate, the German representative called for more states to submit themselves to the compulsory jurisdiction of the International Court of Justice and suggested that 'treaties could, as a rule, contain dispute settlement clauses that provide for an independent adjudication of disputes'.[109] Similarly, Germany supported the UN's reform of its internal administration of justice from a one-tier administrative review into a two-tier, formal UN Dispute Tribunal and UN Appeals Tribunal composed of formally trained judges. Thomas Fitschen, a German diplomat who was representing Germany in the relevant negotiations, has called this reform a major achievement 'to take the rule of law within the Organization to a new level'.[110] Such statements reflect the German tradition of the *Rechtsstaat* that emphasises the importance of formal institutions, especially of courts, as rule of law safeguards.

Germany's support for international courts has also been backed by practical action and financial contributions. Germany played an important role in the negotiations of the Rome Statute. This included, crucially, support for the International Criminal Court as an independent entity and not a 'permanent ad hoc tribunal' under the control of the Security Council, as had been favoured by the US and the other permanent members of the Security Council.[111] German diplomat Hans-Peter Kaul, who later served as judge on the International Criminal Court from 2003 to 2014, played a key role in the negotiations, especially between 1996 and 1998, shaping important parts of the Rome Statute, such as the focus on core crimes and the strict application of the *nullum crimen sine lege* principle, now enshrined in Articles 11, 22 and 24 of the Rome Statute.[112] After the International Criminal Court had taken up its work, Germany was the International Criminal Court's biggest financial contributor, accounting for 20 per cent of the Court's budget in 2003.[113] Between 2002 and 2023, there had always been a German judge on the International Criminal Court and it

[108] UN Doc S/PV.4833, p 16.

[109] Statement by Peter Wittig on behalf of Germany, 'Open Debate on the promotion and strengthening of the rule of law in the maintenance of international peace and security', 29 June 2010, UN Doc S/PV.6347(Resumption1) at p 19.

[110] T Fitschen, 'Reforming the system of administration of justice at the United Nations – A short history' in H Buss et al (eds), *Handbook on the Internal Justice System at the United Nations* (United Nations System Staff College, 2014) 7, 20.

[111] R Steinke, *The Politics of International Criminal Justice: German Perspectives from Nuremberg to The Hague* (Hart Publishing, 2012) 100–11.

[112] C Kreß, 'Versailles – Nürnberg – Den Haag: Deutschland Und Das Völkerstrafrecht' (2006) *JuristenZeitung* 981, 987.

[113] See numbers in T Ingadottir and C Romano, 'The Financing of the International Criminal Court' in T Ingadottir (ed), *The International Criminal Court: Recommendations on Policy and Practice* (Brill, 2003) 47, 50, 54.

came as somewhat of a shock when Germany failed to secure sufficient votes for her candidate in 2023.[114] Germany has also provided practical and ideological support for other international courts. For example, it donated the premises for the International Tribunal for the Law of the Sea in Hamburg, with a substantial contribution of the City of Hamburg.[115] On the regional level, Germany supported the various declarations adopted at the Council of Europe's high-level conferences that aimed at reforming the European Court of Human Rights in view of the Court's increasingly unmanageable caseload and strengthening the Court vis-à-vis the backlash that it has suffered in view of increasing populist and nationalist movements across different European states.[116]

As shown in chapter one, the prevalent understanding of the rule of law in Germany today is a thick understanding of the rule of law that is imbued with substantive values, including importantly the protection of human rights. Such an understanding is also clearly discernible in Germany's support for the rule of law at the global level. In 2019, the German Federal Government adopted for the first time an interministerial strategy for promoting the rule of law, which explicitly states that Germany 'actively engages to defend the understanding that ... the rule of law is linked to respect for and upholding of human rights'.[117] Germany is a state party to all core human rights treaties negotiated under the auspices of the United Nations, with the exception of the International Convention on the Protection of the Rights of All Migrant Workers and Members of Their Families, which has not been ratified by any EU Member State.[118] It regularly provides state reports to the treaty monitoring bodies and the Universal Periodic Review,[119] and has also accepted individual complaints in the UN human rights treaty-monitoring bodies.[120] At the regional

[114] 'IStGH ohne deutsche Richterin', interview with Prof. Dr. Stefanie Bock, *Neue Juristische Wochenschrift*, 28 February 2024, available at rsw.beck.de/aktuell/daily/magazin/detail/njw-interview-2024-9-istgh-ohne-deutsche-richterin.

[115] International Tribunal for the Law of the Sea, 'Seat', available at www.itlos.org/en/main/general-information/seat-of-the-tribunal/.

[116] For an overview of the high-level conferences from Interlaken to Brighton and Copenhagen see LR Glas, 'From Interlaken to Copenhagen: What Has Become of the Proposals Aiming to Reform the Functioning of the European Court of Human Rights?' (2020) 20 *Human Rights Law Review* 121.

[117] German Federal Foreign Office, Strategy of the Federal Government for promoting the rule of law in the fields of crisis prevention, conflict resolution and peacebuilding, 2019, available at peacelab.blog/uploads/Rechtsstaatsförderung-EN-WEB.pdf, at p 7. On the strategy see section B.iii below).

[118] See ratification status at indicators.ohchr.org.

[119] For an overview of Germany's participation in UN human rights mechanisms see *Deutsches Institut für Menschenrechte*, 'Menschenrechtsabkommen', www.institut-fuer-menschenrechte.de/menschenrechtsschutz/deutschland-im-menschenrechtsschutzsystem/vereinte-nationen/vereinte-nationen-menschenrechtsabkommen, and 'Deutschland im UPR', www.institut-fuer-menschenrechte.de/menschenrechtsschutz/deutschland-im-menschenrechtsschutzsystem/vereinte-nationen/vereinte-nationen-menschenrechtsrat/upr-deutschland-2018.

[120] For various decades, Germany had not ratified the Optional Protocol to the International Covenant on Economic, Social and Cultural Rights, which enables individual complaints. After a lengthy civil society-led campaign, the Federal Government deposited its instrument of ratification on

level, it is a party to the European Convention on Human Rights since its entry into force in 1953, including submission to the jurisdiction of the European Commission on Human Rights and the ECtHR since 1955.[121] Germany did not ratify, however, Protocol No 16 to the Convention for the Protection of Human Rights and Fundamental Freedoms, which allows the ECtHR to render advisory opinions on questions of principle relating to the interpretation or application of ECHR rights upon request from a country's highest courts and tribunals.[122] Nonetheless, the high ratification rate of regional and international human rights instruments and submission to individual complaints mechanisms testify to Germany's generally high commitment to international human rights protection, including through courts and quasi-judicial bodies.

In recent years, Germany has increasingly expressed support for a 'rules-based international order'. This terminology is shared by other, primarily western states, and was adopted inter alia by the G7.[123] At the same time, this very terminology has been criticised by other states, perhaps most vocally by the Russian Federation, which sees the use of this terminology as an attempt to replace international law in order 'to camouflage a striving to invent rules depending on changes in the political situation'.[124] There has been some uncertainty as to whether the terms 'rules-based order' and rule of law (or international rule of law) are to be understood as synonyms, or whether they denote different concepts.[125] But it seems clear that the 'rules-based order' that Germany, alongside other states, advocates needs to be understood as a concept that is broader than the mere adherence to rules of positive, international law, and comprises a set of values and other norms that are broadly congruent with a liberal, human rights-driven version of global order; values that Germany posits as universal.[126] This includes sets of pragmatic rules that are non-legal

20 April 2023, and the Optional Protocol entered into force on 20 July 2023. See also *Deutsches Institut für Menschenrechte*, 'Umsetzung des Sozialpakts in Deutschland', www.institut-fuer-menschenrechte.de/menschenrechtsschutz/deutschland-im-menschenrechtsschutzsystem/vereinte-nationen/vereinte-nationen-menschenrechtsabkommen/umsetzung-sozialpakt-in-deutschland.

[121] See declarations under Arts 25 and 44 of 5 July 1955, available at www.coe.int/en/web/conventions/by-member-states-of-the-council-of-europe?module=declarations-by-treaty&numSte=005&codeNature=0.

[122] Protocol No 16 to the Convention for the Protection of Human Rights and Fundamental Freedoms (CETS No 214).

[123] See G7 Foreign Ministers Joint Communiqué, Toronto, April 23, 2018, available at www.g7.utoronto.ca/foreign/180423-communique.html.

[124] Quoted after S Talmon, 'Rules-based order v. international law?', available at gpil.jura.uni-bonn.de/2019/01/rules-based-order-v-international-law/.

[125] A recent statement by Germany in the Security Council suggests that the Foreign Office is using the terms somewhat synonymously: the statement delivered on 12 January 2023, at an open debate on the promotion and strengthening of the rule of law in the maintenance of international peace and security, the German representative opened her speech by stating: 'Germany believes that the *rule of law among nations* lies at the core of our national interests' (UN Doc S/PV.9241 (Resumption 1) p 20, whilst the original version, posted on the German Permanent Representation's website, states: 'Germany believes that the *rules-based international order* and international law lie at the core of our national interest.' See new-york-un.diplo.de/un-en/-/2573086 (emphasis added).

[126] On this understanding see J Dugard, 'The Choice before Us: International Law or a "Rules-Based International Order"?' (2023) 36 *Leiden Journal of International Law* 223.

in character, but considered to complement international law. Germany has used such rules for example in the context of the conflict surrounding the South China Sea, when it issued Policy Guidelines for the Indo-Pacific – a move that has been criticised as brushing over the significant disagreement as to the precise content and legal force of norms that ought to regulate this specific context.[127]

B. Supporting the Rule of Law Abroad: Rule of Law Assistance

With the general rise of rule of law efforts, rule of law assistance has become more prominent in Germany's foreign policy since the early 1990s and has increased since. As of 2019, roughly ten per cent of Germany's official development assistance (€1.9 billion) were spent in the sector 'state and civil society in general', of which roughly €127 million were spent on 'development of legal and court systems' and some €68 million on 'human rights'. It is difficult to say which projects in adjacent sectors might be counted as rule of law assistance as definitions are often contingent on funding sources and partners' preferences.[128] Germany's rule of law understanding in development cooperation is pragmatic and primarily concerned with competences: rule of law assistance aimed at stabilising a post-conflict setting is within the overall competence of the German Federal Foreign Office with civilian projects often carried out or supervised by the Ministry of Development Cooperation and/or the Ministry of Justice, whereas rule of law assistance in countries that have relatively stable state structures falls under the purview of the Ministry of Development Cooperation or the Ministry of Justice.[129] We will first discuss German rule of law assistance in post-conflict settings, using the example of Afghanistan, to then proceed to rule of law assistance in stabilised settings as part of Germany's development cooperation. The last section addresses Germany's recent efforts to streamline their assistance activities across ministries and to provide a greater level of coherence.

i. Rule of Law Assistance in Post-conflict Settings: Afghanistan

Rule of law assistance in post-conflict settings is usually carried out in complex actor constellations. Germany does not act in a vacuum here but depends on multilateral action at various levels, including the EU, the NATO, and the UN. Different legal arrangements are possible. Germany is a member of various

[127] M Jorgensen, 'The Jurisprudence of the Rules-Based Order: Germany's Indo-Pacific Guidelines and the South China Sea Code of Conduct', KFG Working Paper Series 2021, No 49, Berlin Potsdam Research Group 'The International Rule of Law – Rise or Decline?', available at papers.ssrn.com/sol3/papers.cfm?abstract_id=3847800.

[128] All statistics taken from M Kötter, 'Rechtsstaatsförderung in der deutschen auswärtigen Politik' in M Kötter et al (eds), *Rechtsstaatsförderung – Handbuch für Forschung und Praxis* (Kohlhammer, 2022) 1, 5 and annex 1, based on the Organisation for Economic Co-Operation and Development's CRS-data.

[129] ibid 7.

international organisations and supports, for example, UN rule of law assistance through its regular (assessed) and voluntary contributions. German government agencies also act as partners in the implementation of international mandates, and German experts can be seconded to international organisations. Last, Germany is an actor in its own right and different federal ministries have provided rule of law assistance in post-conflict settings.

Perhaps one of the most important rule of law assistance efforts by Germany to date was carried out in Afghanistan. It also set an important precedent and was key in shaping new assistance strategies across different federal ministries, which we discuss below. Germany's experience in Afghanistan illustrates the challenges that rule of law assistance in complex settings faces, but also how rule of law ideals from a specific culture – in the case of Germany, a well-functioning administration bound by law, and a formal, hierarchically ordered court system as the main dispute settlement mechanism – are deeply engrained in the kind of expertise that is provided, yet are not easily transferrable to other contexts.

Germany's rule of law assistance in Afghanistan, particularly its assistance to Afghanistan's justice sector reform, took place in a setting with a multiplicity of international, regional, and national actors. Following the US-led invasion of Afghanistan in September 2001, German support started in the winter of that same year, when the country hosted a group of Afghan high-ranking nationals in Bonn, Germany, in the presence of the UN Special Representative for Afghanistan, to discuss Afghanistan's way forward after the overthrow of the Taliban Government. This conference resulted in the 'Agreement on Provisional Arrangements in Afghanistan Pending the Re-establishment of permanent government institutions' (also known as 'Bonn Agreement'), which provided for an interim authority until a Constitutional Assembly, the Constitutional Loya Jirga, was established.[130] The Bonn Agreement requested inter alia international assistance in the establishment and training of new Afghan security and armed forces, the establishment of an interim UN-mandated force to assist in the maintenance of security, and urged the international community to provide rehabilitation, recovery, and reconstruction assistance to Afghanistan. While this implied some form of rule of law assistance, the Bonn Agreement did not contain the term 'rule of law', and no definition was ever agreed upon between the various international actors and the Afghan Government.[131] Security Council resolution 1386 authorised the International Security Assistance Force for Afghanistan (ISAF), and Germany, after a vote from the German Parliament, which is required by German constitutional law for any use of military force, participated in ISAF.[132] In addition to the military presence, a multitude of

[130] Contained in UN Doc S/2001/1154.

[131] A Wiik and F Lachenmann, 'The Law Behind Rule of Law Promotion in Fragile States: The Case of Afghanistan' (2018) 9 *Goettingen Journal of International Law* 171, 174.

[132] See Decision by the German Parliament on the Participation of German military troops in ISAF, Afghanistan, Decision of 21 December 2001, BT Drs 14/7930, and further mandates renewed

organisations, both as part of multilateral assistance and via bilateral agreements, started to offer civilian assistance, resulting in a convolution of state and non-state actors and very little streamlining.[133]

Germany has been the second-largest donor on rule of law assistance projects in Afghanistan after the US.[134] As part of its engagement with ISAF, Germany led two Provincial Reconstruction Teams (PRTs) in Kunduz and Faisabad, starting in 2003 and 2004, respectively.[135] One of Germany's main areas of activity within ISAF was the security sector reform of the Afghan National Police, first through the German Police Project Team and then since 2007 also as part of the EU police mission EUPOL, with a focus on training police trainers for a multiplying effect as well as on police-judicial cooperation.[136] All activities, including two police training centers in Kunduz and Faisabad, were handed over to the Afghan authorities in 2013 and 2014, as ISAF wound down. In addition to Germany's military engagement, German authorities and non-governmental organisations conducted various civilian rule of law assistance projects focusing on the justice sector and administration reform under the auspices of three different ministries (Foreign Affairs, Ministry of the Interior, Ministry of Development Cooperation). These ministries were involved with programming, financing, and implementing a great variety of projects, typically in cooperation with non-governmental organisations, foundations, and other non-state actors. As of 2018, the German Government co-operated with no fewer than 83 German, international, and Afghan non-governmental organisations, often in projects involving capacity building and training of Afghan public servants and lending expertise on legislative projects and administrative reform.[137] After the Taliban takeover in 2021, Germany suspended all official bilateral cooperation with Afghanistan, including its rule of law assistance, as it does not recognise the Taliban Government. The German Ministry of Development Cooperation continues to provide humanitarian assistance exclusively to local organisations.[138]

While no comprehensive empirical study evaluating Germany's rule of law assistance in Afghanistan from 2002 onwards exists, there is a general perception that rule of law assistance in Afghanistan has fallen short of its proclaimed

annually, available at www.bundestag.de/webarchiv/Ausschuesse/ausschuesse18/a12/auslandseinsaetze/auslandseinsaetze/isaf_bisherige_mandate-247448.

[133] W Plessmann and TJ Röder, 'Koordinierung des Justizaufbaus in Afghanistan (2002–2014)' in Kötter et al (n 128) 75–80.

[134] B Zahir Hellali, 'Justizaufbau und Rechtsverständnis in Afghanistan (seit 2001)' in Kötter et al (n 128) 156. Germany was also the third largest provider of troops in the NATO mission, see S Destradi, 'Germany's Engagement in Afghanistan' in R Harshé and D Tripathi (eds), *Afghanistan Post-2014* (Routledge, 2015).

[135] K Brummer and S Fröhlich, 'Einleitung: Zehn Jahre Deutschland in Afghanistan' in K Brummer and S Fröhlich (eds) *Zehn Jahre Deutschland in Afghanistan* (VS Verlag, 2011) 3.

[136] Destradi (n 134).

[137] Wiik and Lachenmann (n 131) 177 et seq.

[138] See Federal Ministry for Economic Cooperation and Development, Afghanistan, 2023, www.bmz.de/en/countries/afghanistan.

aims and expectations.[139] For German observers of rule of law assistance, the case of Afghanistan shows that coordination both within the German Federal Government, but also on-site, is key to successfully providing rule of law assistance.[140] Afghani observers have also pointed out that German assistance lacked clear funding criteria, did not sufficiently enable local organisations, did not sufficiently focus on anti-corruption measures and in some instances, fostered corruption instead of curbing it.[141] Similarly, German rule of law assistance focused primarily on formal justice institutions, such as courts and administrative officials, whereas Afghanistan has a long tradition of alternative dispute resolution and informal dispute settlement mechanisms, a factor that was largely overlooked by German and other international actors.[142] Rule of law assistance did not sufficiently build on existing legal and societal structures, but instead followed donor perspectives – it was supply-instead of demand-driven – and often conceptualised by foreign experts who applied their own background instead of taking into account the local context.[143] This shows that rule of law values from one country are not easily transferrable to other contexts and that rule of law assistance ought to be cautious when introducing specific justice institutions in vastly different cultural contexts.

In 2023, the first-ever interministerial evaluation of Germany's civilian engagement in Afghanistan was issued, covering the years 2013 through 2021.[144] The evaluation clearly states that Germany's aim in assisting Afghanistan had been to build a 'democratic state based on the rule of law', that Germany, along with the international community, had failed to achieve this aim, and that it would not have been achieved any time soon even without the Taliban's takeover. The evaluation assessed Germany's assistance activities at three levels (political decision-making level; executive ministerial decision-making level; and operative implementation level) and along five criteria (relevance; coherence; effectiveness/impact; sustainability/long-term effects; efficiency).[145] The main conclusions are rather sobering: Germany overestimated its possibilities and did not properly assess the contextual factors in Afghanistan; in some instances, it cooperated with corrupt elites and thus fostered corruption; there was no coherent strategy and a lack of coordination at all three levels; there was no adaptation to changing circumstances or apparent challenges. As a consequence, the evaluation recommends inter alia better coordination at the strategic decision-making

[139] Wiik and Lachenmann (n 131) 180.

[140] Plessmann and Röder (n 133).

[141] See L Saeed, 'International Rule of Law Assistance: Learning from Failures in Afghanistan', available at peacelab.blog/2019/05/international-rule-of-law-assistance-learning-from-failures-in-afghanistan.

[142] Hellali (n 134).

[143] See for a similar assessment with examples, Wiik and Lachenmann (n 131) 180–81.

[144] C Hartmann et al, 'Ressortgemeinsamer Evaluierungsbericht Finale Version Afghanistan' (2023), available at www.auswaertiges-amt.de/blob/2635532/4f24e7a53e139d4f7c9759af33f379c4/231212-ressortgemeinsamer-bericht-afg-data.pdf.

[145] ibid ch 2.

levels, more interministerial strategising and coordination as well as regular evaluation, and more systematic assessment of potential negative effects.[146]

ii. Rule of Law Assistance in Bilateral Development Cooperation: Germany's Rule of Law Dialogues

Whilst rule of law assistance in post-conflict settings is primarily carried out in the context of larger, multilateral state-building efforts, Germany also carries out rule of law assistance as part of its bilateral development cooperation. Since 1990, Germany's development cooperation has increasingly focused on building governance structures in different countries. Such assistance was in part influenced by global governance debates and the numerous World Summits that took place throughout the 1990s on topics that traditionally belonged to the domestic realm of states.[147] Another important factor was the dissolution of the Soviet Union, which was followed by various German rule of law assistance projects in Central, Eastern, and Southeastern European as well as Central Asian countries, starting in the early 1990s. Germany offered newly independent former Soviet states rule of law assistance, both as part of its development cooperation under the auspices of the German Ministry for Development Cooperation and implemented through the German Technical Cooperation Agency (GTZ, now GIZ), and as legal policy under the auspices of the Ministry of Justice.[148] The Ministry of Justice created an independent non-profit organisation, the German Foundation for International Legal Cooperation (*Institut für rechtliche Zusammenarbeit*, IRZ), which was to implement legal assistance projects in Central, Eastern and Southeastern Europe.[149]

Germany's bilateral assistance projects were soon integrated into a broader European and international context: in Central Asia and the South Caucasus, the Council of Europe and the Organisation for Economic Cooperation and Development are important actors,[150] whereas in Central, Eastern, and Southeastern Europe, German assistance activities were integrated into the EU effort aimed at assisting countries wanting to join the EU.[151] In both regions, German rule of law assistance was aimed at facilitating the transition from

[146] ibid ch 10.

[147] S Wege and M Nowak, 'Entwicklungspolitik Im Wiedervereinten Deutschland Zwischen 1990 Und 2015' in W Gieler and M Nowak (eds), *Staatliche Entwicklungszusammenarbeit in Deutschland: Eine Bestandsaufnahme des BMZ 1961–2021* (Springer, 2021) 273, 274–275.

[148] J Trappe, 'Unterstützung der Transformationen in Mittel-, Ost- und Südosteuropa (seit 1992)' in Kötter et al (n 128) 55; J Deppe, 'Unterstützung der Transformationen in Südkaukasus und Zentralasien (seit 1992)' in Kötter et al (n 128) 60. The GIZ and the Ministry of Development Cooperation were the main actors in Central Asia and the South Caucasus region, whereas the IRZ and the Ministry of Justice were focusing primarily on Eastern, Central and Southeastern Europe.

[149] See www.irz.de/index.php/en/about-us. The IRZ also became influential in central Asia, but only after 2006, see Deppe (n 148) 64.

[150] ibid 61 and 67.

[151] Trappe (n 148) 58–59; on the rule of law as a requirement for new EU Member States see section I.A.ii).

a planned economy to a market economy through the establishment of legal institutions that followed the model of the liberal constitutional state, including separation of powers, codified laws, and a legal profession trained in applying these new laws. This was to be achieved through advice to ministries and other parts of the administration as well as to Parliaments and courts, expert advice on legislative projects, and the setting up of different educational projects, both through cooperation between universities as well as through a professional visiting program.[152] The IRZ's professional visiting program, where legal professionals from other countries come to Germany and get immersed into the everyday workings of German legal institutions (courts and administration), exists to this day. In this context, universities and research institutions, such as the Max Planck Institutes, but also foundations, such as the Konrad-Adenauer-Foundation, became important implementing actors in addition to the GIZ and the IRZ.[153]

Unlike in post-conflict settings, where the primary aim is typically to achieve stability and maintain peace and security in the short- to mid-term, rule of law assistance at the bilateral level and in countries that have stable state structures pursues long-term goals of entrenching specific legal institutions and fostering a liberal legal culture in the target countries. This type of rule of law assistance is inextricably linked with the idea of a market economy and aims at fostering an environment that is conducive to the market economy and that attracts foreign investment. As observers point out, German rule of law assistance has had a great impact on the development of private law institutions and codes in various countries.[154] Rule of law assistance in this sense reflects a deep commitment of German public institutions to ideals of a liberal market economy, whilst also emphasising legality and legal technique: German lawyers take a certain pride in German doctrinal technique and it is often considered one of Germany's assets to be 'exported' through rule of law assistance projects. This is underlined by the numerous academic and academia-adjacent institutions that work in the field of rule of law assistance.

We can also observe these ideals (and perhaps limits in promoting them) in one of Germany's earliest and perhaps most prominent rule of law assistance projects: the 'rule of law dialogues' with China. In 1994, the German Development Agency (GIZ, at the time GTZ) initiated a 'rule of law cooperation project' with the Chinese Government, and the rule of law dialogues were formalised in the 2000 'German-Chinese Agreement on Exchange and Co-operation in the Legal Field', since then under the auspices of the German Ministry of Justice. Initially, the primary aim of rule of law cooperation was to create a legal framework that would provide security and predictability

[152] Trappe (n 148); Deppe (n 148).

[153] Trappe (n 148) 56.

[154] Trappe (n 148) 57; Deppe (n 148) 67, who also mentions Germany's impact on public law, less so on criminal law (focusing on Central Asia and South Caucasus).

for foreign investors.[155] Here, we see a similarity with rule of law assistance in former Soviet States, which was also aimed at creating a legal framework to enable functioning market economies. Since 2000, the rule of law dialogues are primarily viewed as a platform for communication and better exchange of ideas, while Chinese partners have formulated one of the aims of the rule of law dialogues to 'help China become a rule of law state'.[156]

The rule of law dialogues comprise different formats, including high-level annual conferences, roundtables amongst government officials, legal consulting on different legislative projects in China, cooperation between Chinese and German law faculties, and a large-scale translation project, funded by the German Academic Exchange Service, which resulted in the translation of several German legal textbooks into Chinese.[157] It is noteworthy that the rule of law dialogue, while explicitly named a 'dialogue' to cater to the Chinese wish for genuine exchange on an equal footing,[158] comprises a considerable transfer dimension from Germany to China, but not vice versa: translations of legal textbooks from German into Chinese, funded by the German Academic Exchange service, are plentiful,[159] and Chinese commentators state that many of these books are today standard reference texts in Chinese legal education and practice.[160] Similarly to other rule of law assistance efforts, the rule of law dialogues also included legal consulting on legislative projects, and it appears that many suggestions made by German legal experts were accepted by Chinese lawmakers and integrated into Chinese law.[161] Last, one key component of the program has been the training of judges in German-style methodology, specifically on interpretation and subsumption, which has been characterised by one German commentator as educating Chinese judges in interpreting laws not only in a predictable but also in the 'correct' manner.[162] This statement reflects German actors' belief in German legal technique to be adequate and lead to correct results irrespective of context, and also underlines that the German conception of the dialogues was not so much thought of as reciprocal, but rather a one-directional transfer of skills.

[155] M Spitzkatz, 'Rechtskooperation mit China (seit 1984)' in Kötter et al (n 128) 49, 49.

[156] X Gao and B Gao 'The German-Chinese "Rule of Law Dialogue": Influence and Outlook' (2014) 47 *Verfassung und Recht in Übersee / Law and Politics in Africa, Asia and Latin America* 392, 394.

[157] ibid.

[158] Spitzkatz (n 155) 54.

[159] On the genre of the German legal textbook (*Lehrbuch*) as a peculiar combination of theoretical and doctrinal accounts, see C Möllers and H Birkenkötter, 'Towards a New Conceptualism in Comparative Constitutional Law, or Reviving the German Tradition of the Lehrbuch' (2014) 12 *International Journal of Constitutional Law* 603.

[160] Gao and Gao (n 156) 398.

[161] Gao and Gao (n 156) 402, provide the example of the Chinese Government Information Disclosure Regulation, which was based on the German Freedom of Information Act (*Informationsfreiheitsgesetz*).

[162] Spitzkatz (n 155) 51.

Overall, the results of Germany's rule of law assistance in states with stable structures are viewed with mixed feelings by most practitioners and experts. Absent a counterfactual, it is difficult to assess the impact of German rule of law assistance on local institutions, and in addition, German entities act in concert with others, making it impossible to disaggregate which actor had what kind of effect in each situation.[163] German actors have also overestimated their impact in relation to the relatively short time span of their assistance projects. As one commentator puts it with regard to Eastern, Central, and Southeast Europe, there was a widespread belief when the IRZ was founded initially for a decade, that a decade would be sufficient to 'complete the transformation processes' in the target countries.[164] This has proven to be unrealistic, as it takes time to entrench a different legal culture. In the case of China specifically, one criticism is the lack of progress with regard to human rights. While the German side has sought to include human rights dialogues into the rule of law dialogues, this has not been very successful and has led to criticism in German media that despite huge investments, no real progress in terms of human rights protection was achieved in China.[165] Chinese observers have noted that perhaps the biggest obstacle to implementing a German-style rule of law state in China is a lack of consensus within China of whether it should transform itself into a rule of law state in the meaning of western countries, given the country's own cultural and legal tradition that emphasises stability, loyalty and development as primary values.[166] As China has become more assertive in recent years, it has become clear that Germany's vision of a 'rule of law dialogue' that is in many ways a one-way transfer from Germany to China is no longer realistic. This is reflected in the recent 'Strategy on China' by the Federal Government, which states that 'China has changed. As a result of this and China's political decisions, we need to change our approach to China' and explicitly states that it wishes 'to reposition the Human Rights Dialogue [only held at very irregular intervals] together with the Rule of Law Dialogue.'[167] This underlines once more that Germany advocates a substantive conception of the rule of law in its international rule of law endeavours that views the rule of law as inextricably linked to both human rights, specifically civil and political rights.

iii. Germany's 2019 Common Strategy on Rule of Law Assistance

In 2019, the German Federal Government adopted a cross-departmental 'Strategy of the Federal Government for promoting the rule of law' to provide a

[163] See ibid 54; Deppe (n 148) 67.
[164] Trappe (n 148) 59.
[165] Spitzkatz (n 155) 54.
[166] Gao and Gao (n 156) 410. Generally on the rule of law in China see E Pils, *Rule of Law in China* (Hart Publishing, forthcoming – in this book series).
[167] German Federal Foreign Office, 'Strategy on China of the Government of the Federal Republic of Germany' (2023) 9, 21.

conceptual framework and common guidance to all federal ministries involved in rule of law assistance, ie, the Foreign Office, the Ministry for Development Cooperation, and the Ministry of Justice.[168] This strategy emerged from a prior interministerial set of guidelines, the 2017 Guidelines on Crisis Prevention.[169] The 2017 Guidelines on Crisis Prevention were hailed as a milestone in German security policy, as they were the result of a yearlong debate that had started around 2013/14, in response to a general feeling that Germany was lacking a clear vision on how to position itself internationally in security matters and a lack of results in countries such as Afghanistan.[170] The 2017 Guidelines were the outcome of a two-year-long consultation process organised by the Global Public Policy Institute, a Berlin-based think tank, which brought together experts and practitioners from different implementing organisations, ministries, and academia at an unprecedented scale.[171] The Guidelines identify the rule of law as one primary field of action of state building, understood as comprising reform of the legal and judicial sector, dispute settlement mechanisms, the promotion of human rights and equal participation of all groups in society, and the prevention of international law crimes and transitional justice.[172] This understanding of the rule of law once again reflects Germany's tradition of combining a focus on substantive values, especially human rights, on the one hand, with an emphasis on the judicial sector and dispute settlement through law on the other hand.

The Guidelines also announced the establishment of an interministerial working group for the drafting of an interministerial strategy for promoting the rule of law.[173] As mentioned in the previous sections, there are typically at least three ministries involved in rule of law assistance projects: the Foreign Office, the Ministry for Development Cooperation, and the Ministry of Justice, sometimes also the Ministry of the Interior and the Ministry of Defence, as far as police and/or military action is concerned. Therefore, rule of law assistance debates amongst German policy actors had often been primarily concerned with questions of competence, without necessarily addressing theoretical debates on what the rule of law might mean.[174]

[168] German Federal Government, Strategy Rule of Law (n 117).

[169] German Federal Government, 'Guidelines on Preventing Crises, Resolving Conflicts, Building Peace' (2017), www.auswaertiges-amt.de/blob/1214246/057f794cd3593763ea556897972574fd/preventing-crises-data.pdf.

[170] On the shortcomings of Germany's assitance activities in Kosovo and Afghanistan from a practitioner's perspective see W Nachtwei, 'Lehren aus deutschen Krisenengagements gibt es reichlich – aber auch Lernfortschritte?' (2019) 3 *SIRIUS – Zeitschrift für Strategische Analysen* 362.

[171] Amongst other things, the Federal Foreign Office financed a policy dialogue throughout 2016 that comprised 27 events with over 1,800 participants and an online blog called *PeaceLab*, see Guidelines on Crisis Prevention (n 169) p 15 and the debate at peacelab.blog/debatte/peacelab-2016.

[172] The five fields of action of 'German engagement to promote peace in partner countries' are: legitimate politics, security, rule of law, economy and vital natural resources, and government revenue and public services, see Guidelines on Crisis Prevention (n 169) p 75, for the understanding of the rule of law see ibid p 93.

[173] ibid p 96.

[174] Kötter et al (n 128) 7.

The 2019 Rule of Law Strategy aims at providing more conceptual coherence amongst the ministries. It explicitly places its understanding of the rule of law in recent German history and defines it as 'limit[ing] and commit[ting] state authority to safeguarding individual freedoms and material justice, in particular by recognising fundamental rights, ensuring the administration is subject to the law and effectively protecting individual rights by maintaining the independence of the courts'.[175] This 'specific understanding of the concept of the rule of law' is understood as being explicitly German, but is then put into the context of international rule of law definitions, particularly Kofi Annan's shared understanding of the rule of law in the UN system,[176] as well as 'relevant terminology used by the Council of Europe, the EU and the OSCE',[177] although this relevant terminology is neither identified nor further specified throughout the document.

Assisting in building the rule of law is seen both as an aim in and of itself as well as a means to achieving other aims, most importantly crisis prevention and sustainable development, as well as fighting corruption and promoting human rights and democracy. The strategy contains several guiding principles that are intended to provide structure to rule of law assistance measures for the short, medium, and long term, which includes a commitment to cooperation with other international and local actors, including civil society, context sensitivity, local ownership and the no-harm principle, and a human rights-based approach.[178] Specific assistance measures that are mentioned in the strategy are consultations on constitutional reforms, federalism, and decentralisation as well as legal education, especially of judges and other public officials, both through the secondment of experts and dialogues.[179]

Overall, the strategy does not introduce new elements, but rather reads like a summary of previous rule of law assistance activities in conflict and non-conflict settings. As such, it is characterised by a tension. On the one hand, the strategy advocates a specific, German understanding of the rule of law that is substantive in its emphasis on individual rights protection and privileges formal courts as the best way to protect individual rights. On the other hand, one 'lesson learned' from previous rule of law assistance activities is that local context needs to be considered, such as the above-mentioned alternative justice systems instead of

[175] German Federal Government, Strategy Rule of Law (n 117) p 6.

[176] 'The "rule of law" is a concept at the very heart of the Organization's mission. It refers to a principle of governance in which all persons, institutions and entities, public and private, including the State itself, are accountable to laws that are publicly promulgated, equally enforced and independently adjudicated, and which are consistent with international human rights norms and standards. It requires, as well, measures to ensure adherence to the principles of supremacy of law, equality before the law, accountability to the law, fairness in the application of the law, separation of powers, participation in decision-making, legal certainty, avoidance of arbitrariness and procedural and legal transparency.' See, 'The rule of law and transitional justice in conflict and post-conflict societies', Report of the Secretary-General of 23 August 2004, UN Doc S/2004/616, para 6.

[177] German Federal Government, Strategy Rule of Law (n 117) p 7.

[178] ibid ch 2.2.

[179] ibid ch 3.

formal courts in Afghanistan. This is visible in the strategy as well: the strategy highlights problems with informal justice systems, including failure to implement human rights or procedural standards, as well as the exclusion of minority groups,[180] but fails to show how these problems might be overcome without doing away with such existing systems altogether. Instead, the strategy recommends that 'efforts should be made to create formal links to legitimate public courts or administrative bodies'.[181] Intentionally or not, the adjective 'legitimate' in conjunction with courts suggests that informal justice systems, as opposed to public courts or administrative bodies, are not to be seen as legitimate. As a consequence, the strategy's commitment to local ownership and context sensitivity rings hollow. A similar tension is visible where the strategy emphasises the importance of local ownership, ie, 'that people involved in measures can identify with them', but also underlines that 'this must be carefully balanced with the interests of the donor institution'.[182] While the strategy stops short of explicitly spelling out the tensions that exist between competing visions of the rule of law, it is clear that it promotes a German vision of the rule of law that can be in tension with other, competing conceptions. Because this tension is not clearly spelt out, there is then a lack of clear guidance for operationalisation, a criticism that has been voiced elsewhere with regard to the Guidelines on Crisis Prevention and the resulting strategies, including the rule of law strategy, as a whole.[183]

Rule of law assistance is today a core element of Germany's development cooperation and its programmes on good governance and sustainable development, yet, efforts to design a coherent, clearly discernible *German* approach to the topic is a relatively new endeavour.[184] While Germany has long considered itself to be well-positioned as an 'honest broker' due to the fact that it was at the receiving end of rule of law assistance after World War II,[185] efforts to achieve conceptual and operational coherence date back less than a decade. Rather, rule of law assistance was built in a piecemeal fashion and insufficient interministerial coordination. The results of rule of law assistance have not been entirely satisfactory: in addition to the difficulty of measuring to what extent rule of law assistance has led to more stable state structures or a more deeply entrenched legal culture, there are clear cases where German (and international) rule of law assistance has failed to bring about stability.

[180] German Federal Government, Strategy Rule of Law (n 117) p 14.
[181] ibid p 15.
[182] ibid p 16.
[183] G Kurtz, 'Präventive Außenpolitik braucht überprüfbare Strategien: Die Bundesregierung stärkt die zivile Krisenprävention, (DGAP-Standpunkt, 27)', Forschungsinstitut der Deutschen Gesellschaft für Auswärtige Politik e.V. 2019, nbn-resolving.org/urn:nbn:de:0168-ssoar-64475-2.
[184] Kötter et al (n 128) 5.
[185] ibid 4.

III. CONCLUSION

This chapter has shown that the German rule of law discourse is today inextricably interwoven with European rule of law debates, both within the Council of Europe and the EU. Germany has actively shaped the rule of law notions in both institutions, and is subject to its monitoring mechanisms. Those mechanisms, as well as the ECtHR's jurisprudence, have had an impact on Germany's domestic rule of law notion; the interaction between the European and the national levels is of a very dynamic nature.

Beyond European institutions, Germany advocates a rule of law notion that is closely linked to its tradition and is substantive, considering the protection of human rights as an integral part of the rule of law, whilst emphasising the importance of judicial review, formal court systems, and trained legal professionals. It supports this rule of law notion both in multilateral fora as well as through rule of law assistance. Rule of law assistance is today a core part of Germany's development cooperation and of crisis prevention; yet, there is little to no impact of these activities on the domestic rule of law discourse in Germany.

6

The Rechtsstaat *in the Digital World*

DIGITALISATION HAS CHANGED and continues to change the social and legal realities in most countries – and Germany is no exception to that. In this last chapter, we outline how these changes influence the rule of law practice in Germany. We first show the impact of digitalisation on the rule of law experience today (I). We then assess the structural effect of digitalisation on the *Rechtsstaatsprinzip* as a legal principle (II). In terms of an outlook, we end the chapter by reflecting on the future challenges that digitalisation causes for the rule of law in Germany (III).

I. IMPACT OF DIGITALISATION ON THE RULE OF LAW EXPERIENCE IN GERMANY

From the perspective of the addressees of law in Germany, digitalisation comes with advantages and disadvantages for certain aspects of the rule of law. This section gives an overview of the rule of law experience in the country as it is impacted by digitalisation.

To start with, digitalisation can enhance the accessibility of law and of (both private and public) legal services. This access-enhancing effect of digitalisation has several dimensions.

First, in terms of access to legal resources, it is now possible for most Germans to access the content of legal acts online, with digitalisation thus lowering the information barrier. The same is true for certain judicial decisions. While only a fraction of judicial decisions are made available online in Germany, and many of them still are only accessible via paid services, the higher courts and the FCC make their decisions available on their website, and some private platforms also provide free access to certain decisions.[1] This provides people with direct access to legal norms and judicial decisions. It also enhances the de facto transparency of state institutions and governance.

Further, legal tech has enhanced access to legal services in certain areas of law. Most prominently, for airline passengers whose flights were delayed or cancelled, digital platforms offer automatised assessment and enforcement of passenger

[1] An example of a free private platform is www.openjur.de.

rights under the Air Passengers Rights Regulation of the EU.[2] Another example is tenancy law, a field in which legal tech companies offer, inter alia, ready-made online tools to fight a rental increase, illegal clauses in rental contracts or the termination of rental contracts. Such digital services make rights enforcement easier and more accessible to large parts of the population. Moreover, such digital services are especially impactful in a legal order as that of Germany which allows for group or class actions before courts only exceptionally and in restricted areas of law. Legal tech provides an alternative to such actions. It is also worth noting that the Federal High Court (*Bundesgerichtshof*) has, in several decisions, paved the way for such digital legal services. Although 'classical' law firms often oppose such services and some regional courts challenged the court's liberal approach to legal tech,[3] the *Bundesgerichtshof* has permitted most of the services of such platforms.[4]

Finally, digitalisation can also increase access to administrative services when these services are provided online. In Germany, the digitalisation of public administration is, however, a challenging endeavour. The digitalisation of the public administration has been initiated by E-Government Acts (*E-Government-Gesetze*) on the federal and *Länder* level (since 2013).[5] These acts make it possible for the federal administration, the *Länder* administration, and the communal administration to offer electronic services to the citizens. Moreover, the Online Access Act (*Onlinezugangsgesetz*) has even obliged the administration to provide, until the end of 2022, around 600 services digitally via their websites. The administration, however, did not live up to this obligation. By early 2024, only between 172 and 264 services were digitally available in the *Länder* administrations.[6] The reasons for this slow process of digitalisation are manifold.[7] To start with, due to the federal structure of Germany, the competence for digitalising the public administration is dispersed among the many *Länder* authorities as well as the federal level. As a result, the *Länder* each took individual approaches to digitalising the administrative services, including which technical programmes and formats to use. This has led to incompatibilities between the different formats used by different authorities in Germany.

[2] Regulation (EC) No 261/2004 of the European Parliament and of the Council of 11 February 2004 establishing common rules on compensation and assistance to passengers in the event of denied boarding and of cancellation or long delay of flights, and repealing Regulation (EEC) No 295/91.

[3] Eg, *Landgericht* Berlin, decision of 5 August 2021, 67 S 75/21.

[4] See, eg, *Bundesgerichtshof*, decision of 27 November 2019, VIII ZR 285/18; decision of 30 March 2022, VIII ZR 256/21.

[5] Generally on e-governance in Germany, A Guckelberger, *Öffentliche Verwaltung im Zeitalter der Digitalisierung* (Nomos, 2019). See also M Martini, 'Transformation der Verwaltung durch Digitalisierung' (2017) *Die öffentliche Verwaltung* 443; A Guckelberger, 'E-Government: Ein Paradigmenwechsel in Verwaltung und Verwaltungsrecht?' (2019) 78 VVDStRL 235; H Kube, 'E-Government: Ein Paradigmenwechsel in Verwaltung und Verwaltungsrecht?' (2019) 78 VVDStRL 289.

[6] Information about the status has been made available at dashboard.digitale-verwaltung.de/.

[7] They are assessed eg, by Guckelberger, Öffentliche Verwaltung (n 5) 161–173.

Further, the federal structure also posed a legal obstacle to implementing the e-government approach. As a principle, the Basic Law stipulates a strict separation between the exercise of competences of the federal and the *Länder* level. To make the cooperation that is required by an e-government legally possible, a specific provision – Article 91c – had to be introduced in the Basic Law (see also below at II). In addition, the population was initially rather hesitant to use the early attempts of e-governance. This includes the online function of the ID card and other functions requiring a so-called electronic signature as an authentication tool. With regard to the online function of the ID card that has been available since 2010, a study showed in 2021 that only 7 per cent of ID holders used this function.[8] A key reason for this reluctance is that, for most people, there were still too few situations in daily life in which this function might be relevant.

Similarly, the digitalisation of the judiciary has so far been a rather slow process. For a long time, many actors within the judiciary have been opposed to moving away from traditional organisational tools. As an example, the introduction of the electronic file in the judiciary (*E-Akte*) that is meant to fully replace the paper file has only very recently picked up pace. In 2017, a legal act stipulated the introduction of the electronic file in all courts and public prosecutor's offices, an aim that must be reached at the latest by the end of 2026. In 2022, in some *Länder*, several courts already worked exclusively with the electronic file. In others, however, introducing this tool has been slow.[9] The digitalisation process has been fuelled somewhat by the circumstances during the COVID-19 pandemic. The hardware and software infrastructure has been improved. For example, court hearings by video-conferencing technology have become more widespread[10] – a fact that has even inspired the Minister for Justice to introduce a draft law on enhancing the use of videoconference technology before courts.[11]

A second set of impacts on the rule of law experience is rather negative for the individuals concerned. To start with, a problematic effect of digitalisation relates to the effectiveness of rule enforcement in cyberspace. Like many other countries, Germany struggles to enforce the applicable law regarding acts that occur on the Internet. This concerns criminal law but also other areas of law such as, inter alia, copyright law, data protection regulation, and the rules on the protection of private and family life. Regarding criminal law, one of the

[8] See a summary of the representative study conducted in July and August 2021 by PricewaterhouseCoopers available at www.personalausweisportal.de/SharedDocs/kurzmeldungen/Webs/PA/DE/2021/10_pwc_studie.html.

[9] V Heeger, 'E-Akte: Wo steht die deutsche Justiz?', *Tagesspiegel*, 14 June 2022, available at background.tagesspiegel.de/digitalisierung/e-akte-wo-steht-die-deutsche-justiz.

[10] On video-conferencing and other impacts of the pandemic for the digitalisation of the judiciary: H Müller and B Windau, 'Pandemie als Digitalisierungsschub für die Justiz?' (2021) *Deutsche Richterzeitung* 332.

[11] The draft law is available at www.bmj.de/SharedDocs/Gesetzgebungsverfahren/DE/2022_Videokonferenztechnik.html?nn=110490.

issues that are also prominently discussed among the general public is the fact that, for the most part, the police and public prosecutors do not investigate – effectively or at all – statements on the Internet that are prohibited by criminal law such as death threats, incitement, hate speech or the use of prohibited signs and symbols.[12] Such offences have a predominantly right-wing and/or extremist background which makes the lack of law enforcement in the digital sphere a structural problem for the democratic and rule of law-based state. And especially for persons who are victims of acts such as death threats, there is often little that they can do to counter such acts if the police are not able or willing to investigate the identity of the offender. One of the various reasons for this issue is lacking personnel for the large amount of offences committed on the Internet.[13] But other factors play a role as well. For example, such statements often take place on platforms owned by private companies that are not always willing to provide the necessary data.

This involvement of third parties, such as digital platforms and search engines, also impacts how and to what extent individuals can enforce their fundamental rights in the digital sphere. A salient example is a case that has been prominently decided by the FCC in 2019: the case of a person who wanted to oblige an internet search engine to eliminate certain search results about this person.[14] The person, the CEO of a company, was the subject of a TV programme which accused this person of unfair treatment vis-à-vis an employee. Several years later, this TV programme still came up as a result when searching for the name of the CEO on Google. The issue in this type of case is the potential three-party relationship among three fundamental rights holders: the search engine's freedom to conduct a business; the broadcasting company's freedom of expression and freedom of the press; and the individual concerned and their right to private and family life and to the protection of personal data under EU law as well as their personality rights under the German Basic Law. In the case at hand and a parallel case decided on the same day, the Court established the so-called 'right to be forgotten' for such circumstances. After a certain time has elapsed and depending on the specific circumstances of the case, a search engine can be obliged to delete personal information from the search results for an individual. In a parallel case decided on the same day, the Court also established the (alternative) right of the affected person that the media outlet inhibits the searchability of such information via a general search engine such as Google.[15] These decisions strengthen the personality rights of individuals in the digital sphere. And they have provided individuals with two options to enforce these rights, with the result of mitigating the enforceability issue in the digital sphere at least for this type of cases.

[12] TP Holterhus, 'Rechtsstaat', *Informationen zur politischen Bildung* no 351 (2/2022) 47–51.
[13] On this and other reasons, Holterhus (n 12) 51.
[14] FCC, decision of 6 November 2019, 1 BvR 276/17.
[15] FCC, decision of 6 November 2019, 1 BvR 16/13.

Further, a tool that is at best ambivalent from the perspective of the rule of law is predictive policing. This term describes the use of algorithms to predict future illegal or dangerous behaviour of individuals in order for state authorities to take measures to prevent such behaviour. In Germany, predictive policing has been used since 2014 in some fields of executive activity. In several *Länder*, the police use predictive policing to determine where burglaries or car thefts will be likely to take place.[16]

Although predictive policing might contribute to an effective enforcement of law and, from this perspective, can be beneficial for the rule of law practice in Germany, it also bears risks for other elements of the rule of law.[17] As research on predictive policing in other countries has shown, the algorithms used can lead to the discrimination of certain social groups.[18] Legally, such discriminatory algorithms are not permissible. Both German constitutional law with its non-discrimination clause in Article 3 of the Basic Law and EU law with Article 21 of the Fundamental Rights Charta and Article 11(3) of the EU-Directive 2016/680 regarding non-discrimination in the context of profiling require that AI and other digital tools be designed and used in a non-discriminatory manner. Moreover, such tools can infringe upon data protection rights. This can, for example, be the case when the data used for predictive policing is combined with data from video surveillance infrastructure.[19] Such a combination would lead to an intensified impact on fundamental rights.

Initially, predictive policing in Germany did not use personal data. The algorithms only analysed area-specific data. For this form of predictive policing, it has been argued that this would not affect fundamental rights.[20] This form of data use was different from the use of both personal and area-specific data that has been characteristic of predictive policing in the US for some time now. More recently, however, authorities broadened predictive policing in Germany to include the use of personal data. This has given rise to judicial review of these measures. As a result, the use of data for preventive police action has been assessed by the FCC. In a decision of 2023, the FCC decided that the legislation in the *Länder* Hesse and Hamburg regarding automated data analysis for the prevention of criminal acts is unconstitutional.[21] The legislation in

[16] I Härtel, 'Digitalisierung im Lichte des Verfassungsrechts – Algorithmen, Predictive Policing, autonomes Fahren' (2019) *Landes- und Kommunalverwaltung* 49, 54. See also T Singelnstein, 'Predictive Policing: Algorithmenbasierte Straftatprognosen zur vorausschauenden Kriminalintervention' (2018) *Neue Zeitschrift für Strafrecht* 1; T Knobloch, *Vor die Lage kommen: Predictive Policing in Deutschland* (Stiftung Neue Verantwortung/BertelsmannStiftung, 2018) 13–15.

[17] See generally, Härtel (n 16).

[18] Eg, R Richardson, JM Schultz and K Crawford, 'Dirty data, bad predictions: How civil rights violations impact police data, predictive policing systems, and justice' (2019) 94 *New York University Law Review* 15; AD Selbst, 'Disparate impact in big data policing' (2018) 52 *Georgia Law Review* 109.

[19] Härtel (n 16) 54–55.

[20] ibid 54; Knobloch (n 16) 5.

[21] FCC, decision of 16 February 2023, 1 BvR 1547/19, 1 BvR 2634/20.

question allowed to link previously unconnected automated databases in analysis platforms and permitted systematic access of data across sources through searches. It authorised the police to process stored personal data through automated data analysis or interpretation in order to prevent serious criminal acts or to avert dangers to certain legal interests. The FCC decided that the reviewed legal provisions 'violate the general right of personality (Art. 2(1) in conjunction with Art. 1(1) of the Basic Law) in its manifestation as the right to informational self-determination because they do not contain thresholds that are appropriate to the severity of interference resulting from the authorised data analysis/interpretation measures'.[22]

This jurisprudence reflects the constitutional barriers to digital tools enabling predictive and preventive police activity in Germany. In its earlier decisions on electronic profiling and searches (*Rasterfahndung*) in 2006 and on automatic licence plate recognition of vehicles in 2008 and 2018, the FCC had already established restrictive conditions for such preventive measures. To start with, the Court decided that electronic profiling cannot be used as a general preventive measure.[23] According to the Court, electronic profiling is only permissible

> if there is a specific danger to high-ranking legal interests such as the existence or security of the Federation or a Land or life, limb or liberty of the person. Such electronic profiling is impermissible if it serves as a purely precautionary measure before a danger to public security arises. … [S]uch measures require further facts indicating the existence of a specific danger, such as the danger of a terrorist attack being prepared or carried out.[24]

The Court has thus limited the circumstances in which such measures can be used. For the Court, this is required by the principle of proportionality which only allows for proportionate limitations of the right to informational self-determination.

With regard to the automatic licence plate recognition of vehicles, the FCC took a similar approach. In its first decision on the matter in 2008, it decided that the police could not use automatic recognition as a general precautionary measure.[25] Rather, it required the existence of a specific danger. Here again, the constitutional law basis for this jurisprudence is the right to informational self-determination. In this first decision, the Court only considered this right to be affected by automatic licence plate recognition whenever the licence plate was not immediately deleted without further analysis.[26] However, in 2018, the FCC adopted a more restrictive approach and now considers the right to informational self-determination to be affected by an automatic licence

[22] Para 173.
[23] FCC, decision of 4 April 2006, 1 BvR 518/02.
[24] ibid.
[25] FCC, decision of 11 March 2008, 1 BvR 2074/05.
[26] ibid.

plate recognition 'even if the result is a 'no match' and the data is deleted immediately'.[27] The Court also qualified the conditions under which such a recognition is possible. It stated that

> [g]iven the weight of its interference, automatic number plate recognition must serve to protect legal interests of at least considerable weight, or comparably weighty public interests. The range of number plate information in police database records used for cross-checking must be limited in relation to the specific purpose of the automatic number plate recognition.[28]

The FCC thus limited the use of this tool further, strengthening its restrictive approach to such preventive and surveillance-related measures.

All of the above-mentioned decisions that concern the right to informational self-determination go back to a key judgment of 1983, which has laid the foundation for the rather restrictive approach in German constitutional law and practice towards data processing. This judgment concerned a general population census that the FRG wanted to undertake this year. The original plan involved public officials going from door to door to count the population and to gather certain additional information such as, inter alia, marital status, religion, professional qualifications, source of income, and workplace. In this case, the FCC established the right to informational self-determination as a key constitutional basis for data protection in Germany. This right, which is not explicitly mentioned in the Basic Law, is constructed by reference to the general right of personality under Article 2(1) in conjunction with the protection of human dignity under Article 1(1) of the Basic Law. According to the Court, it 'encompasses the protection of the individual against the unlimited collection, storage, use and sharing of their personal data'.[29] On this basis, the Court set up several conditions under which this right may be restricted. This includes a statutory basis which is in line with the requirement of legal clarity and the principle of proportionality. The Court stated:

> A societal order, and its underlying legal order, would not be compatible with the right to informational self-determination if citizens were no longer able to tell who knows what kind of personal information about them, at what time and on which occasion.[30]

In sum, the rule of law experience in Germany has benefited from digitalisation, especially regarding increased and simplified access opportunities to law and legal services for the general public. This benefit contrasts with several risks for the rule of law, among which the enforcement issue in cyberspace constitutes a major rule of law deficiency. This is a deficiency that will likely continue to be a

[27] FCC, decision of 18 December 2018, 1 BvR 142/15.
[28] ibid.
[29] Para 147.
[30] Para 146.

significant challenge in the future. In comparison, the jurisprudence of the FCC that addresses novel issues created by digitalisation manages to counter, at least to some extent, the challenges to fundamental rights protection that the use of digital tools both by private and public actors can constitute.

II. STRUCTURAL IMPACT ON THE *RECHTSSTAATSPRINZIP*[31]

After this overview of the practical impact of digitalisation on the rule of law experience in Germany, we focus more closely on the legal dimension of this development. In the German legal discourse, the *Rechtsstaatprinzip* is an important reference point for assessing developments associated with digitalisation. When addressing these developments, observers often argue that digitalisation negatively affects *Rechtsstaatlichkeit*.[32] For some, there is even a 'danger of erosion' of this principle by digitalisation.[33] In this section, we examine whether and to what extent digitalisation does in fact impact core elements of the *Rechtsstaatsprinzip*. The elements of the *Rechtsstaatsprinzip* considered here are the guarantee of legal protection (*Rechtsschutzgarantie*), the binding effect of law for all public authorities (*Rechtsbindung*), the principle of proportionality, and the separation of powers.

A. Legal Protection Guarantee

The guarantee of legal protection is the first element of the rule of law principle most prominently concerned by the digitalisation of administrative processes and decisions. In the context of the e-government initiative (see above) and further automation of administrative actions, several aspects of this guarantee are relevant. They are outlined in turn.

[31] This section is based on section IV.1. of one of the authors' following article in German: D Burchardt, 'Strukturelle Auswirkungen der Digitalisierung auf das öffentliche Recht' (2023) *Die öffentliche Verwaltung* 935.

[32] See, eg, H-J Papier, 'Herausforderungen des Rechtsstaats im Zeitalter der Digitalisierung' in C Bär, T Grädler and R Mayr (eds), *Digitalisierung im Spannungsfeld von Politik, Wirtschaft, Wissenschaft und Recht* (Springer, 2018) 171; T Siegel, 'Digitalisierung des Verwaltungsrechts – Reformbedarf im Verwaltungsverfahrensgesetz?' (2023) *Neue Zeitschrift für Verwaltungsrecht* 193; HP Bull, 'Über die rechtliche Einbindung der Technik – Juristische Antworten auf Fragen der Technikentwicklung' (2019) 58 *Der Staat* 57; Kube (n 5); Guckelberger, Öffentliche Verwaltung (n 5); L Guggenberger, 'Einsatz künstlicher Intelligenz in der Verwaltung' (2019) *Neue Zeitschrift für Verwaltungsrecht* 844; A Windoffer, 'Herausforderungen der Digitalisierung aus der Perspektive der öffentlichen Verwaltung' in C Bär, T Grädler and R Mayr (eds), *Digitalisierung im Spannungsfeld von Politik, Wirtschaft, Wissenschaft und Recht* (Springer, 2018) 363; J Englisch and M Schuh, 'Algorithmengestützte Verwaltungsverfahren – Einsatzfelder, Risiken und Notwendigkeit ergänzender Kontrollen' (2022) 55 *Die Verwaltung* 155.

[33] Papier (n 32) 172.

A first aspect is the requirement to provide reasons for administrative decisions, a requirement that, inter alia, serves for preparing a potential judicial action against a negative decision. In the context of automated administrative acts, it has been possible since the 1970s within the framework of the Administrative Procedures Act not to accompany acts by a statement of grounds 'when the authority issues identical administrative acts in considerable numbers or with the help of automatic equipment and individual cases do not merit a statement of grounds'.[34] This norm was, however, designed as an exception. With increasing automation, there is a risk that this norm might de facto become the rule and thus undermine the general requirement to provide reasons for administrative decisions. This would reduce constitutional rule of law standards. Yet, since grounds for administrative acts can increasingly be created on a case-by-case basis using text-generating AI, it is possible to counteract this danger through technology.[35] The fact that even human decision-makers provide such grounds on an ex-post basis makes it possible to use AI to draw up such grounds.[36] Further, the provisions of the EU General Data Protection Regulation (GDPR) regarding the requirement to give reasons for decisions must also be observed. These provisions apply to the majority of partially or fully automated administrative decisions relating to the evaluation of personal data.[37] The GDPR goes even further than the Administrative Procedures Act. In addition to a general justification, the administrative authority must provide information about the method and criteria of the decision-making process, including the algorithm used.[38] As long as these requirements are implemented, the legal protection guarantee of the *Rechtsstaatsprinzip* is fulfilled.

Another aspect relevant to the guarantee of legal protection is the right of the participants in administrative proceedings to inspect the documents connected with the proceedings. Initially, legal scholars controversially discussed whether the inspection of documents according to the Administrative Procedures Act[39] only covers physical documents or also includes electronic files.[40] However, as the implementation of e-government increases, it will be difficult to argue that this provision should be interpreted in a restrictive manner.[41] Rather, this provision is likely to generally apply to electronic files as well. In addition, the E-Government Acts of the federal states and the Federal Government contain

[34] Section 39(2) 2 No 3 (Alt 2) Administrative Procedures Act (*VwVfG*).

[35] On AI-generated statements of grounds, T Wischmeyer, 'Künstliche Intelligenz und neue Begründungsarchitektur' in M Eifert (ed), *Digitale Disruption und Recht* (Nomos, 2020) 73.

[36] Also pointing to this ex-post nature, Wischmeyer (n 35) 78.

[37] U Stelkens, in P Stelkens, HJ Bonk and M Sachs (orig eds and ed), *VwVfG*, 10th edn (CH Beck, 2023), § 39, para 98.

[38] See Arts 13(2)(f), 14(2)(g) and 15(1)(h) GDPR.

[39] Section 29 Administrative Procedures Act.

[40] On this discussion, Siegel (n 32) 197.

[41] On the rule of law requirement of a right to inspect documents, see also Kube (n 5) 300.

special provisions regarding the inspection of electronic documents.[42] To the extent that these acts require electronic file management, the modalities of access to these files are also regulated. In this respect, constitutional standards regarding the *Rechtsstaatsprinzip* are maintained.

Further, the relationship between the right to be heard in administrative proceedings and digitalisation is ambivalent.[43] On the one hand, the hearing can take place in electronic form already under the current version of the Administrative Proceedings Act.[44] This form is potentially easier to access for those involved. On the other hand, when administrative decisions are not only partially but fully automated, it is – at least prima facie – challenging to integrate a hearing into this decision-making. With automation in the classic form, the technical process often leaves no room for hearing the individuals concerned. Accordingly, the Administrative Proceedings Act provides that it is possible to omit the hearing for administrative acts that are 'issued with the help of automatic devices'.[45] As with the requirement to give reasons, there is a risk that this norm, which was created as an exception, will become the rule as automation becomes more widespread. This would render the right to be heard ineffective.[46] However, with newer forms of automation, particularly those using AI, it will be easier to integrate a hearing into the decision-making process. Conducting a hearing in this context is therefore primarily a technical question as it seems conceivable within the legal framework to allow for an AI-based hearing. In view of the *Rechtsstaatsprinzip*, a hearing remains necessary even when administrative decisions are fully automated.[47]

An additional aspect that can affect the guarantee of legal protection is the lack of transparency in the decision-making processes when using AI. For example, in its decision on passenger data records, the CJEU stated that 'given the opacity which characterises the way in which artificial intelligence technology works', it may be impossible to identify the reason why a given program arrives at a given result, which 'may deprive the data subjects … of their right to an effective judicial remedy enshrined in Article 47 of the Charter'.[48] Beyond this specific context, lacking transparency of AI algorithms also generally affects the transparency of administrative processes. Such transparency is, however, a requirement of the rule of law. Accordingly, within the scope of application of the GDPR, Article 5(1)(a) GDPR explicitly requires a transparent manner

[42] Eg, Section 8 EGovG Bund; Section 9 EGovG Berlin; Section 34 EGovG Bayern; Section 8 EGovG Baden-Würtemberg; Section 8 EGovG Bremen; Section 7(6) EGovG Brandenburg.

[43] In detail on the right to a hearing in the context of the E-Government Acts, Guckelberger, Öffentliche Verwaltung (n 5) 589 et seq.

[44] Section 28 Administrative Procedures Act; see also Siegel (n 32) 196; Guckelberger, Öffentliche Verwaltung (n 5) 590.

[45] Section 28(2) (No 4) Administrative Procedures Act. See Stelkens (n 37), § 35a VwVfG para 51.

[46] See Guckelberger, Öffentliche Verwaltung (n 5) 594.

[47] Siegel (n 32) 198–199; Guckelberger, Öffentliche Verwaltung (n 5) 592.

[48] CJEU, decision of 21 June 2022, C-817/19, ECLI:EU:C:2022:491, para 195.

of data processing that is understandable for the data subject. In German administrative law, there is a further basis for such a transparency requirement. Traditionally, administrative lawyers have classified algorithms as administrative regulations (*Verwaltungsvorschriften*).[49] As a result, the rules on administrative regulations would also apply to algorithms. If one assumes that administrative regulations must generally be made transparent, then algorithms must also be made transparent.[50]

B. Binding Effect of Law for All Public Authorities

The binding effect of law on public authorities is a further element of the *Rechtsstaatsprinzip* that can be affected in the context of digitalisation. There is a particular risk when administrative actions are automated. The administration must ensure that, when using AI, the binding effect of the law is fully implemented. For self-learning AI, observers see a risk that AI could independently adjust the regulatory content of a legal norm when implementing this norm. In this scenario, the AI would determine itself 'which results are undesirable and need to be corrected'.[51] It is thus argued that the legislator must not 'completely relinquish control … over the specific regulatory content'.[52] Even if there is no general right to a human decision, there is a right 'that the use of AI is carried out in a legally compliant manner'.[53] This requirement is not limited to the procedural framework that applies to automated administrative actions, but must also cover substantive law.

C. Principle of Proportionality

The principle of proportionality, as a further element of the *Rechtsstaatsprinzip*, is particularly relevant concerning partially or fully automated administrative actions. The question here is to what extent an automated decision can realise the balancing of affected rights and interests that the proportionality assessment requires. For administrative procedural law, the legislator has limited fully automated administrative decisions to decisions without discretion or margin

[49] On this classification, Guckelberger, E-Government (n 5) 269.

[50] Guckelberger, E-Government (n 5) 269–270. However, arguing that such transparency cannot be unlimited considering the freedom of profession and the right to property of the companies that develop these programmes, W Werner, 'Schutz durch das Grundgesetz im Zeitalter der Digitalisierung' (2019) *Neue Juristische Online Zeitschrift* 1041, 1043.

[51] Stelkens (n 37), § 35a VwVfG para 47.

[52] Guggenberger (n 32) 846. See also Stelkens (n 37), § 35a VwVfG para 47; Guckelberger, Öffentliche Verwaltung (n 5) 512 et seq; Windoffer (n 5) 371.

[53] G Hornung, in F Schoch and J-P Schneider (eds), *Verwaltungsrecht, VwVfG – Kommentar*, 3rd edn (CH Beck, 2022) § 35a VwVfG, para 46.

of appreciation (Section 35a Administrative Procedure Act). For decisions that leave room for administrative discretion or margin of appreciation, the legislator wants to ensure that human beings within the administration assess the proportionality of the decision. The legislator assumed that such a proportionality assessment cannot (yet) be part of an automated decision if this decision concerns situations with high divergencies among individual cases. In turn, for situations with little case divergence, standardised proportionality assessments can be included in the algorithm – a fact that arguably shapes the scope of Section 35a.[54] This means that where proportionality can be ensured by providing an abstract balancing of rights and interests, the *Rechtsstaatsprinzip* does not constitute an obstacle to automatising administrative decisions. But particularly for discretionary decisions, one would need to use an algorithm that goes beyond mere standardisation and that provides a case-by-case balancing – otherwise, a human decision would be required in these cases. More generally, critics point to a problem of 'routinization and schematization' when AI is used for the exercise of public authority.[55] In this context, it will be important to keep track of AI's increasing capabilities for individualisation and normative decision-making.[56] In any event, the *Rechtsstaatsprinzip* requires that the principle of proportionality also be implemented in such decision-making.

D. Separation of Powers

Another element of the *Rechtsstaatsprinzip* that is impacted by a digitalised exercise of public authority is the principle of separation of powers. This is the case for the horizontal and vertical separation of powers.

With regard to the vertical separation of powers, digitalisation poses a challenge for the federal structure within which public authority is exercised.[57] In Germany, due to the federal structure of the state, a so-called 'mixed administration' (*Mischverwaltung*), a situation in which the authorities of the federal and the *Länder* level fulfil a certain function together, is in principle not permissible. In the context of digitalisation, there is, however, a need for cooperation between the federal and *Länder* governments as well as among the *Länder*.

[54] On the possibility to standardise certain types of cases as point of reference for this provision, Guckelberger, E-Government (n 5) 265.

[55] For the context of automated judicial decision-making, Bull (n 32) 76.

[56] Eg, A Balagopalan et al, 'Judging facts, judging norms: Training machine learning models to judge humans requires a modified approach to labelling data' (2023) 9 *Science Advances*, DOI: 10.1126/sciadv.abq0701. In contrast, critical on normative legal decision-making by AI, D Timmermann and K Gelbrich, 'Können Algorithmen subsumieren?' (2022) *Neue Juristische Wochenschrift* 25.

[57] On the impact of digitalisation on the federal structures of Germany, see also W Bernhardt, 'Digitalisierung im Spannungsfeld der grundgesetzlichen Kompetenzträger' in C Bär, T Grädler and R Mayr (eds), *Digitalisierung im Spannungsfeld von Politik, Wirtschaft, Wissenschaft und Recht* (Springer, 2018) 1, 9 et seq; Härtel (n 16).

To make this cooperation possible, the legislator had to amend the constitutional law. Article 91c was introduced into the Basic Law in 2009 in order to authorise cooperation concerning the planning, construction, and operation of information technology systems. Further, this regulation was supplemented in 2017 with paragraph 5, which creates a competence basis for regulating access by means of information technology to the administrative services, so as to implement the goal of an e-government. These provisions limit the vertical separation of powers to some extent.

Regarding the horizontal separation of powers, digitalisation has only begun to influence this principle, yet with great potential to change it in a structural manner in the future. One practice that has already been discussed as a separation of powers problem is the storage of judicial data by the administration. It has been argued that, in order to prevent an inadmissible intertwining of the judiciary and the executive, it is important that executive actors do not have access to this data.[58] The horizontal separation of powers is further weakened when public functions that are assigned to different branches of government are outsourced, at least indirectly, to the same group of private actors. When software developers and programmers in IT companies determine the process and content of (partially or fully) automated administrative decisions by creating algorithms and, at the same time, also design (partially) automated instruments used in judicial decision-making, these private actors hold de facto regulatory power for executive and judicial exercise of public authority simultaneously. Such overlaps can also occur regarding the legislative branch. This is the case when the legislator specifies the exact content of algorithms – which some observers already demand today, given the increasing regulatory effect that algorithms have.[59] Because of the technical expertise required to do that, the legislator will need input from the same private actors from the IT sector as in the executive and judicial context so that the branches of power merge to some extent, at least on a de facto level.

Another question that is important concerning the separation of powers is who assumes responsibility for the exercise of public authority. This is relevant when it comes to controlling partially or fully automated processes. If public actors cannot control such processes at all or if they can only check selected decisions with regard to selected aspects, this would amount to further shifting de facto power to the private actors who are technically in charge of the IT systems used.[60] In such situations, it is impossible for public actors to assume their responsibility as required by the rule of law.[61]

[58] FCC, decision of 17 January 2013, 2 BvR 2576/11. See also *Bernhardt* (n 57) 7.

[59] On legislation in relation to AI, E Reimer, 'Einfluss der Digitalisierung auf die Rechtsetzung' in J Hey (ed), *Digitalisierung im Steuerrecht* (Otto Schmidt Verlag, 2019) 97.

[60] On this issue in the context of the tax administration, Kube (n 5) 317–318.

[61] ibid.

This overview shows that digitalisation has significant effects on several elements of the *Rechtsstaatsprinzip*. However, these effects primarily concern and require adapting the rule of law guarantees to the digital context. In contrast, there is, at least so far, no evidence that the *Rechtsstaatsprinzip* will be structurally undermined by digitalisation. Nonetheless, certain elements of the *Rechtsstaatsprinzip* might be at risk in light of future developments – a risk that the next section addresses in more detail.

III. FUTURE CHALLENGES TO THE RULE OF LAW POSED BY DIGITALISATION

In this last section, we highlight certain future challenges that digitalisation causes for the rule of law in Germany.

The first aspect that will shape the rule of law practice in an increasingly digitalised world is the progressing automatisation of administrative decision-making and potentially also of (parts of judicial) decision-making. Regarding automated administrative decisions, the rule of law concerns mentioned in section II above will become more prominent. The outlined issues regarding transparency and proportionality of decision-making as well as procedural guarantees are likely to become more widespread as automated decision-making is used in more areas of administrative law. They are, however, 'classical' legal questions that can be addressed if the legislator adapts the legal framework to the technical development. In contrast, the above-mentioned impact on structural principles such as the separation of powers might be more difficult to address. As influence of private actors from the IT sector on the three branches of power increases, there is a risk that the traditional separation of powers will be undermined in the long run. It is to be expected that the development will continue the trajectory that the legislation both on the domestic and the EU level has taken so far.

As to automated decision-making within the judiciary, the prognosis seems less clear. To start with, in the German judiciary, automated or assisted decision-making has, in contrast to other countries, not been realised in rights-sensitive areas of law such as criminal law yet. For example, programmes such as COMPAS (Correctional Offender Management Profiling for Alternative Sanctions), a programme that is used in the US to assist judges when they decide whether a convicted person should receive a sentence on parole, do not exist in Germany yet. If such programmes are used in the future, they will come with certain risks for the rule of law. As has been shown for COMPAS, such programmes are prone to be biased to the disadvantage of certain social groups.[62] In this regard, the

[62] J Angwin, J Larson, S Mattu and L Kirchner, 'Machine Bias' *ProPublica*, 23 May 2016, www.propublica.org/article/machine-bias-risk-assessments-in-criminal-sentencing.

Rechtsstaatsprinzip in German constitutional law as well as the non-discrimination clause of Article 3 of the Basic Law will require state authorities to ensure that within the judicial procedure, no discriminating algorithms are used.

Automatisation and AI-based tools have already been used in certain areas of law.[63] In so-called mass proceedings with many similar cases, programmes are used to analyse and categorise the content of court files.[64] For example, Bavaria uses the System SMART for such a categorisation of legal documents and for creating meta data for these documents.[65] In other *Länder*, speech recognition technology is used before civil courts to draw up the minutes of the proceedings and AI assists in the calculation of spousal and child maintenance.[66]

Based on this experience, actors within the judiciary as well as within the government contemplate to broaden the use of automatisation and AI-based tools before courts. In a position paper of 2022, the presidents of the high courts of the *Länder* as well as of the *Bundesgerichtshof* have outlined the potential use of such tools in the future.[67] They emphasise that such tools be primarily used for decisions that have a formulaic character and do not involve the balancing of rights or interests. As examples, they mention, inter alia, cost decisions in civil cases, part of the decision on legal aid, insolvency law and the law of foreclosure and the judicial review of general terms and conditions (*AGB*) in private contracts.[68] In addition, academic proposals include, inter alia, prognostic assistance technology for the decision about whether a person should be put in custody awaiting trial and for the sentencing decision.[69] But the position paper also points to legal limits for using such tools. The core of the judicial functions such as the development of jurisprudential guidelines is seen as reserved to human actors.[70] Further, according to the paper, the use of AI must be transparent and access to courts cannot only be made available by AI-based means.[71] The paper also stresses the risk of discrimination that comes with the use of algorithms as well as possible issues relating to the performance review and general supervision of judges.[72] Within the academic discussion, additional concerns are that automatisation of judicial decisions might create the impression among the

[63] See generally, D Nink, *Justiz und Algorithmen* (Duncker & Humblot, 2021) 161–165.

[64] JJ Vasel, 'Künstliche Intelligenz in der Justiz' (2023) *Legal Tech – Zeitschrift für die digitale Anwendung* 179, 179.

[65] ibid.

[66] Vasel (n 64) 180.

[67] 'Einsatz von KI und algorithmischen Systemen in der Justiz, Grundlagenpapier zur 74. Jahrestagung der Präsidentinnen und Präsidenten der Oberlandesgerichte, des Kammergerichts, des Bayerischen Obersten Landesgerichts und des Bundesgerichtshofs vom 23. bis 25. Mai 2022 in Rostock', available at www.justiz.bayern.de/media/images/behoerden-und-gerichte/oberlandesgerichte/nuernberg/einsatz_von_ki_und_algorithmischen_systemen_in_der_justiz.pdf.

[68] At pp 28–31.

[69] Nink (n 63) 397–415.

[70] At p 10.

[71] At pp 10, 14, 15.

[72] At p 18, 20, 23. On the risk of discrimination, see also Nink (n 63) 167–176.

parties before a court that it does not provide individual justice anymore, which might in turn lead to a reduced acceptance of the judiciary.[73]

Further, the government suggested not only the above-mentioned draft law on enhancing the use of videoconference technology before courts but also an automated protocol in criminal proceedings. According to a draft law of 2023, court proceedings shall be recorded and the audio recording shall be automatically transferred into a text document using transcription software.[74] Moreover, AI regulation that is relevant for the judicial context has also taken place on the EU level. The general Artificial Intelligence Act constitutes a major step in this development.[75] In fact, the EU is a very active regulatory forum for digitalisation-related matters in general. As a result, the legal framework applicable in Germany will be significantly shaped by EU legal acts in the future.

A digitalisation-specific challenge for judicial independence is related to concerns about a 'transparent judge'. First, such 'transparency' is discussed as a result of social media and digitalised sources of information about judges.[76] Here, the fact that personal and other information about judges is potentially available to a large number of people is seen as a risk that certain actors might pressure judges in order to obtain a favourable judicial decision. Second, beyond the mere availability of information about judges, digital tools and especially AI-based technology can make 'profiling' of judges possible. This bears a risk for actors to manipulate outcomes in legal cases. Inter alia to counter this risk, France adopted legislation in 2019 that prohibits such profiling.[77] Although this legislation is arguably too far-reaching as it prohibits a broad range of academic research on judicial decision-making,[78] the above-mentioned position paper by the presidents of the high courts of the *Länder* and of the *Bundesgerichtshof* suggests that such profiling should also be banned in Germany.[79]

Moreover, in the discussion about digitalisation and the rule of law in Germany, observers have raised concerns regarding a potential challenge that is inspired by the practice in certain autocratic regimes. With the example of

[73] Vasel (n 64) 183.

[74] 'Gesetzentwurf der Bundesregierung Entwurf eines Gesetzes zur digitalen Dokumentation der strafgerichtlichen Hauptverhandlung', available at www.bmj.de/SharedDocs/Gesetzgebungsverfahren/DE/2022_DokHVG_Hauptverhandlungsdokumentationsgesetz.html?nn=110040. See also M van Hattem and P Bafteh, 'Aktuelle Gesetzesvorhaben zur weiteren Digitalisierung der deutschen Gerichtsbarkeit' (2023) *MMR Zeitschrift für IT-Recht und Recht der Digitalisierung* 100.

[75] Regulation (EU) 2024/1689 of 13 June 2024. See in particular Art 9-15 and Annex III (8)(a).

[76] Eg, K Kuchenbauer, 'Der gläserne Richter – Big-Data-Analyse als Mittel zur Vorhersehbarkeit richterlicher Entscheidungen?' (2021) 76 *JuristenZeitung* 647–655.

[77] LOI n° 2019-222 du 23 mars 2019 de programmation 2018–2022 et de réforme pour la justice, Art 33: 'Les données d'identité des magistrats et des membres du greffe ne peuvent faire l'objet d'une réutilisation ayant pour objet ou pour effet d'évaluer, d'analyser, de comparer ou de prédire leurs pratiques professionnelles réelles ou supposes.'

[78] On this critique, eg, M Langford and MR Madsen, 'France Criminalises Research on Judges', *Verfassungsblog*, 22 June 2019, available at verfassungsblog.de/france-criminalises-research-on-judges/, DOI: 10.17176/20190622-232658-0.

[79] At p 42.

China in mind, digitalisation is seen as a potential tool for extensive and intrusive surveillance of the entire population.[80] In Germany, this is an especially sensitive issue for several reasons. To start with, Germany's historical experience makes it very sensitive to all forms of mass surveillance. As we have outlined in chapter three, the GDR had an all-encompassing and very intrusive surveillance apparatus, the *Stasi*. This is an important historical experience that has shaped the perception of the German public with regard to potential surveillance by the state. Moreover, in the FRG before reunification, there was also strong resistance against all forms of data gathering and potential surveillance by state authorities. A key aspect in this regard is the decision of the FCC of 1983 on the population census (see above).[81] Based on this jurisprudence, an all-encompassing surveillance of the population's movements and actions via digital and AI-supported means would violate the human dignity core of the right to informational self-determination.[82]

In addition to the above-mentioned challenges that emanate from the use of digital tools by public actors, a second set of challenges for the rule of law stems from private actors. Importantly, digital technologies play an increasing role in propagating anti-rule of law discourse. As we have outlined in chapter four of this book, this discourse has become prominent in the context of the migration and COVID-19 crises during the last decade. This includes anti-institutional conspiracy narratives as well as a rejection of the German state structure as a whole.[83] And the spreading of 'classical' right-wing extremism challenges democratic structures and institutions of the *Rechtsstaat*. Extremism and anti-rule of law discourse are significantly fuelled by digitalisation – a situation that is likely to become even more prominent in the future. The domestic intelligence services on the state and federal level, the services 'for the protection of the constitution' (*Verfassungsschutz*), have pointed to this issue.[84] A considerable part of the population has developed a mistrust of traditional media – and as a result, the discourse has shifted to social media platforms and alternative messenger services. Here, discourse happens in so-called echo chambers, that is, among groups of persons who share similar world views and thus reinforce each other's opinions. The head of the domestic intelligence service in Saxony has called this 'digital extremism'.[85] This development can be explained by a phenomenon that social psychologists have described as 'attitude polarization'.[86] In Germany, like

[80] Mentioning this risk, eg, Holterhus (n 12) 53.
[81] FCC, decision of 15 December 1983, 1 BvR 209/83.
[82] Härtel (n 16) 56.
[83] On so-called *Reichsbürger* and *Selbstverwalter*, see Report on the Protection of the Constitution 2023 (*Verfassungsschutzbericht*), www.verfassungsschutz.de/EN/home/home_node.html.
[84] On the federal level, Report on the Protection of the Constitution 2023 (n 83).
[85] D-M Christian, President of the *Landesamtes für Verfassungsschutz Sachsen*, statement as quoted in '"Digitaler Extremismus" alarmiert Verfassungsschutz', *n-tv online*, 21 February 2023, www.n-tv.de/politik/Digitaler-Extremismus-alarmiert-Verfassungsschutz-article23932331.html.
[86] DG Myers and H Lamm, 'The polarizing effect of group discussion' (1975) 63 *American Scientist* 297.

in many other countries, this is a serious challenge both for the present and the future. Moreover, right-wing extremists are using digital communication and networking in a professionalised manner. This includes, inter alia, general social media platforms such as Twitter/X or Facebook, podcasts on platforms such as Spotify, as well as alternative social media and messenger services such as 'vk' and 'Telegram'.[87] The 2023 Report on the Protection of the Constitution of the Federal Intelligence Service points not only to the potential for further radicalisation in such fora but also to the fact that it is very difficult for the authorities to detect and prevent terrorist activities coordinated via these tools.[88] In this respect, the rule of law risk is thus two-fold.

IV. CONCLUSION

The overview in this chapter has shown that, with the digital age, the *Rechtsstaatsprinzip* has entered a new era. Both in terms of the rule of law experience of people in Germany and in terms of legal challenges, digitalisation has significantly impacted the rule of law practice and legal guarantees. Although there is no 'erosion' of the *Rechtsstaat* (yet) as some may fear, the German *Rechtsstaat* is still in the process of adapting to the novel possibilities and challenges that digitalisation both of public and private actions entails. Considering the challenges that might still lie ahead, whether this adaption will succeed seems a crucial question for the fundamental structures of the German *Rechtsstaat*.

[87] On these examples, Ministry of the Interior of the state of Rhineland-Palatinate at mdi.rlp.de/themen/verfassungsschutz/rechtsextremismus/rechtsextremismus-im-internet.

[88] Report on the Protection of the Constitution 2023 (n 83) 53.

Bibliography

'Verfassungsrichter: Corona-Regeln sind "Stresstest" für Demokratie', *Berliner Zeitung*, 3 April 2021, www.berliner-zeitung.de/news/verfassungsrichter-corona-regeln-sind-stresstest-fuer-demokratie-li.150311.

'Koch geht auf den Bau', *Die Tageszeitung*, 29 October 2010, available at taz.de/!5133155/.

'Köhler sieht DDR als Unrechtsstaat. Bundespräsident geht nach Wiederwahl auf Distanz zu Schwan', *Leipziger Volkszeitung*, 25 May 2009.

'IStGH ohne deutsche Richterin', Interview with Prof. Dr. Stefanie Bock, *Neue Juristische Wochenschrift*, 28 February 2024, available at rsw.beck.de/aktuell/daily/magazin/detail/njw-interview-2024-9-istgh-ohne-deutsche-richterin.

'"Digitaler Extremismus" alarmiert Verfassungsschutz', *n-tv online*, 21 February 2023, www.n-tv.de/politik/Digitaler-Extremismus-alarmiert-Verfassungsschutz-article23932331.html.

'Schröder To Build Putin's Pipeline', *SPIEGEL International*, 12 December 2005, available at www.spiegel.de/international/letter-from-berlin-schroeder-to-build-putin-s-pipeline-a-389965.html.

'Gerhard Schröder soll in Gazprom-Aufsichtsrat einziehen', *SPIEGEL Online*, 4 February 2022, available at www.spiegel.de/ausland/gerhard-schroeder-soll-in-gazprom-aufsichtsrat-einziehen-a-12350b39-af36-4e52-ad4b-47fecb894cfd.

'Welche Affären die Union gerade beschäftigen', *Sueddeutsche Zeitung*, 26 March 2021, available at www.sueddeutsche.de/politik/cdu-csu-korruptionsaffaere-ueberblick-1.5240578.

'Gesine Schwan, "Vorsicht! Ich bin die andere!" SPD-Präsidentschaftskandidatin Gesine Schwan sprach mit dem Tagesspiegel über ihre Bewerbung fürs Schloss Bellevue', *Tagesspiegel*, 17 May 2009, available at www.tagesspiegel.de/politik/vorsicht-ich-bin-die-andere-1759957.html.

'Kretschmer zu radikalen Corona-Protesten: "Rechtsstaat muss handeln, bevor es Tote gibt"', *Tagesspiegel*, 7 January 2022, available at www.tagesspiegel.de/politik/rechtsstaat-muss-handeln-bevor-es-tote-gibt-8017159.html.

Abendroth W, 'Zum Begriff des demokratischen und sozialen Rechtsstaates im Grundgesetz der Bundesrepublik Deutschland' in M Buckmiller, J Perels and U Schöler (eds), *Wolfgang Abendroth, Gesammelte Schriften – Band 2: 1949–1955* (Offizin Verlag Hannover, 2008).

Adams KA, 'What Is Just: The Rule of Law and Natural Law in the Trials of Former East German Border Guards' (1992–1993) 29 *Stanford Journal of International Law* 271.

Ambos K, 'The German Public Prosecutor as (no) judicial authority within the meaning of the European Arrest Warrant: A case note on the CJEU's judgment in OG (C-508/18) and PI (C 82/19 PPU)' (2019) 10 *New Journal of European Criminal Law* 399.

Amelung K, 'Nochmals: § 34 StGB als öffentlichrechtliche Eingriffsnorm?' (1978) *Neue Juristische Woschenschrift* 623.

Angwin J, Larson J, Mattu S and Kirchner L, 'Machine Bias' *ProPublica* 23 May 2016, www.propublica.org/article/machine-bias-risk-assessments-in-criminal-sentencing.

Aust S, *Der Baader-Meinhoff-Komplex* (Goldmann Verlag, 1998).

Bäcker C, *Gerechtigkeit im Rechtsstaat – Das Bundesverfassungsgericht an der Grenze des Grundgesetzes* (Mohr Siebeck, 2015).

——, 'Rechtsstaat' in M Sellers and S Kirste (eds), *Encyclopedia of the Philosophy of Law and Social Philosophy* (Springer Netherlands, 2020) 1.

Badura P, *Das Verwaltungsrecht Des Liberalen Rechtsstaates* (Schwartz, 1967).

Bahr E, 'Die DDR war nicht der einzige Unrechtsstaat im Ostblock', *Frankfurter Allgemeine Zeitung*, 16 May 2015.

Bähr O, *Der Rechtsstaat: eine publicistische Skizze* (Wigand, 1864).

Baer S, 'The Rule of – and Not by Any – Law. On Constitutionalism' (2018) 71 *Current Legal Problems* 335.

Baer S and Markard N, in H v Mangoldt, F Klein, C Starck (orig eds), *Grundgesetz: Kommentar* (CH Beck, 2018), Art 3 (2,3), 451.

Bakardjieva Engelbrekt A, Moberg A and Nergelius J (eds), *Rule of Law in the EU – 30 Years After the Fall of the Berlin Wall* (Hart Publishing, 2021).

Balagopalan A et al, 'Judging facts, judging norms: Training machine learning models to judge humans requires a modified approach to labelling data' (2023) 9 *Science Advances*, DOI: 10.1126/sciadv.abq0701.

Baldus M, 'Gefahrenabwehr in Ausnahmelagen – Das Luftsicherheitsgesetz auf dem Prüfstand' (2006) *Neue Zeitschrift für Verwaltungsrecht* 532.

Barczak T, *Der nervöse Staat* (Mohr-Siebeck, 2020).

Bast J and Möllers C, 'Dem Freistaat zum Gefallen: über Udo Di Fabios Gutachten zur staatsrechtlichen Beurteilung der Flüchtlingskrise', *Verfassungsblog*, 16 January 2016, verfassungsblog.de/dem-freistaat-zum-gefallen-ueber-udo-di-fabios-gutachten-zur-staatsrechtlichen-beurteilung-der-fluechtlingskrise/.

Bates E, *The Evolution of the European Convention on Human Rights – From Its Inception to the Creation of a Permanent Court of Human Rights* (Oxford University Press, 2010).

Baumann K, 'Das Urteil des BVerfG zum Luftsicherheitseinsatz der Streitkräfte' (2006) *Juristische Ausbildung* 447.

Benvindo JZ, *Rule of Law in Brazil: The Legal Construction of Inequality* (Hart Publishing, 2022).

Berg W, 'Der Rechtsstaat und die Aufarbeitung der vor-rechtsstaatlichen Vergangenheit' (1992) 51 VVDStRL 46.

Bernhardt W, 'Digitalisierung im Spannungsfeld der grundgesetzlichen Kompetenzträger' in C Bär, T Grädler and R Mayr (eds), *Digitalisierung im Spannungsfeld von Politik, Wirtschaft, Wissenschaft und Recht* (Springer, 2018) 1.

Bielefeldt H, *Gefahrenabwehr im demokratischen Rechtsstaat. Zur Debatte um ein 'Feindrecht'* (German Institute for Human Rights, 2008).

Birkenkötter H, 'The United Nations and the Rule of Law' in M Sevel (ed), *Handbook on the Rule of Law* (Routledge, forthcoming).

Blankenburg E, 'Changes in Political Regimes and Continuity of the Rule of Law in Germany' in H Jacob (ed), *Courts, law, and politics in comparative perspective* (Yale University Press, 1996) 249.

Böckenförde EW, 'Entstehung und Wandel des Rechtsstaatsbegriffs' in H Ehmke, C Schmid and H Scharoun (eds), *Festschrift Für Adolf Arndt Zum 65. Geburtstag* (Europäische Verlagsanstalt, 1969) 53.

——, 'Der verdrängte Ausnahmezustand' (1978) *Neue Juristische Wochenschrift* 1881.

——, 'Rechtsstaat oder Unrechtsstaat?', *Frankfurter Allgemeine Zeitung*, 12 May 2015, available at www.faz.net/aktuell/feuilleton/debatten/war-die-ddr-ein-unrechtsstaat-13587574.html.

Boom SJ, 'The European Union after the Maastricht Decision: Will Germany Be the "Virginia of Europe?"' (1995) 43 *American Journal of Comparative Law* 177.

Brandenburger M, 'Stasi-Unterlagen-Gesetz und Rechtsstaat' (1995) 28 *Kritische Justiz* 351.

Brummer K and Fröhlich S (eds) *Zehn Jahre Deutschland in Afghanistan* (VS Verlag, 2011).

Brunner G, *Einführung in das Recht der DDR*, 2nd edn (CH Beck, 1979).

Bull HP, 'Über die rechtliche Einbindung der Technik – Juristische Antworten auf Fragen der Technikentwicklung' (2019) 58 *Der Staat* 57.

Burchardt D, 'Der Grundsatz richterlicher Unabhängigkeit: eine verhaltensbezogene Perspektive' (2022) 70 *Jahrbuch des Öffentlichen Rechts* 453.

——, 'Strukturelle Auswirkungen der Digitalisierung auf das öffentliche Recht' (2023) *Die öffentliche Verwaltung* 935.

Buschmann M, 'Wenn das Recht bloßes Herrschaftsinstrument Ist – Noch immer löst der Begriff "Unrechtsstaat" bei einigen ein Störgefühl aus – aber was war die DDR sonst?', *Frankfurter Allgemeine Zeitung*, 14 June 2023, availabe at www.faz.net/aktuell/politik/staat-und-recht/wenn-das-recht-blosses-herrschaftsinstrument-ist-18963690.html.
Calliess C, 'Sicherheit im freiheitlichen Rechtsstaat' (2002) *Zeitschrift für Rechtspolitik* 1.
Carré de Malberg R, *Contribution à la théorie générale de l'État* (Sirey, 1920–1922).
Carothers T, 'The Rule of Law Revival' (1998) 77 *Foreign Affairs* 95.
Carsten ES and Rautenberg EC, *Die Geschichte der Staatsanwaltschaft in Deutschland*, 3rd edn (Nomos, 2015).
Closa C and Kochenov D (eds), *Reinforcing Rule of Law Oversight in the European Union* (CUP, 2016).
Coman R, *The Politics of the Rule of Law in the EU Polity Actors, Tools and Challenges* (Palgrave, 2022).
Craig PP, 'Formal and Substantive Conceptions of the Rule of Law: An Analytical Framework' (1997) *Public Law* 467.
Cruz Villalón P, 'Rule of (German) Law?: On Legal Hegemony in the EU', *Verfassungsblog*, 12 December 2020, verfassungsblog.de/rule-of-german-law/.
Dahs H, 'Das "Anti-Terroristen-Gesetz" – eine Niederlage des Rechtsstaats' (1976) *Neue Juristische Wochenschrift* 2145.
Depenheuer O, *Selbstbehauptung des Rechtsstaats* (Schöningh, 2007).
Depenheuer O and Grabenwarter C (eds) *Der Staat in der Flüchtlingskrise: zwischen gutem Willen und geltendem Recht*, 2nd edn (Schöningh, 2017).
Derlien HU, 'German Unification and Bureaucratic Transformation' (1993) 14 *International Political Science Review* 319.
Destradi S, 'Germany's Engagement in Afghanistan' in R Harshé and D Tripathi (eds), *Afghanistan Post-2014* (Routledge, 2015).
Detjen S and Steinbeis M, *Die Zauberlehrlinge: der Streit um die Flüchtlingspolitik und der Mythos vom Rechtsbruch* (Klett-Cotta, 2019).
Deutscher Bundestag (ed), *Materialien der Enquete-Kommission 'Aufarbeitung von Geschichte und Folgen der SED-Diktatur in Deutschland'*, vol 4: Recht, Justiz und Polizei im SED–Staat (Nomos, 1995).
Di Fabio U, 'Migrationskrise als föderales Verfassungsproblem – Gutachten im Auftrag des Freistaates Bayern', 8 January 2016, available at img.welt.de/bin/di-fabio-gutachten-150937063.pdf.
Dreier H, 'Gustav Radbruch und die Mauerschützen' (1997) 52 *JuristenZeitung* 421.
——, 'Rechtsstaat, Demokratie und Föderalismus in der Corona-Pandemie' (2021) *Die Öffentliche Verwaltung* 229.
Dugard J, 'The Choice before Us: International Law or a "Rules-Based International Order"?' (2023) 36 *Leiden Journal of International Law* 223.
Duguit L, *L'État, le droit objectif et la loi positive* (Fontemoing, 1901).
Dürig G, Herzog R and Scholz R (orig eds), *Grundgesetz-Kommentar*, 99th EL (CH Beck, 2022).
——, *Grundgesetz-Kommentar*, 100th EL (CH Beck, 2023).
Eisele J and Trentmann C, 'Die Staatsanwaltschaft – "objektivste Behörde der Welt"?' (2019) *Neue Juristische Wochenschrift* 2365.
Englisch J and Schuh M, 'Algorithmengestützte Verwaltungsverfahren – Einsatzfelder, Risiken und Notwendigkeit ergänzender Kontrollen' (2022) 55 *Die Verwaltung* 155.
Erb V, 'Notwehr als Menschenrecht – Zugleich eine Kritik der Entscheidung des LG Frankfurt am Main im "Fall Daschner"' (2005) *Neue Zeitschrift für Strafrecht* 593.
Fitschen T, 'Reforming the system of administration of justice at the United Nations – A short history' in H Buss et al (eds), *Handbook on the Internal Justice System at the United Nations* (United Nations System Staff College, 2014) 7.
Forsthoff E, 'Begriff und Wesen des sozialen Rechtsstaates' (1973) 12 VVDStRL 1.

Fraenkel E, *The Dual State: A Contribution to the Theory of Dictatorship*, E Shils, E Lowenstein, KE Knorr and J Meierhenrich (transl) (Oxford University Press, 2017).
——, *Der Doppelstaat*, 5th edn (Europäische Verlagsanstalt, 2019).
Frowein J, 'The Transformation of Constitutional Law through the European Convention on Human Rights' (2008) 41 *Israel Law Review* 489.
Gallon J and Mangold AK, 'Grundrechte und Rechtsstaat in der Krise: Hat sich die Verfassungsordnung während der Corona-Pandemie bewährt?' (2023) 9 *Politikum* 12.
Gao X and Gao B, 'The German-Chinese "Rule of Law Dialogue": Influence and Outlook' (2014) 47 *Verfassung und Recht in Übersee / Law and Politics in Africa, Asia and Latin America* 392.
Glas LR, 'From Interlaken to Copenhagen: What Has Become of the Proposals Aiming to Reform the Functioning of the European Court of Human Rights?' (2020) 20 *Human Rights Law Review* 121.
Gneist R, *Der Rechtsstaat und die Verwaltungsgerichte in Deutschland* (Springer, 1879).
Goodman M, 'After the Wall The Legal Ramifications of the East German Border' (1996) 29 *Cornell International Law Journal* 727.
González Hauck S, '*Weiße* Deutungshoheit Statt Objektivität: Der 'objektive Dritte' Und Die Systematische Abwertung Rassismuserfahrener Perspektiven' (2022) 42 *Zeitschrift für Rechtssoziologie* 153.
Götz H, 'Das Urteil gegen Daschner im Lichte der Werteordnung des Grundgesetzes' (2005) *Neue Juristische Wochenschrift* 953.
Gowder P, *The Rule of Law in the United States: An Unfinished Project of Black Liberation* (Hart Publishing, 2021).
Gramm C, 'Der wehrlose Verfassungsstaat?' (2006) *Deutsches Verwaltungsblatt* 653.
Grimm D, *Deutsche Verfassunsgeschichte 1776–1866* (Suhrkamp, 1988).
Grogan J, 'States of Emergency', *Verfassungsblog*, 26 May 2020, verfassungsblog.de/states-of-emergency/.
——, 'Power and the COVID-19 Pandemic – Introduction & List of Contributions: #PowerandPandemic', *Verfassungsblog*, 22 February 2021, verfassungsblog.de/power-and-the-covid-19-pandemic/.
Guckelberger A, 'E-Government: Ein Paradigmenwechsel in Verwaltung und Verwaltungsrecht?' (2019) 78 VVDStRL 235.
——, *Öffentliche Verwaltung im Zeitalter der Digitalisierung* (Nomos, 2019).
Guggenberger L, 'Einsatz künstlicher Intelligenz in der Verwaltung' (2019) *Neue Zeitschrift für Verwaltungsrecht* 844.
Häberle P and Kotzur M, *Europäische Verfassungslehre*, 8th edn (Nomos, 2016).
Habermas J, *Between Facts and Norms*, W Rehg (transl) (MIT Press, 1996).
Hailbronner K and Thym D, 'Grenzenloses Asylrecht? Die Flüchtlingskrise als Problem europäischer Rechtsintegration' (2016) *Juristenzeitung* 753.
Hallstein W, *Europäische Reden*, T Oppermann (ed) (Deutsche Verlags-Anstalt, 1979).
Hansack R, *Unrechtsstaat DDR – Zur Genesis des Terminus politicus Unrechtsstaates nach der Transformation 1989* (Peter Lang, 2015).
Härtel I, 'Digitalisierung im Lichte des Verfassungsrechts – Algorithmen, Predictive Policing, autonomes Fahren' (2019) *Landes- und Kommunalverwaltung* 49.
van Hattem M and Bafteh P, 'Aktuelle Gesetzesvorhaben zur weiteren Digitalisierung der deutschen Gerichtsbarkeit' (2023) *MMR Zeitschrift für IT-Recht und Recht der Digitalisierung* 100.
Hawel M, 'Dämmerung des demokratischen Rechtsstaats?' (2009) *Kritische Justiz* 64.
Hecker W, 'Die Entscheidung des Bundesverfassungsgerichts zum Luftsicherheitsgesetz' (2006) 39 *Kritische Justiz* 179.
Heeger V, 'E-Akte: Wo steht die deutsche Justiz?', *Tagesspiegel*, 14 June 2022, available at background.tagesspiegel.de/digitalisierung/e-akte-wo-steht-die-deutsche-justiz.
Heinig HM, *Der Sozialstaat im Dienst der Freiheit* (Mohr-Siebeck, 2008).
——, 'The Political and the Basic Law's *Sozialstaat* Principle – Perspectives from Constitutional Law and Theory' (2011) 12 *German Law Journal* 1887.

Heinig HM et al, 'Why Constitution Matters – Verfassungsrechtswissenschaft in Zeiten der Corona-Krise' (2020) *JuristenZeitung* 861.
Heller H, *Rechtsstaat oder Diktatur?* (Mohr Siebeck, 1930).
Herbert U and Schönhage J, 'Vor dem 5. September. Die "Flüchtlingskrise" 2015 im historischen Kontext' (2020) 30–32 *Aus Politik und Zeitgeschichte* 27.
Herzberg RD, 'Folter und Menschenwürde' (2005) *Juristenzeitung* 321.
Heuer UJ and Riege G, *Der Rechtsstaat – eine Legende? Erfahrungen zweier Rechtswissenschaftler 1990/91 in Volkskammer und Bundestag* (Nomos, 1992).
Heuer UJ (ed), *Die Rechtsordnung der DDR. Anspruch und Wirklichkeit* (Nomos, 1995).
Heuschling L, *État de droit, Rechtsstaat, Rule of Law* (Dalloz, 2002).
Hillgruber C, 'Der Staat des Grundgesetzes – nur "bedingt abwehrbereit"?' (2007) *JuristenZeitung* 209.
Hoeck J, *Verwaltung, Verwaltungsrecht und Verwaltungsrechtsschutz in der Deutschen Demokratischen Republik* (Duncker & Humblot, 2003).
Hofmann G, 'Schäubles Nachtlektüre' (2007) 33 *Die Zeit* 7.
Holterhus T, *Der Rechtsstaat* (Bundeszentrale für Politische Bildung, 2022).
Homann U, *Herausforderungen an den Rechtsstaat durch Justizunrecht: die Urteile bundesdeutscher Gerichte zur strafrechtlichen Aufarbeitung von NS- und DDR-Justizverbrechen* (Berliner Wissenschafts-Verlag, 2003).
Hörner J, 'The rise of the AfD after Cologne poses a serious challenge for Merkel's policy on refugees', 27 January 2016, blogs.lse.ac.uk/europpblog/2016/01/27/the-rise-of-the-afd-after-cologne-may-force-merkel-to-change-course-on-refugees.
Huber PM, 'Rechtsstaat' in M Herdegen et al (eds), *Handbuch des Verfassungsrechts* (Munich, CH Beck, 2021) 383.
van Husen P, 'Die Entfesselung der Dritten Gewalt' (1952/53) 78 *Archiv des öffentlichen Rechts* 49.
Humphreys S, *Theatre of the Rule of Law. Transnational Legal Intervention in Theory and Practice* (Cambridge University Press, 2010).
Immisch L, *Der sozialistische Richter in der DDR und seine Unabhängigkeit* (Peter Lang, 1997).
Ingadottir T and Romano C, 'The Financing of the International Criminal Court' in T Ingadottir (ed), *The International Criminal Court: Recommendations on Policy and Practice* (Brill, 2003).
Isensee J, 'Aussprache' (1992) 51 VVDStRL 134.
Jacobson AJ and Schlink B (eds), *Weimar: A Jurisprudence of Crisis* (University of California Press, 2002).
Jakobs G, 'Kriminalisierung im Vorfeld einer Rechtsgutsverletzung' (1985) 97 *Zeitschrift für die gesamte Strafrechtswissenschaft* 751.
——, 'Bürgerstrafrecht und Feindstrafrecht' (2004) *Onlinezeitschrift für Höchstrichterliche Rechtsprechung zum Strafrecht* 88.
Jarass HD and Pieroth B, *Grundgesetz für die Bundesrepublik Deutschland: Kommentar*, 17th edn (CH Beck, 2022)
——, *Grundgesetzkommentar*, 16th edn (CH Beck, 2020).
Jeschke M, 'Modelle einer selbstverwalteten Dritten Gewalt in Europa' (2010) 93 *Kritische Vierteljahresschrift für Gesetzgebung und Rechtswissenschaft* 233.
Jestaedt M and Lepsius O (eds), *Verhältnismäßigkeit – Zur Tragfähigkeit eines verfassungsrechtlichen Schlüsselkonzepts* (Mohr Siebeck, 2015).
Johst D, 'Die Entdeckung des Unrechtsstaates' in W Konitzer (ed), *Moralisierung des Rechts. Kontinuitäten und Diskontinuitäten nationalsozialistischer Normativität* (Campus, 2014) 127.
Jorgensen M, 'The Jurisprudence of the Rules-Based Order: Germany's Indo-Pacific Guidelines and the South China Sea Code of Conduct', KFG Working Paper Series 2021, No 49, Berlin Potsdam Research Group "The International Rule of Law – Rise or Decline?", available at papers.ssrn.com/sol3/papers.cfm?abstract_id=3847800.

Jürgensen S and Orlowski F, 'Critique and Crisis: The German Struggle with Pandemic Control Measures and the State of Emergency', *Verfassungsblog*, 19 April 2020, verfassungsblog.de/critique-and-crisis-the-german-struggle-with-pandemic-control-measures-and-the-state-of-emergency/.

Kaiser AB, *Ausnahmeverfassungsrecht* (Mohr-Siebeck, 2020).

Kant I, *Metaphysik der Sitten* (Nicolovius, 1797).

——, 'The metaphysics of morals' in MJ Gregor (trans), *Practical Philosophy* (Cambridge University Press, 1996).

Kelemen RD, 'Europe's Other Democratic Deficit: National Authoritarianism in Europe's Democratic Union' (2020) 52 *Government & Opposition* 211.

——, 'The European Union's authoritarian equilibrium' (2020) 27 *Journal of European Public Policy* 481.

Keller H and Stone Sweet A (eds), *A Europe of Rights: The Impact of the ECHR on National Legal Systems* (Oxford University Press, 2008).

Keller H and Walther R, 'The Bell of Görgülü Cannot Be Unrung – Can it?' (2020) *Global Community Yearbook of International Law and Jurisprudence* 83.

Keller I, *Strafrechtliche Aufarbeitung von DDR-Justizunrecht* (Peter Lang, 2013).

Kelsen H, *Reine Rechtslehre. Einleitung in Die Rechtswissenschaftliche Problematik* (Mohr Siebeck, reissue 2008, orig 1934).

Kingreen T, 'Der Demokratische Rechtsstaat in der Corona-Pandemie' (2021) *Neue Juristische Wochenschrift* 2766.

Klafki A, 'Kontingenz des Rechts in der Krise – Rechtsempirische Analyse gerichtlicher Argumentationsmuster in der Corona-Pandemie' (2021) 69 *Jahrbuch des öffentlichen Rechts* 593.

Kluth W, 'Systemische Mängel im deutschen Rechtsstaat wegen fehlender Unabhängigkeit der Staatsanwaltschaften?' (2019) *Neue Juristische Wochenschrift* 1175.

Knobloch T, *Vor die Lage kommen: Predictive Policing in Deutschland* (Stiftung Neue Verantwortung/BertelsmannStiftung, 2018).

Kochenov DV and Grabowska-Moroz B, 'The Loss of Face for Everyone Concerned. EU Rule of Law in the Context of the "Migration Crisis"' in V Stoyanova and S Smet (eds), *Migrants' Rights, Populism and Legal Resilience in Europe* (Cambridge University Press, 2022) 115.

Koehler D, *Right-Wing Terrorism in the 21st Century: The 'National Socialist Underground' and the History of Terror from the Far-Right in Germany* (Routledge, 2016).

Kommers DP and Miller RA, *The Constitutional Jurisprudence of the Federal Republic of Germany*, 3rd edn (Duke University Press, 2012).

Kötter M et al (eds), *Rechtsstaatsförderung – Handbuch für Forschung und Praxis* (Kohlhammer, 2022).

Kramer B, 'Die Selbstverwaltung der Dritten Gewalt' (2009) *Neue Juristische Wochenschrift* 3079.

Kraut GM, *Rechtsbeugung? Die Justiz der DDR auf dem Prüfstand des Rechtsstaates* (CH Beck, 1997).

Kreß C, 'Versailles – Nürnberg – Den Haag: Deutschland Und Das Völkerstrafrecht' (2006) *JuristenZeitung* 981.

Krever T, 'The Legal Turn in Late Development Theory: The Rule of Law and the World Bank's Development Model' (2011) 52 *Harvard International Law Journal* 287.

Kube H, 'E-Government: Ein Paradigmenwechsel in Verwaltung und Verwaltungsrecht?' (2019) 78 VVDStRL 289.

Kuchenbauer K, 'Der gläserne Richter – Big-Data-Analyse als Mittel zur Vorhersehbarkeit richterlicher Entscheidungen?' (2021) 76 *JuristenZeitung* 647.

Kunig P, *Das Rechtsstaatsprinzip: Überlegungen Zu Seiner Bedeutung Für Das Verfassungsrecht Der Bundesrepublik Deutschland* (Mohr Siebeck, 1986).

Künzler A, 'Judicial Legitimacy and the Role of Courts: Explaining the Transitional Context of the German Border Guard Cases' (2012) 32 *Oxford Journal of Legal Studies* 349.

Kurtz G, 'Präventive Außenpolitik braucht überprüfbare Strategien: Die Bundesregierung stärkt die zivile Krisenprävention, (DGAP-Standpunkt, 27)', Forschungsinstitut der Deutschen Gesellschaft für Auswärtige Politik e.V. 2019, nbn-resolving.org/urn:nbn:de:0168-ssoar-64475-2.

Landfried C, 'The Selection Process of Constitutional Court Judges in Germany' in K Malleson and PH Russell (eds), *Appointing Judges in an Age of Judicial Power* (University of Toronto Press, 2006) 196.

Langford M and Madsen MR, 'France Criminalises Research on Judges', *Verfassungsblog*, 22 June 2019, available at verfassungsblog.de/france-criminalises-research-on-judges/.

Laskowski S, 'Unrecht-Strafrecht-Gerechtigkeit: Die Probleme des Rechtsstaats mit dem DDR-Unrecht' (1994) *Juristische Arbeitsblätter* 151.

Lautenbach G, *The Concept of the Rule of Law and the European Court of Human Rights* (Oxford University Press, 2013).

Lepsius O, 'Das Luftsicherheitsgesetz und das Grundgesetz' in F Roggan (ed), *Mit Recht für Menschenwürde und Verfassungsstaat* (Berliner Wissenschaftsverlag, 2006) 47.

——, 'Vom Niedergang grundrechtlicher Denkkategorien in der Corona-Pandemie', *Verfassungsblog*, 6 April 2020, verfassungsblog.de/vom-niedergang-grundrechtlicher-denkkategorien-in-der-corona-pandemie/.

——, 'Partizipationsprobleme und Abwägungsdefizite im Umgang mit der Corona-Pandemie' (2021) 69 *Jahrbuch des öffentlichen Rechts* 705.

Linke T, 'BVerfGE 115, 118' in J Menzel and R Müller-Terpitz (eds), *Verfassungsrechtsprechung*, 3rd edn (Mohr Siebeck, 2017) 766.

Lohmann U, 'Sozialistischer Rechtsstaat, Unrechtsstaat oder … ? Versuch einer Charakterisierung von Staat und Recht in der DDR' in U Lohmann (ed), *Zur Staats- und Rechtsordnung der DDR – Juristische und sozialwissenschaftliche Beiträge 1977–1996* (VS Verlag für Sozialwissenschaften, 2015) 405.

Löw K (ed), *10 Jahre Deutsche Einheit* (Duncker & Humblot, 2001).

Lübbe-Wolff G, 'Rechtsstaat und Ausnahmerecht' (1980) 11 *Zeitschrift für Parlamentsfragen* 110.

MacCormick DN, 'Der Rechtsstaat und die Rule of Law' (1984) *JuristenZeitung* 65.

Maier W, 'Wie unabhängig sind Staatsanwälte in Deutschland?' (2003) *Zeitschrift für Rechtspolitik* 387.

Majer D, 'Die Überprüfung von Richtern und Staatsanwälten in der ehemaligen DDR' (1991) 24 *Zeitschrift für Rechtspolitik* 171.

Mangold AK, 'The Persistence of National Peculiarities:' (2014) 21 *Indiana Journal of Global Legal Studies* 223.

——, 'Von Homogenität zu Vielfalt. Die Entstehung von Antidiskriminierungsrecht als eigenständigem Rechtsgebiet in der Berliner Republik' in T Duve and S Ruppert (eds), *Rechtswissenschaft in der Berliner Republik* (Suhrkamp, 2018) 461.

——, 'Germany and COVID-19: A Most Eventful Year', *Verfassungsblog*, 7 April 2021, verfassungsblog.de/germany-and-covid-19-a-most-eventful-year/.

v Mangoldt H, Klein F and Starck C (orig eds), *Grundgesetz Kommentar*, 7th edn (2018).

Marsch N, Vilain Y and Wendel M (eds), *Französisches und Deutsches Verfassungsrecht: Ein Rechtsvergleich* (Springer, 2015).

Martini M, 'Transformation der Verwaltung durch Digitalisierung' (2017) *Die öffentliche Verwaltung* 443.

Martini S, 'Die Pluralität von Rule-of-Law-Konzeptionen in Europa und das Prinzip einer europäischen Rule of Law' in M Kötter and GF Schuppert (eds), *Normative Pluralität Ordnen: Rechtsbegriffe, Normenkollisionen Und Rule of Law in Kontexten dies- und jenseits des Staates* (Nomos, 2009) 303.

Marxen K and Werle G, *Die strafrechtliche Aufarbeitung von DDR-Unrecht – Eine Bilanz* (de Gruyter 1999).

Mayer FC, 'The Ultra Vires Ruling: Deconstructing the German Federal Constitutional Court's PSPP decision of 5 May 2020' (2020) 16 *European Constitutional Law Review* 733.

Mayer O, *Deutsches Verwaltungsrecht, Band I* (Duncker & Humblot, 1895).
——, *Deutsches Verwaltungsrecht*, 3rd edn (Duncker & Humblot, 1924).
McAdams AJ, 'The Honecker Trial: The East German Past and the German Future' (1996) 58 *Review of Politics* 53.
Meierhenrich J, *The Remnants of the Rechtsstaat* (Oxford University Press, 2018).
——, '*Rechtsstaat* versus the Rule of Law' in J Meierhenrich and M Loughlin (eds), *The Cambridge Companion to the Rule of Law* (Cambridge University Press, 2021) 39.
Mertin H, 'Selbstverwaltung der Justiz als Verfassungsauftrag?' (2002) *Zeitschrift für Rechtspolitik* 332.
Möller H and Kocka J, in Deutscher Bundestag (ed), *Materialien der Enquete-Kommission "Aufarbeitung von Geschichte und Folgen der SED-Diktatur in Deutschland"*, vol 9 (1995).
Möllers C, *Gewaltengliederung: Legitimation und Dogmatik im nationalen und internationalen Rechtsvergleich* (Mohr Siebeck, 2005).
——, *The Three Branches: A Comparative Model of Separation of Powers* (Oxford University Press, 2013).
——, 'Rechtsstaat' in U Kischel and H Kube (eds), *Handbuch des Staatsrechts. Neuausgabe Band II* (CF Müller, forthcoming) 517.
Möllers C and Birkenkötter H, 'Towards a New Conceptualism in Comparative Constitutional Law, or Reviving the German Tradition of the Lehrbuch' (2014) 12 *International Journal of Constitutional Law* 603.
Müller H and Windau B, 'Pandemie als Digitalisierungsschub für die Justiz?' (2021) *Deutsche Richterzeitung* 332.
Müller I, 'Neuestes und allerneustes Strafprozeßrecht' (1978) *Kritische Justiz* 301.
——, 'Die DDR – ein Unrechtsstaat?' (1992) *Neue Justiz* 281.
von Münch I, 'Rechtsstaat versus Gerechtigkeit?' (1994) 33 *Der Staat* 165.
von Münch I and Kunig P (eds), *Grundgesetz-Kommentar*, 7th edn (2021).
Murswiek D, 'Die Corona-Waage – Kriterien für die Prüfung der Verhältnismäßigkeit von Corona-Maßnahmen' (2021) *Neue Zeitschrift für Verwaltungsrecht* 281.
Myers DG and Lamm H, 'The polarizing effect of group discussion' (1975) 63 *American Scientist* 297.
Nachtwei W, 'Lehren aus deutschen Krisenengagements gibt es reichlich – aber auch Lernfortschritte?' (2019) 3 *SIRIUS – Zeitschrift für Strategische Analysen* 362.
Neumann FL, *Behemoth: The Structure and Practice of National Socialism, 1933–1944* (Ivan R. Dee, reissue 2009, org 1942).
Niedernhuber T, 'How Much Independence is Necessary to Issue a European Arrest Warrant?' (2020) 10 *European Criminal Law Review* 5.
Nink D, *Justiz und Algorithmen* (Duncker & Humblot, 2021).
Nussberger A, *The European Court of Human Rights* (Oxford University Press, 2020).
Offe C and Poppe U, 'Transitional Justice in the German Democratic Republic and in Unified Germany' in A Czarnota, M Krygier and W Sadurski (eds), *Rething the Rule of Law after Communism* (CEU Press, 2005) 239.
Papier HJ, 'Zur Selbstverwaltung der Dritten Gewalt' (2002) *Neue Juristische Wochenschrift* 2585.
——, 'Eklatantes Politikversagen in der Flüchtlingskrise', *Handelsblatt*, 12 January 2016, www.handelsblatt.com/politik/deutschland/ex-verfassungsrichter-papier-eklatantes-politikversagen-in-der-fluechtlingskrise/12818088.html.
——, 'Herausforderungen des Rechtsstaats im Zeitalter der Digitalisierung' in C Bär, T Grädler and R Mayr (eds), *Digitalisierung im Spannungsfeld von Politik, Wirtschaft, Wissenschaft und Recht* (Springer, 2018) 171.
Pech L, '"A Union Founded on the Rule of Law": Meaning and Reality of the Rule of Law as a Constitutional Principle of EU Law' (2010) 6 *European Constitutional Law Review* 359.
Perels J, 'Der Soziale Rechtsstaat Im Widerstreit: Zur Verfassungsinterpretation Wolfgang Abendroths Aus Anlass Seines 100. Geburtstags' (2006) 39 *Kritische Justiz* 295.

Petersen N, 'Alexy and the "German" Model of Proportionality: Why the Theory of Constitutional Rights Does Not Provide a Representative Reconstruction of the Proportionality Test' (2020) 21 *German Law Journal* 163.

Pichl M, *Law statt Order. Der Kampf um den Rechtsstaat* (Suhrkamp, 2024).

Pieroth B, 'Der Rechtsstaat und die Aufarbeitung der vor-rechtsstaatlichen Vergangenheit' (1992) 51 VVDStRL 91.

——, 'Historische Etappen des Rechtsstaats in Deutschland' (2011) 33 *Juristische Ausbildung* 729.

Plener U (ed), *Die Treuhand – der Widerstand in Betrieben der DDR – die Gewerkschaften (1990–1994). Tagung vom 2. April 2011 in Berlin (NORA 2011).*

Polgári E, 'Hungary: "Gains and Losses" – Changing the Relationship with the European Court of Human Rights' in P Popelier, S Lambrecht and K Lemmens (eds), *Criticism of the European Court of Human Rights* (Intersentia, 2016) 295.

Pötter W, 'Die aktuellen Probleme des Richterstandes im Lichte der historischen Betrachtung' in *Die Unabhangigkeit des Richters: ein Cappenberger Gespräch* (Grote 1969).

Prinz S, 'Die Linkspartei und der Unrechtsstaat DDR. Der Preis der Macht. Die Koalition "frisst ihre Kinder"' (2015) 464 *Politische Studien* 44.

Putzer M, *Gerichte, Terror und Verfahren* (Mohr Siebeck, 2015).

Quint PE, 'Judging the Past: The Prosecution of East German Border Guards and the GDR Chain of Command' (1999) 61 *The Review of Politics* 303.

Radbruch G, 'Gesetzliches Unrecht und übergesetzliches Recht' (1946) 1 *Süddeutsche Juristenzeitung* 105.

Ramelsberger A, 'Der wehrhafte Rechtsstaat? Da lachen ja die braunen Brüder', *Süddeutsche Zeitung*, 15 December 2021.

Rautenberg EC, 'Deutscher Widerstand gegen weisungsunabhängige Staatsanwaltschaft' (2016) *Zeitschrift für Rechtspolitik* 38.

Reimer E, 'Einfluss der Digitalisierung auf die Rechtsetzung' in J Hey (ed), *Digitalisierung im Steuerrecht* (Otto Schmidt Verlag, 2019) 97.

Reinschmidt G, 'Zur Legitimationsfrage bei der Richterwahl' (1972) *Zeitschrift für Rechtspolitik* 160.

Richardson R, Schultz JM and Crawford K, 'Dirty data, bad predictions: How civil rights violations impact police data, predictive policing systems, and justice' (2019) 94 *New York University Law Review* 15.

Rieß P, 'Die Durchführung der Hauptverhandlung ohne Angeklagten' (1975) *Juristenzeitung* 265.

Roesler J, 'Nur den Anforderungen des Marktes verpflichtet? Autokratische Züge und demokratische Ansätze der Treuhandprivatisierung', available at www.bpb.de/themen/deutschlandarchiv/54068/nur-den-anforderungen-des-marktes-verpflichtet/.

Röhner C, *Ungleichheit und Verfassung. Vorschlag für eine relationale Rechtsanalyse* (Velbrück 2019).

Roggemann H, 'Gerichtlicher Verwaltungsrechtsschutz in der DDR' (1989) 44 *JuristenZeitung* 579.

Rosenau H, *Tödliche Schüsse im staatlichen Auftrag: Die strafrechtliche Verantwortung von Grenzsoldaten für den Schußwaffengebrauch an der deutsch- deutschen Grenze* (Nomos, 1998).

Rottleuthner H, 'Steuerung der Justiz in der DDR' (1992) 75 *Kritische Vierteljahresschrift für Gesetzgebung und Rechtswissenschaft* 237.

Rottleuthner H and Baer A (eds), *Steuerung der Justiz in der DDR – Einflussnahme der Politik auf Richter, Staatsanwälte und Rechtsanwälte* (Bundesanzeiger, 1994).

Rudolphi HJ, 'Strafprozeß im Umbruch' (1976) 9 *Zeitschrift für Rechtspolitik* 165.

Saeed L, 'International Rule of Law Assistance: Learning from Failures in Afghanistan', available at peacelab.blog/2019/05/international-rule-of-law-assistance-learning-from-failures-in-afghanistan.

Sälter G, 'Der Rechtsstaat und das Grenzregime der DDR – Die strafrechtliche Verfolgung der Grenzdelikte in der Bundesrepublik' in J Ganzenmüller (ed) *Recht und Gerechtigkeit – Die strafrechtliche Aufarbeitung von Diktaturen in Europa* (Böhlau, 2017) 115.

Saurer J, 'Die Globalisierung des Verhältnismässigkeitsgrundsatzes' (2012) 51 *Der Staat* 3.

Scheuing DH, 'Europäische Union und Rechtsstaatlichkeitsgebot' in H Scholler (ed), *Die Sicherung des Rechtsstaatsgebotes im modernen europäischen Recht – anhand von Garantien im Recht der Europäischen Union sowie in Russland und Deutschland* (Duncker & Humblot, 2011) 27.

Scheuner U, 'Der Rechtsstaat und die soziale Verantwortung des Staates: Das Wissenschaftliche Lebenswerk von Robert von Mohl' (1979) *Der Staat* 1.

Schmalz D, 'Review of: Der Staat in Der Flüchtlingskrise. Zwischen Gutem Willen Und Geltendem Recht by Otto Depenheuer and Christoph Grabenwarter' (2016) 49 *Kritische Justiz* 260.

Scholz R, 'Wider die Relativierung: Die DDR war ein Unrechtsstaat', *Frankfurter Allgemeine Zeitung*, 1 June 2015.

Schlink B, 'Rechtsstaat und revolutionäre Gerechtigkeit', Lecture at Humboldt University Berlin 1994, available at edoc.hu-berlin.de/handle/18452/2273.

——, 'Proportionality in Constitutional Law: Why Everywhere But Here?' (2012) 22 *Duke Journal of Comparative & International Law* 291.

Schmedes HJ, 'Mehr Transparenz wagen? Zur Diskussion um ein gesetzliches Lobbyregister beim Deutschen Bundestag' (2009) 3 *Zeitschrift für Parlamentsfragen* 543.

Schmidt-Aßmann E, 'Der Rechtsstaat' in J Isensee and P Kirchhof (eds), *Handbuch des Staatsrechts*, vol 2, 3rd edn (CF Müller, 2004) 541.

Schmitt C, *Constitutional Theory*, J Seitzer (transl and ed) (Duke University Press, 2008).

——, 'Nationalsozialismus und Rechtsstaat' (1934) in C Schmitt (ed), *Gesammelte Schriften 1933–1936: Mit Ergänzenden Beiträgen aus der Zeit des Zweiten Weltkriegs* (Duncker und Humblot, 2021).

Schoch F and Schneider JP (eds), *Verwaltungsrecht, VwVfG – Kommentar*, 3rd edn (CH Beck, 2022).

Schöneburg V, 'Recht im nazifaschistischen und im "realsozialistischen" deutschen Staat – Diskontinuitäten und Kontinuitäten' (1992) *Neue Justiz* 49.

Schröder M, 'Staatsrecht an den Grenzen des Rechtsstaates: Überlegungen zur Verteidigung des Rechtsstaates in außergewöhnlichen Lagen' (1978) *Archiv des öffentlichen Rechts* 121.

Schröder R (ed), *Zivilrechtskultur der DDR*, vol 14 (Duncker & Humblot, 1999–2008).

Schulte-Kellinghaus T, 'Die begrenzte Macht der Dritten Gewalt – Zur Notwendigkeit der Selbstverwaltung der Gerichte' (2008) *Zeitschrift für Rechtspolitik* 205.

Selbst AD, 'Disparate impact in big data policing' (2018) 52 *Georgia Law Review* 109.

Sendler H, 'Editorial' (1991) *Neue Justiz* 137.

——, 'Über Rechtsstaat, Unrechtsstaat und anderes – Das Editorial der Herausgeber im Meinungsstreit' (1991) *Neue Justiz* 379.

Siegel T, 'Digitalisierung des Verwaltungsrechts – Reformbedarf im Verwaltungsverfahrensgesetz?' (2023) *Neue Zeitschrift für Verwaltungsrecht* 193.

Sieveking K, *Die Entwicklung des sozialistischen Rechtsstaatsbegriffs in der DDR: eine Studie zur Auseinandersetzung mit dem Rechtsstaat in der SBZ-DDR zwischen 1945 und 1968* (Nomos, 1975).

Singelnstein T, 'Predictive Policing: Algorithmenbasierte Straftatprognosen zur vorausschauenden Kriminalintervention' (2018) *Neue Zeitschrift für Strafrecht* 1.

Sobota K, *Das Prinzip Rechtsstaat – Verfassungs- und verwaltungsrechtliche Aspekte* (Mohr Siebeck, 1997).

Söllner A, 'Jürgen Habermas und die kritische Theorie des gegenwärtigen Rechtsstaates – Versuch einer wissenschaftsgeschichtlichen Einordnung' (1982) 10 *Leviathan* 97.

Sommermann KP, *Die Deutsche Verwaltungsgerichtsbarkeit*, 3rd edn (Deutsches Forschungsinstitut für öffentliche Verwaltung, 1994).

Spendel G, 'Luftsicherheitsgesetz und Bundesverfassungsgericht – Eine notwendige Kritik' (2006) *Recht und Politik* 131.

Stahl FJ, *Die Philosophie des Rechts*, 2nd edn (JCB Mohr, 1847).

——, *Die Philosophie des Rechts, Zweiter Band: Rechts- und Staatslehre auf der Grundlage christlicher Weltanschauung* 5th edn (JCB Mohr, 1878).

Starck C, 'Der Rechtsstaat in der politischen Kontroverse' (1978) *JuristenZeitung* 746.

——, 'Der Rechtsstaat und die Aufarbeitung der vor-rechtsstaatlichen Vergangenheit' (1992) 51 VVDStRL 9.

Steinitz K, 'Die Treuhandanstalt und der wirtschaftliche Absturz Ostdeutschlands' in U Plener (ed), *Die Treuhand – der Widerstand in Betrieben der DDR – die Gewerkschaften (1990–1994). Tagung vom 2. April 2011 in Berlin* (NORA, 2011) 15.

Steinke R, *The Politics of International Criminal Justice: German Perspectives from Nuremberg to The Hague* (Hart Publishing, 2012).

——, 'Die Enthemmten', *Süddeutsche Zeitung*, 12 December 2021, availabe at www.sueddeutsche.de/meinung/coronaleugner-telegram-maske-protest-rechtsstaat-1.5485284.

——, *Vor dem Gesetz sind nicht alle gleich. Die neue Klassenjustiz* (Berlin Verlag, 2022).

Stelkens P, Bonk HJ and Sachs M (orig eds and ed), *VwVfG*, 10th edn (CH Beck, 2023).

Stolleis M, *Sozialistische Gesetzlichkeit – Staats- und Verwaltungsrechtswissenschaft in der DDR* (CH Beck, 2009).

——, *Geschichte des öffentlichen Rechts in Deutschland*, vol 4 (CH Beck, 2012).

——, 'Rechtsstaat und Unrechtsstaat im 20. Jahrhundert' in C Starck (ed), *Recht und Willkür* (CH Beck, 2012) 47.

——, *Öffentliches Recht in Deutschland: Eine Einführung in Seine Geschichte (16.-21. Jahrhundert)* (CH Beck, 2014).

——, 'Die soziale Programmatik der Weimarer Reichsverfassung' in H Dreier and C Waldhoff (eds), *Das Wagnis der Demokratie* (CH Beck, 2018) 195.

Talmon S, 'Rules-based order v. international law?', available at gpil.jura.uni-bonn.de/2019/01/rules-based-order-v-international-law/.

Tamanaha BZ, *On the Rule of Law. History, Politics, Theory* (Cambridge University Press, 2004).

Tatham AF, *Central European constitutional courts in the face of EU membership: The influence of the German model in Hungary and Poland* (Brill, 2013).

Thränhardt D, 'Die Asylkrise 2015 als Verwaltungsproblem' (2020) 30–32 *Aus Politik und Zeitgeschichte* 37.

Thym D, 'Der Rechtsstaat und die deutsche Staatsgrenze', *Verfassungsblog*, 22 January 2016, verfassungsblog.de/der-rechtsstaat-und-die-deutsche-staatsgrenze/.

——, 'Der Rechtsbruch-Mythos und wie man ihn widerlegt', *Verfassungsblog*, 2 May 2018, verfassungsblog.de/der-rechtsbruch-mythos-und-wie-man-ihn-widerlegt/.

Timmermann D and Gelbrich K, 'Können Algorithmen subsumieren?' (2022) *Neue Juristische Wochenschrift* 25.

Tischbirek A, 'A Double Conflict of Laws: The Emergence of an EU "Staatskirchenrecht"?' (2019) 20 *German Law Journal* 1066.

Tomassini F, 'Right, Morals and the Categorical Imperative' (2023) 114 *Kant-Studien* 513.

Tomuschat C, 'Europe – a Common Constitutional Space' in B de Witte and C Forder (eds), *The Common law of Europe and the Future of Legal Education* (Kluwer, 1992) 133.

Ullerich R, *Rechtsstaat und Rechtsgemeinschaft im Europarecht* (Nomos, 2011).

Vasel JJ, 'Künstliche Intelligenz in der Justiz' (2023) *Legal Tech – Zeitschrift für die digitale Anwendung* 179.

Waldron J, 'Is the Rule of Law an Essentially Contested Concept (in Florida)?' (2002) 21 *Law and Philosophy* 137.

——, 'Kant's Theory of State' in P Kleingeld (ed), *Toward Perpetual Peace and Other Writings on Politics, Peace, and History* (Yale University Press, 2017) 179.

Wassermann R, 'Wieviel Unrecht macht einen Staat zum Unrechtstaat?' (1997) *Neue Juristische Wochenschrift* 2152.

Wege S and Nowak M, 'Entwicklungspolitik Im Wiedervereinten Deutschland Zwischen 1990 Und 2015' in W Gieler and M Nowak (eds), *Staatliche Entwicklungszusammenarbeit in Deutschland: Eine Bestandsaufnahme des BMZ 1961–2021* (Springer, 2021) 273.

Welcker CT, *Die Letzten Gründe von Recht, Staat und Strafe: Philosophisch und nach den Gesetzen der merkwürdigsten Völker rechtshistorisch entwickelt* (Heyer, 1813).

Wendel M, 'Comparative reasoning and the making of a common constitutional law: EU-related decisions of national constitutional courts in a transnational perspective' (2013) 11 *International Journal of Constitutional Law* 981.

Wendel M, 'Enforcing the independence of national courts by means of EU law standards, procedures and actors as exemplified by the crisis of the Polish judiciary' in K Meier, A Lorenz and M Wendel (eds), *Rule of Law and the Judiciary* (Nomos, 2023) 123.

Werner W, 'Schutz durch das Grundgesetz im Zeitalter der Digitalisierung' (2019) *Neue Juristische Online Zeitschrift* 1041.

Wihl T, *Aufhebungsrechte. Form, Zeitlichkeit und Gleichheit der Grund- und Menschenrechte* (Velbrück, 2019).

——, 'Rechtsstaatlichkeit' in M Festl (ed), *Handbuch Liberalismus* (JB Metzler, 2021) 183.

Wiik A and Lachenmann F, 'The Law Behind Rule of Law Promotion in Fragile States: The Case of Afghanistan' (2018) 9 *Goettingen Journal of International Law* 171.

Will R, 'Der deutsche Rechtsstaat in Zeiten des rechtsextremen Terrors' in Institut für Friedensforschung und Sicherheitspolitik an der Universität Hamburg (ed), *OSZE Jahrbuch 2012* (Nomos, 2013) 183.

Willoweit D, 'Unrechtsstaat, Rechtsstaat – eine richtige Alternative?' in HG Hockerts (ed), *Koordinaten deutscher Geschichte in der Epoche des Ost-West-Konflikts* (Oldenbourg Wissenschaftsverlag, 2004) 245.

——, *Deutsche Verfassungsgeschichte*, 7th edn (CH Beck, 2013).

Winkler D, 'Verfassungsmäßigkeit des Luftsicherheitsgesetzes' (2006) *Neue Zeitschrift für Verwaltungsrecht* 536.

Windoffer A, 'Herausforderungen der Digitalisierung aus der Perspektive der öffentlichen Verwaltung' in C Bär, T Grädler and R Mayr (eds), *Digitalisierung im Spannungsfeld von Politik, Wirtschaft, Wissenschaft und Recht* (Springer, 2018) 363.

von Winterfeld A, 'Terrorismus – "Reform" ohne Ende?' (1977) *Zeitschrift für Rechtspolitik* 265.

Wischmeyer T, 'Künstliche Intelligenz und neue Begründungsarchitektur' in M Eifert (ed), *Digitale Disruption und Recht* (Nomos, 2020) 73.

Wittreck F, *Die Verwaltung der Dritten Gewalt* (Mohr-Siebeck, 2006).

Zacher H, 'Das soziale Staatsziel' in J Isensee and P Kirchhof (eds), *Handbuch des Staatsrechts*, vol 1 (, CF Müller, 1987) 1045.

Zöller MA, 'Diskussion um neue Rechtsextremisten-Datei: Wer alles weiß, soll nicht alles dürfen', *LTO*, 21 November 2011, available at www.lto.de/recht/hintergruende/h/diskussion-um-neue-rechtsextremisten-datei-wer-alles-weiss-soll-nicht-alles-duerfen/.

Index

Introductory Note

References such as '178–79' indicate (not necessarily continuous) discussion of a topic across a range of pages. Wherever possible in the case of topics with many references, these have either been divided into sub-topics or only the most significant discussions of the topic are listed. Because the entire work is about the 'rule of law', the use of this term (and certain others which occur constantly throughout the book) as an entry point has been restricted. Information will be found under the corresponding detailed topics. Cross-references in a form such as 'courts *see also individual courts*' direct the reader to headings in a particular class (e.g. in this case 'FCC (Federal Constitutional Court') rather than a specific '*individual courts*' entry.

www.ingramcontent.com/pod-product-compliance
Ingram Content Group UK Ltd.
Pitfield, Milton Keynes, MK11 3LW, UK
UKHW020816290926
15470UKWH00003B/1190

9 781509 969296